COMPASS

All-in-one Integrated Skills and Grammar

Sue Frame

OXFORD
UNIVERSITY PRESS

OXFORD
UNIVERSITY PRESS

Oxford University Press is a department of the University of Oxford.
It furthers the University's objective of excellence in research, scholarship,
and education by publishing worldwide. Oxford is a registered trade mark of
Oxford University Press in the UK and in certain other countries.

Published in Canada by
Oxford University Press
8 Sampson Mews, Suite 204,
Don Mills, Ontario M3C 0H5 Canada

www.oupcanada.com

Catalogage avant publication de Bibliothèque et Archives Canada

Frame, Sue, auteur
Compass 2 : all-in-one integrated skills and grammar / Sue Frame.

ISBN 978-0-19-902256-4 (couverture souple)

1. Anglais (Langue)–Manuels pour francophones.   2. Anglais
(Langue)–Problèmes et exercices.   I. Titre.   II. Titre: Compass two.

PE1129.F7F6295 2017   428.2'441   C2016-907600-8

Oxford University Press is committed to our environment.
Wherever possible, our books are printed on paper which comes from
responsible sources.

Printed and bound in the United States of America

1 2 3 4 — 20 19 18 17

Acknowledgements

I would like to thank the entire team at OUP, and in particular David Coombes, for their dedication and support. I'd also like to extend untold thanks to my editor, Nicola Balfour, whose encouragement, attention to detail, and sense of humour contributed to making this such a rewarding experience.

I'd like to dedicate this book to my two sons, Lewis and Arnaud, who keep me grounded and put up with my "distracted" moments. I wish Helen and Nana had been able to see this project come to fruition. This is for you four.

Sue Frame

Oxford University Press Canada would like to express appreciation to the English teachers who generously offered feedback about *Compass* at various stages of the development process. Their feedback was instrumental in helping to shape and refine the book.

Annick Bilodeau Cégep de Sainte-Foy
Heather Boyle Cégep de Baie Comeau
Judith Campbell Collège de Maisonneuve
Alexa Eason Collège de Rosemont
Ryan Fisher Cégep Garneau
Sandra Gasparini Collège de Bois-de-Boulogne
Barry G. Glebe Collège de Maisonneuve
Alan E. Hall Cégep Édouard-Montpetit
Jerry Johnson Cégep Édouard-Montpetit
Sherry Kent Cégep Saint-Jean-sur-Richelieu
Izabela Kubinska Collège de Valleyfield
Chiara Laricchiuta Collège Ahuntsic
Viviane Mahy Cégep Limoilou
Felix Maranda Castonguay Cégep Lévis-Lauzon
Caroline Orton Cégep du Vieux Montréal
Xuelian (Lotus) Wei Cégep André-Laurendeau

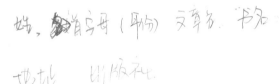

ABOUT THE AUTHOR

Sue Frame has been teaching at Cégep Marie-Victorin since 1996 and has also taught ESL in the UK and France. She holds an MA in English and French and a BEd in ESL/FLS from McGill University.

Compass: How to Use the Book

Book Structure

Six theme-based **Skills** units provide contemporary, high interest, Canadian and international readings, listenings, and watchings.

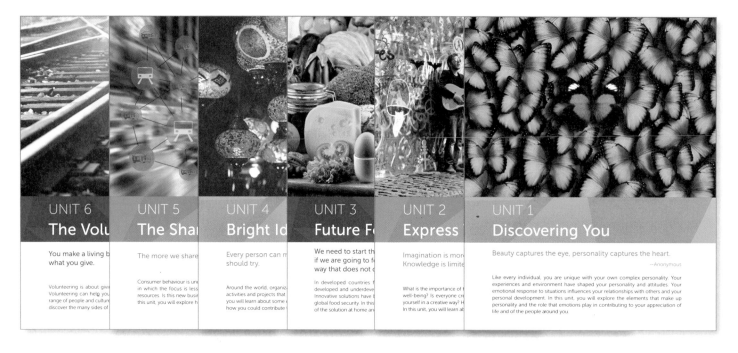

UNIT 6
The Volu

You make a living by what you give.

Volunteering is about givi Volunteering can help you range of people and cultures discover the many sides of

UNIT 5
The Shar

The more we share

Consumer behaviour is und in which the focus is less resources. Is this new busin this unit, you will explore h

UNIT 4
Bright Id

Every person can m should try.

Around the world, organiza activities and projects that you will learn about some how you could contribute

UNIT 3
Future F

We need to start thi if we are going to fe way that does not c

In developed countries f developed and underdeve Innovative solutions have global food security. In thi of the solution at home an

UNIT 2
Express

Imagination is more Knowledge is limite

What is the importance of well-being? Is everyone cre yourself in a creative way? H In this unit, you will learn ab

UNIT 1
Discovering You

Beauty captures the eye, personality captures the heart.

—Anonymous

Like every individual, you are unique with your own complex personality. Your experiences and environment have shaped your personality and attitudes. Your emotional response to situations influences your relationships with others and your personal development. In this unit, you will explore the elements that make up personality and the role that emotions play in contributing to your appreciation of life and of the people around you.

A concise, comprehensive in-book **Learning Strategies** section for Writing, Speaking, Reading, and Listening helps students become independent, successful learners.

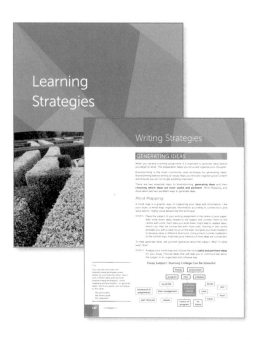

Fourteen **Grammar Guide** chapters cover all the key grammar points and give students hundreds of practice activities.

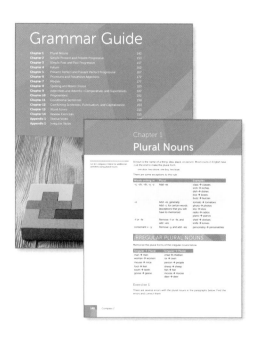

Skills Unit Features

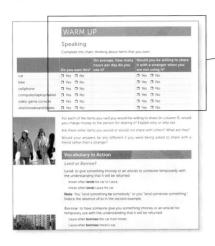

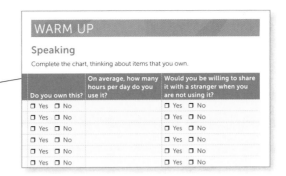

Interesting **Warm Up** activities trigger prior knowledge and get students involved with unit's theme.

Warm Up activities practice all four skills!

Exceptional Vocabulary Development!

Vocabulary Activities before texts, audios and videos ensure students are more successful with reading, listening, and watching activities.

Vocabulary In Action helps students with commonly confused and useful words.

Theme-related words and expressions help students expand their vocabulary base.

Reading, Listening, and Watching

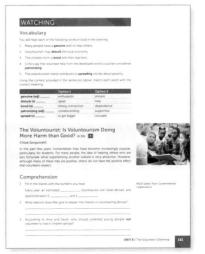

Stimulating readings, audios, and videos
Authentic, high-interest and level-appropriate readings, audios and videos from Canadian and international sources

Speaking, Pronunciation, and Writing

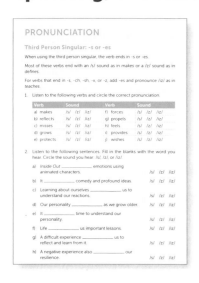

Pronunciation practice
Points in each chapter improve students' speaking skills and develop more confident speakers.

Highly communicative
Four to six speaking activities in every skills unit and communication activities in every grammar chapter.

Exceptional Writing support Writing activities take students step by step from writing structured paragraphs to well-developed essays.

Learning Strategies

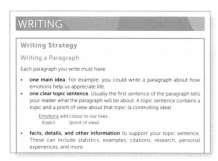

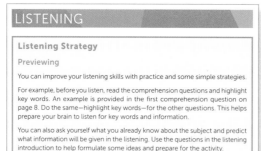

Carefully chosen **Learning Strategies** in each skills unit makes learning easier, quicker, and more enjoyable.

Learning strategies help students become independent and successful learners.

Grammar

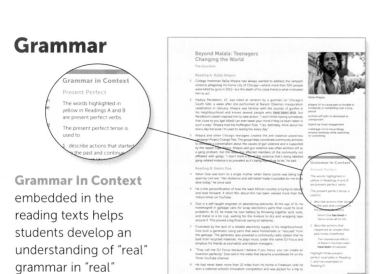

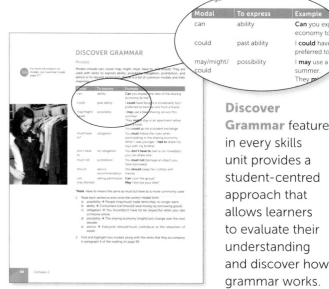

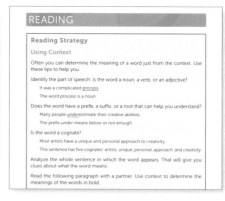

Grammar In Context embedded in the reading texts helps students develop an understanding of "real" grammar in "real" situations.

Discover Grammar feature in every skills unit provides a student-centred approach that allows learners to evaluate their understanding and discover how grammar works.

Compass Online

Compass Online is an easy-to-use website that provides students with hundreds of practice activities related to the content in the student book. Students will improve their English through additional practice in vocabulary, listening, watching, reading, pronunciation, revising and editing, and all aspects of English grammar.

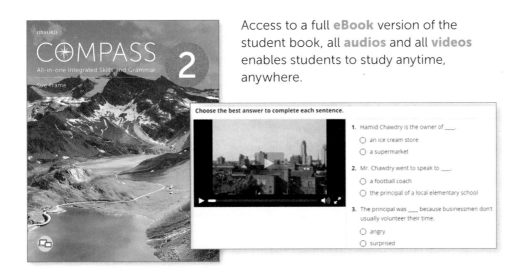

Access to a full **eBook** version of the student book, all **audios** and all **videos** enables students to study anytime, anywhere.

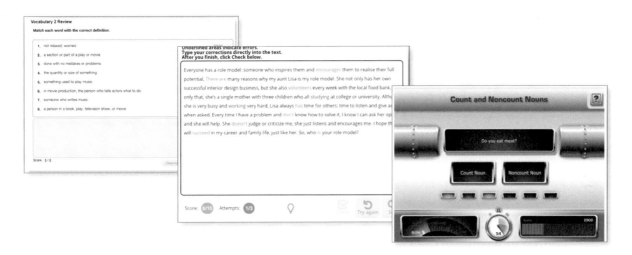

Interactive, self-graded activities, games and tests make learning stimulating and fun!

Instant feedback and access to **charts**, and **tips** develops autonomous learning.

	Chap. 1
Unit Total	
Total Attempts	3
Total Score	16 / 16 100%
Total Seat Time	3 min
Activity 1	View
Attempts	2
	8 / 8

Gradebook allows students and teachers to track progress quickly and easily.

Scope and Sequence

	Reading	Writing	Listening & Watching
UNIT 1 **Discovering You**	• Read about personality traits • Read about the role emotions play in our lives • Complete a quiz on emotional intelligence	• Write a paragraph describing your personality • Write a paragraph describing someone else's personality • Write a summary of a video clip • **Strategy** Writing a Paragraph	• Listen to a report about the importance of emotions • Watch an interview about emotional intelligence • **Strategy** Preparing to Listen
UNIT 2 **Express Yourself**	• Read about how music helps you process emotions • Read about how to nurture creativity • **Strategy** Using Context	• Write a paragraph about music that evokes a memory • Write a paragraph describing your creativity or a creative person • Write about how you deal with stress • Write a paragraph about a six-word memoir or summarize an article about teaching creativity • Write a topic sentence and supporting details	• Watch a video about music therapy • Listen to a report about a university arts workshop for combatting stress
UNIT 3 **Future Food**	• Read about innovative solutions to the global food crisis • Read about the realities of and the potential for 3D printed food	• Write two paragraphs predicting the future of food • Develop an essay outline based on a thesis statement • Write two paragraphs supporting a thesis statement • Summarize the main idea of an article about food • **Strategy** Working from a Thesis Statement	• Watch a report about urban farming • Listen to a report about eating insects
UNIT 4 **Bright Ideas**	• Read about young social activists • Read an interview with Guy Laliberté about improving access to clean water • **Strategy** Scanning	• Write questions to ask an activist • Write a paragraph to support an opinion • Summarize an article • Practise freewriting to capture ideas • Write a paragraph explaining your point of view • Write a response to a video	• Watch a video about the Ocean Cleanup project • Listen to a report about a homeless person with a mission • **Strategy** Predicting
UNIT 5 **The Sharing Economy**	• Read about the sharing economy • Read about a Facebook trading group	• Write a paragraph expressing an opinion on the sharing economy • Write a paragraph explaining the popularity of the sharing economy • Write an opinion essay about the sharing economy • Summarize a report on the sharing economy • Write two paragraphs summarizing a video on the impact of the sharing economy	• Watch a report about the growth of the sharing economy • Listen to a report on the legal issues related to the sharing economy
UNIT 6 **The Volunteer Dilemma**	• Read about the negative side of voluntourism • Read about the impact of the voluntourism industry	• Take notes during an oral presentation • Develop an outline for an opinion essay • Write an opinion essay • Write a paragraph about the activities of a volunteer organization	• Listen to an interview about socially responsible volunteering • Watch a documentary on overseas volunteering trips

Speaking & Pronunciation	Vocabulary	Grammar	Revising & Editing
• Pronounce third person singular: -s and -es • Interview and introduce someone • Prepare for reading by sharing personal opinions on personality • Form simple present questions: describe activity using simple present and present progressive • Interview classmates about emotions • Respond to scenarios related to emotional intelligence • Oral presentation: A personality trait or emotional reaction to modify	• Cognates and false cognates • Learn words related to personality, emotions, and intelligence **Vocabulary in Action** • Participles as adjectives: -ing or -ed?	• Simple present and present progressive **Grammar in Context** • Possessive adjectives • Capitalization	• Revise to correct errors in present tense • Revise to correct errors in possessive adjectives
• Pronounce past tense verb endings: -ed • Outline the role of the arts in your life • Brainstorm benefits of music therapy • Discuss what it means to be creative • Share ideas about student stress • Describe a personal creative project • Oral presentation: A creative person you admire, music therapy, or art therapy	• Figure out definitions from context clues • Use words related to the arts • Form questions using *do*, *don't*, *does*, *is*, and *are* • Write definitions for new vocabulary **Vocabulary in Action** • *To listen to* • *Feel* or *fall*? • *Wish* or *hope*?	• Simple past and past progressive **Grammar in Context** • *Your* or *you're*? • *Its* or *it's*? • Gerund as subject	• Revise to correct errors in the simple past and past progressive
• Pronounce *can* and *can't* • Discuss food challenges and solutions • Share knowledge of urban farming • Present a case for a food solution • Brainstorm and present solutions to food challenges • Talk about food-related opportunities with 3D printing • Conduct a food-preferences interview • Debate an urban farming project • Oral presentation: A food shortage or food waste solution	• Learn words related to food production and sustainability • Use context to determine meaning • Choose between multiple dictionary definitions **Vocabulary in Action** • *Security* or *safety*? • Compound adjectives	• Future **Grammar in Context** • Irregular plurals • Preposition + gerund	• Write an essay introduction • Revise topic sentences
• Pronounce words beginning with *h* • Share ideas on what it means to make a difference • Present an inspirational person • Discuss the issue of homelessness • Describe the personal impact of a report • Oral presentation: someone who is contributing to a local or international community	• Practise words related to social responsibility • Work with word families • Complete a crossword with unit vocabulary **Vocabulary in Action** • *Make* or *do*?	• Present perfect **Grammar in Context** • Present perfect • Apostrophe to indicate possession	• Revise to correct past tense errors and word choice errors
• Pronounce words with silent letters • Solicit opinions from classmates about sharing of goods • Interview classmates about their sharing economy experiences • Negotiate trades in an in-class trading zone • Present and support an opinion for or against the sharing economy • Oral presentation: the services of a collaborative consumption project	• Learn words related to the sharing or exchange of goods and services **Vocabulary in Action** • *Lend* or *borrow*? • Slang	• Modals **Grammar in Context** • Passive voice • Comparative and superlative adjectives	• Write a thesis statement for an essay • Write topic sentences for development paragraphs • Write an essay conclusion • Revise to correct modal errors
• Pronounce words using the correct stress • Discuss volunteer experiences • Brainstorm motivations for and challenges of volunteering • Debate the merits of local and international volunteering • Discuss the effects of volunteer work • Create and present a volunteer recruitment campaign • Oral presentation: An organization providing services locally or abroad	• Use words and expressions related to volunteering **Vocabulary in Action** • *Assist* or *attend*? • Negative prefixes	• The conditional **Grammar in Context** • *Much* or *many*? • Preposition *to* with verbs of movement	• Revise to correct verb tense, spelling, and word choice errors • Write a topic sentence

Contents

SKILLS UNITS

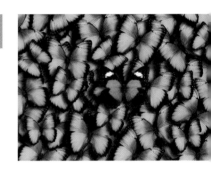

UNIT 3 **Future Food**   39

UNIT 4 **Bright Ideas**   59

UNIT 5　The Sharing Economy   79

UNIT 6　The Volunteer Dilemma   97

Learning Strategies   115

Grammar Guide

Abbreviations Used in the Text	
abbr	abbreviation
adj	adjective
adv	adverb
exp	expression
n	noun
n phr	noun phrase
phr v	phrasal verb
tr	transitive (verb)
v	verb

UNIT 1
Discovering You

Beauty captures the eye, personality captures the heart.

—Anonymous

Like every individual, you are unique with your own complex personality. Your experiences and environment have shaped your personality and attitudes. Your emotional response to situations influences your relationships with others and your personal development. In this unit, you will explore the elements that make up personality and the role that emotions play in contributing to your appreciation of life and of the people around you.

Speaking

A. What kind of person are you? In the table below, write five different adjectives to describe your personality. Think about how you would describe yourself and about how other people might describe you. Use both positive and negative adjectives. Add a brief note to explain why you chose each adjective to describe yourself.

Adjectives	Reasons and examples to support your choice

B. Work with another student to learn about his or her personality. Ask why your partner chose certain adjectives to describe himself or herself.

Form a group of four students and introduce your partner to the group. Remember to explain each of the adjectives used.

EXAMPLE I'd like you to meet Gabrielle. She's very sociable. She loves meeting new people and learning about them. However, she can be too direct and her friends sometimes say she should think before she speaks.

C. Read the list of adjectives in the chart below. With a partner come up with three examples of a behaviour or attitude demonstrated by someone with each trait.

EXAMPLE impatient

How does an *impatient* driver behave? She honks her horn. She speeds up when the traffic light is changing. She makes rude gestures at other drivers.

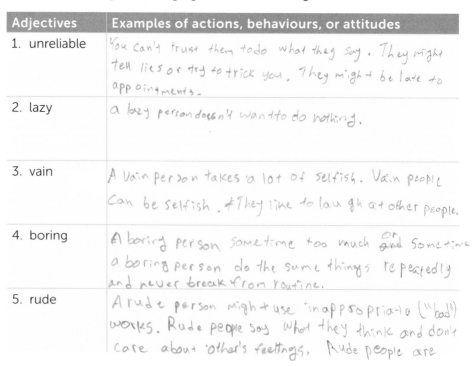

Adjectives	Examples of actions, behaviours, or attitudes
1. unreliable	You can't trust them to do what they say. They might tell lies or try to trick you. They might be late to appointments.
2. lazy	a lazy person doesn't want to do nothing.
3. vain	A vain person takes a lot of selfish. Vain people can be selfish. They like to laugh at other people.
4. boring	A boring person sometime too much and sometime a boring person do the same things repeatedly and never break from routine.
5. rude	A rude person might use inappropriate ("bad") works. Rude people say what they think and don't care about other's feelings. Rude people are

READING

Pre-Reading Activity

How would you describe yourself? Are you a lot like anyone in your family or are you very different? How do your friends and family perceive you?

Discuss the following questions with a partner.

1. What personality traits would you like to have? Why? How could these qualities help you in your personal or professional life, now or in your future?

2. What three adjectives would your friends or family use to describe you? How accurate do you think these observations are? How do you feel about being described that way?

Share your information with another pair of students.

What makes you who you are as a person? There are many ways to categorize personality, but most psychologists have stopped trying to group humanity neatly into types. Instead, they consider personality to include all the individual differences in the ways people tend to think, feel, and behave. Read about personality traits that contribute to your unique nature.

Personality Traits

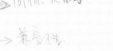

1   Before you can define who you are, you have to understand your personality. Ask yourself some questions, such as "What do I like to do?" or "How do I act in various situations?" When you can answer these questions, you can use the information to discover your personality, and define yourself as an individual.

Types of Personality Traits

2   There are many different personality types, and it is sometimes difficult to classify a person into a single type because there are so many different personality traits you can possess. Personality traits are simply

- actions
- attitudes
- behaviours

Positive Personality Traits

3   Some personality traits are positive. Being honest is one personality trait people should aspire to and one that is appreciated by everyone. It is also important to take responsibility for your actions, have the courage to do what's right in tough situations, and be loyal to your friends and loved ones. Having compassion and understanding will also help you in life. Adaptability and compatibility are great qualities and can help you get along with others, personally and professionally. Finally, having the **drive** to keep going when things are tough, yet showing patience when necessary are also highly positive characteristics.

drive (n) determination

Negative Personality Traits

4   Other personality traits are negative. While it is important to relax and take things easy at times, habitual laziness will prevent you from achieving your goals in life. If you are self-centred, you lack the ability to empathize with

Grammar in Context

Possessive Adjectives

The word highlighted in yellow in paragraph 1 is a possessive adjective.

Possessive adjectives are used to indicate ownership.

I → my

you → your

he → his

she → her

it → its

we → our

you → your

they → their

Possessive adjectives agree with the <u>subject</u>.

<u>Julien</u> gets on well with **his** sister. <u>She</u> likes **her** brother.

Possessive adjectives are invariable.

<u>We</u> are responsible for **our** actions.

Find and highlight five different examples of possessive adjectives in the text.

 To learn more about possessive adjectives, see Grammar Guide page 174.

stingy (adj) cheap or not generous

upbeat (adj) enthusiastic

glare (n) angry look

mood (n) the way a person feels at a particular moment

sulk (v) to keep quiet because you are angry about something

drag on (phr v) to seem long or go slowly

others. Being arrogant and acting superior toward people will not help you make friends either. Similarly, acting thoughtlessly shows that you do not consider other people's feelings and being rude is wholly unnecessary and reveals a very negative character. Finally, even if you do not have much money, being **stingy** is unappealing to others.

5   Here are a few more positive and negative traits to consider.

Positive personality traits	Negative personality traits
• conscientiousness	• dishonesty
• dependability	• possessiveness
• independence	• sarcasm
• intelligence	• irritability
• persistence	• impulsiveness
• competence	• unfriendliness
• confidence	• unreliability
• reliability	• bossiness
• helpfulness	• vulgarity
• imagination	• maliciousness

Determining Personality Types

6   Your personality type can be determined in many ways. You can approach it the scientific way by having a psychologist test and analyze you. A personality test is rather simple. You answer some questions about your likes and dislikes and your goals in life, and a professional can give you a report detailing the type of personality you have.

7   Another way of determining your personality type is to just take a long and deep look at yourself. Asking questions is a great way of discovering who you are. Ask questions like "If a child is hurt and alone, what would I do?" The main thing you want to know is what kind of person you are.

How Do I Create My Personality?

8   Your personality is entirely up to you. It is visible in the actions you take and the decisions you make. Either you are a patient person or not, a responsible person or not. The only way to change your personality is to take active steps to become the person you want to be.

9   Taking up a hobby is a great way to expand your interests and improve your personality. Sports can make you stronger, arts and crafts can make you patient, volunteering can make you more caring. Even reading a book can inspire you to be a better person.

How Can My Personality Affect Others?

10   Being positive and **upbeat** can influence everyone around you, and so can negativity. For example, a friendly smile to a stranger can brighten up their day, as a **glare** can frighten them and cause their **mood** to drop. Remember the famous quote: "Do to others as you would have them do to you."

11   While you may not be able to help it if you are having a bad day or if you don't like doing a particular thing, changing your attitude changes everything. Complaining and **sulking** only makes time **drag on** when doing an unpleasant task. Singing a song in your head or even humming makes it just a little easier to deal with. Being a pleasant person helps every day.

12 Understanding personality traits is a great way to start the journey into self-discovery. If you're **up for** the challenge, you can make positive changes to your personality type.

to be up for (exp) prepared or ready

Comprehension

Answer the following questions. If the answer to a True/False question is False, rewrite the sentence to make it true.

1. What is the main idea of this reading?
   a) Everyone has positive and negative characteristics that are expressed in their actions and attitudes.
   b) To be successful in life, it is important to know yourself and understand your personality.
   c) Understanding yourself, choosing your attitude, and making positive changes are key to personal development. *(circled)*

2. According to the text, what three things combine to make up someone's personality?
   actions, attitudes, behaviours

3. In your own words, give an example from the text of an action, attitude, or behaviour that is positive.
   Courage to do what is right situations and be kind to your friends and loves ones.

4. Find a word in paragraph 3 (positive personality traits) that means *flexibility*.
   adaptability

5. Find a word in paragraph 4 (negative personality traits) that means *think about*.
   consider

6. Describe two different ways you can learn more about your personality. → *have a psychological test and analyse you*
   Answer some questiones about likes or dislikes and your goals in life
   Ask questions is a great way of discovering who you are.

7. Personality cannot be changed. ☐ True ☑ False
   It's can. You can change behaviour (To take active steps

8. "Being positive and upbeat can influence everyone around you, and so can negativity." What supporting details are given to support this point of view?
   Smile to a stranger can brighten up their day. A glare can frighten them and cause their mood to drop.

9. According to the text, what is one example of how changing your attitude can benefit you?
   Singing a song in your head or even humming makes it just a little easier to deal with

10. The text says that a hobby can help develop your personality. Think of a hobby or interest that you have. Explain how this has contributed to your personal development.
    play guitar → make me happy and forget sadness.

Writing

Look back at the chart you completed in the warm up activity on page 2 with adjectives that describe your personality. Are there adjectives from the text you just read that you could now add to that chart to describe your personality more accurately?

Write a paragraph (75–100 words) titled "This Is Me" describing your personality, attitudes, and behaviours. Provide examples to explain your choices. Incorporate some of the new vocabulary you have learned.

EXAMPLE I'm an upbeat person. When I'm faced with a difficult situation, I try to look for the positive side of things and am confident I can find a solution to the problems I'm facing.

VOCABULARY

Cognates and False Cognates

Cognates are words in different languages that have the same origin and a similar meaning (e.g., *société* and *society*). Many English words come from Latin, the same source as most French words. Identifying cognates will help you to understand a text without using a dictionary.

In the first paragraph of the article on page 3, five cognates are underlined. Identify and underline 10 cognates in paragraph 6.

False cognates are words that look or sound similar in different languages, but have a different meaning. *Une librarie* (a bookstore) and *library* (une bibliothèque) are examples of false cognates in French and English.

1. Each of the following sentences has a false cognate. Using a dictionary if necessary, underline the false cognate and write the English word that should be used in the sentence.

    a) Hurry up! The bus won't attend us. _____

    b) The police officer gave the people at the party an advertisement for making too much noise. _____

    c) If you have any questions, you can demand the teacher. _____

    d) The new students seem very sympathetic. _____

    e) I have very sensible skin. _____

2. Now use each of these English words in a sentence that clearly demonstrates the meaning.

    a) attend _____

    b) advertisement _____

    c) demand _____

    d) sympathetic _____

    e) sensible _____

S For tips on how to listen more effectively, see Listening Strategies page 137.

> **Listening Strategy**
>
> Previewing
>
> You can improve your listening skills with practice and some simple strategies.
>
> For example, before you listen, read the comprehension questions and highlight key words. An example is provided in the first comprehension question on page 8. Do the same—highlight key words—for the other questions. This helps prepare your brain to listen for key words and information.
>
> You can also ask yourself what you already know about the subject and predict what information will be given in the listening. Use the questions in the listening introduction to help formulate some ideas and prepare for the activity.

Vocabulary

You will hear each of the following words in bold in the listening.

1. If you're not sure what to do, don't act immediately; **sit on** the problem.

2. He is a very **likeable** person.

3. You should always **take accountability for** your actions.

4. It can be difficult to **navigate** through a crisis.

5. To understand yourself, you need to be **aware** of your emotions.

Using the context provided in the sentences above, match each word with the correct meaning.

	Option 1	Option 2
sit on (exp) _2_	to lower yourself onto a chair	to wait and think before acting
likeable (adj) _2_	generally true	pleasant
take accountability for (exp) _1_	accept responsibility	be willing to pay for
navigate (v) _1_	to work through	to use a map
aware (adj) _1_	conscious of something	know something

Branding Yourself: Emotional Intelligence (5:36) ◀))

Mark Connolly

CBC Edmonton AM

In the previous reading you learned about the importance of attitude and behaviour in influencing and reflecting your personality. What about your emotions? What role do they play in your life? This listening explores how essential emotional reactions are.

Comprehension

Answer the following questions. If the answer to a True/False question is False, rewrite the sentence to make it true.

1. Who first mentioned the topic of emotional intelligence to Lazina Mckenzie?

   _____

2. When did this person talk about the subject?

   _____

3. Everyone can learn interpersonal skills. ☑ True ☐ False

   _____

4. Lazina gives an example to illustrate emotional intelligence in action after a conflict.

   a) What does person A do?

   _____

   b) What does person B do?

   _____

   _____

   _____

5. In discussing high and low emotional intelligence, Lazina refers to a difference in the ability to manage one's own emotions and understand others' emotions, and to move forward from there. ☑ True ☑ False

   _____

6. Lazina suggests questions you can ask yourself to assess and understand your own emotional intelligence in order to improve it. Check all those questions mentioned.

   ☑ How likeable am I?   ☑ How do I deal with conflict?

   ☑ Am I tactful?   ☐ How do others see me?

   ☑ Am I accountable for my actions?   ☐ How do I manage my emotions?

   ☐ How do I deal with other people's emotions?

7. Name five components of communication skills mentioned by Lazina.

   _____

   _____

8. Why is it important to understand what truly motivates you?

   _____

9. What two strategies does Lazina suggest for doing self-analysis of one's emotional intelligence?

   _____

10. How you dress is considered an element of communication. In your own words, explain why and provide two specific examples of how the way someone dressed communicated positively or negatively.

    _____

DISCOVER GRAMMAR

Simple Present and Present Progressive

GG | For more information about the present tenses, see Grammar Guide page 150.

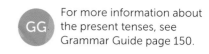

Simple Present

The simple present tense is used

*   to state a fact

    Everyone **experiences** emotions.

*   to describe repeated actions: habits and routines

    I always **cry** when I watch a sad movie.

Key words used with the simple present tense include frequency adverbs such as *always*, *sometimes*, and *never* and expressions of time such as *every day/week/year* or *on Mondays* (referring to every Monday).

Write five to ten questions to learn about a partner's weekly routine. Ask your partner to describe a typical weekday. What time does he or she get up? What does he or she usually eat for breakfast? How does your partner get to college? What classes does he or she have? What does your partner do in the evening?

Present Progressive

The present progressive tense is used

*   to describe actions happening right now

    The teacher is explaining the activity.

*   to talk about actions in a temporary period of time

    She is staying with me while her parents are on vacation.

Key words used with the present progressive tense are words like *right now, at the moment*, and *presently.*

Search online or use your phone or tablet to take a picture of people in a busy place such as the college cafeteria, a shopping mall, or on public transportation. With a partner, describe what people are doing in the photo. Use the simple present and present progressive. Include at least two negative statements.

EXAMPLE   A small group of students at a table are chatting. They seem relaxed and happy but aren't eating very much.

READING

Pre-Reading Activity

Complete the following chart with your own answers. Give details to explain your responses. Then interview two students and note their answers.

Question	You	Student 1	Student 2
What kind of things or events make you happy?	earn more money		
What kind of things or events make you sad?	other people ~~lie~~ lie to me		
When do you get frustrated?	improve English slowly		
What do you do when you are angry?	lose friends accompany me		
Are you an optimist or a pessimist?	It depends.		

involve to the career development in future.

Share your answers with a small group. Are there any items that were mentioned by more than one person?

EXAMPLE Everyone said that they were happy when they spent time with good friends.

Vocabulary

Find the following words in the reading and select the correct meaning according to context.

		Option 1	Option 2
tapestry (n) (para. 2)	1	something made up of many elements ✓	piece of heavy cloth with embroidery or designs
sound (adj) (para. 4)	1	solid, reliable ✓	something that can be heard ✓
regroup (v) (para. 6)	2	form a new group	take time before making another effort ✓
detrimental (adj) (para. 9)	1	damaging, harmful ✓	useful
setback (n) (para. 11)	2	obstacle	temporary problem preventing progress ✓
unsettling (adj) (para. 13)	1	troubling ✓	unbalanced

figurative
literal

Now complete the following sentences using the words from the table above.

1. When people experience a personal ___set back___, they tend to become discouraged.

2. Difficult emotions can be ___unsettling___

3. To appreciate life fully, we must accept the rich ___tapestry___ of emotions and feelings it creates.

4. When you have difficulties, a good friend might offer ___sound___ advice.

5. It is often necessary to take time to ___regroup___ after an emotional event.

6. Suppressing negative feelings can have a ___detrimental___ effect on your health.

Every day, we all experience a range of emotions in our reactions to people, events, and situations. Some of these can be difficult to deal with, but emotions—even negative ones—contribute to our appreciation of life.

What Disney Pixar's Film *Inside Out* Teaches Us about Emotions: Seven Essential Lessons for Embracing Life's Inevitable Highs and Lows

By Kristen Lee

Psychology Today

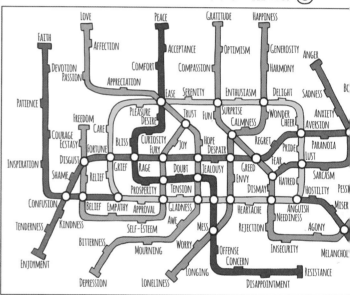

UNDERGROUND MAP OF FEELINGS

1 Disney Pixar's "emotion" picture, *Inside Out* is not only another **endearing** creative masterpiece, it also teaches us some important lessons on the nature of our emotions.

2 It **turns out** that our unique tapestry of emotional responses—whether joy, anger, curiosity, disgust, surprise, sadness, fear, shame, or guilt—all serve a distinctive purpose. Even though we might like to eliminate unfavourable emotions, they serve an important role.

endearing (adj) charming

turn out (phr v) prove to be

flatlined (adj) without variation, <u>not changing</u>

3 The American Psychological Association defines emotion as a "complex feeling state," affecting nearly all facets of our lives." Our responses are influenced by what we perceive to be "personally significant." We experience emotions in a wide variety of ways, according to what stage of life we are in, our unique temperament, and how we view ourselves—and the situations we find ourselves in.

4 *Inside Out*, while appealing largely to a younger audience, offers sound wisdom we can apply to make sense of our emotions—both at work and at home.

5 **Lesson 1: Feelings add colour to our lives.** Life would be boring if our emotions were **flatlined**. We'd lack passion and zest. The wide range of emotions we are capable of experiencing contribute to our human experience and essence: our personality, mood, behaviour, and motivation. Yes, emotions can be raw, messy, and visceral, but they can also be profound, beautiful, and comforting. They all add dimension and flavour.

Grammar in Context

Conjunction: *even though*

We use *even though* to show that one thing is unexpected or surprising, in relation to another thing.

Even though has a similar meaning to *despite* and *in spite of*.

> It is raining. I will go for a walk.
>
> Even though it is raining, I will go for a walk.

Change these sentences by using *even though*.

> Peter is tired. He will go to the party.
>
> Even though Peter _____
>
> She studied hard. She failed the exam.
>
> Even though she _____

Highlight one more example of *even though* in the text.

 For more information on the use of conjunctions, see Grammar Guide page 203.

ride out (phr v) to survive a difficult moment

clobber (v) to hit with force (figurative)

squash (v) to suppress or stop

jump at the chance (exp) seize the opportunity

reckless abandon (n phr) freedom from considering consequences

strive (v) to try very hard

tough pill to swallow (exp) something that is difficult to accept

6 **Lesson 2: We don't always have to think positively.** It's unrealistic to think that we are always going to put an instant positive spin on things. Very often, we may need to pause to think about the situation and work through complex emotions. Our tendency to want a quick fix can help us look for solutions, but it can also be a trap that makes us fight ourselves when we think we "should" have already overcome something and instead find ourselves needing time to regroup and put the pieces together.

7 **Lesson 3: Emotional contrasts are important.** When we've experienced difficult emotions, it can help us appreciate the good moments even more. If we never had to endure rainy days and seasons, we'd have less appreciation for sunny ones once they arrive. In a similar way, it's what makes us enjoy a break after a long and intensive work period.

8 **Lesson 4: Emotional states aren't permanent.** Even though we might think we're forever stuck, feeling states, like weather patterns, are temporary. The winds of change are inevitable. Knowing this can help us learn to appreciate and remember the positive moments and **ride out** the ones that **clobber** us and bring us to our knees.

9 **Lesson 5: Difficult emotions can protect us.** If given the choice to completely **squash** feelings like sadness, rage, and disgust, our first tendency might be to instantly **jump at the chance**. This could be detrimental, because our emotions provide us with all sorts of important information. Our fears or apprehensions often serve us well and prevent us from living with **reckless abandon**.

10 **Lesson 6: Emotions reflect our deeper values and desires.** Feelings reflect what we care about. When we're immersed in sadness or anger during life's changes, it reflects our desire for closeness, connection, and contentment.

11 **Lesson 7: All emotions can be catalysts towards growth.** When we meet a goal or experience success, the energy propels us to keep **striving**. When we make a mistake, or have setbacks, even though it can be a **tough pill to swallow**, the emotions generated can prompt us to take action toward improvement.

12 *Inside Out* provides a poignant reminder that when our emotional responses are strong in one area—whether joy or sorrow, we can't magically switch gears. We also learn that these emotions are intricately connected, and you can't have one without the other.

13 We are inevitably going to have powerful responses to our life circumstances. It takes time and effort to sort out our complex emotions and come to terms with change, loss and stressors. We can't force ourselves to feel a certain way at a given moment, but knowing this can help us remember to make the joyful moments count and recognize that the more unsettling ones can also be useful.

Comprehension

Answer the following questions. If the answer to a True/False question is False, rewrite the sentence to make it true.

1. Which of the following statements best expresses the main idea of the reading?
   a) All emotions, whether positive or negative, are useful if we can learn to accept that the negative ones will pass with time.
   b) Watching the film *Inside Out* is a great way for both children and adults to learn important lessons about emotions.
   c) All the emotions we experience, both positive and negative, contribute to our appreciation of the richness and complexity of life.

2. Find at least three examples the author provides to support the main idea.
   _____
   _____
   _____
   _____

3. Our emotional responses are dependent *only* on our personalities.
   ☐ True   ☑ False
   _____
   _____

4. Why is it not advisable to always think positively?
   Because it's unrealistic
   _____

5. How do difficult emotions protect us?
   Maybe to instantly jump at the chance
   _____

6. How can feeling sad or angry have a positive effect on us?
   Prompt us to take action toward improvement
   _____

7. According to the reading, emotions can . . .

   Check all answers that apply.

   ☑ teach us important lessons   ☐ be switched off
   ☐ be forced   ☑ help us grow
   ☑ require time to be understood   ☑ give us the energy to change

8. Do you agree that even negative emotions like anger or frustration can help us appreciate life more? Why or why not? Explain your answer giving a personal example.
   Yes, I do. Because when the period of frustration in my mind, I feel more happiness when I ride out the
   _____

Participles as Adjectives: -ing or -ed?

The **present participle (-ing)** is used to describe something or someone.

Inside Out is an <u>interesting</u> movie about emotions.

The **past participle (-ed)** is used to describe how people feel about something or someone.

I'm <u>interested</u> in the psychology of emotions.

Choose the correct adjective.

1. Life would be bored/<u>boring</u> without emotions.
2. I'm <u>excited</u>/exciting to learn about the positive role of emotions in our lives.
3. Research on emotional intelligence is very <u>encouraged</u>/encouraging.

PRONUNCIATION

Third Person Singular: -s or -es

When using the third person singular, the verb ends in -s or -es.

Most of these verbs end with an /s/ sound as in *makes* or a /z/ sound as in *defines*.

For verbs that end in -s, -ch, -sh, -x, or -z, add -es and pronounce /iz/ as in *teaches*.

1. Listen to the following verbs and circle the correct pronunciation.

Verb	Sound			Verb	Sound		
a) makes	/s/	/z/	/iz/	f) forces	/s/	/z/	/iz/
b) reflects	/s/	/z/	/iz/	g) propels	/s/	/z/	/iz/
c) misses	/s/	/z/	/iz/	h) feels	/s/	/z/	/iz/
d) grows	/s/	/z/	/iz/	i) provides	/s/	/z/	/iz/
e) protects	/s/	/z/	/iz/	j) wishes	/s/	/z/	/iz/

2. Listen to the following sentences. Fill in the blanks with the word you hear. Circle the sound you hear: /s/, /z/, or /iz/.

a) *Inside Out* _____ emotions using animated characters.   /s/ /z/ /iz/

b) It _____ comedy and profound ideas.   /s/ /z/ /iz/

c) Learning about ourselves _____ us to understand our reactions.   /s/ /z/ /iz/

d) Our personality _____ as we grow older.   /s/ /z/ /iz/

e) It _____ time to understand our personality.   /s/ /z/ /iz/

f) Life _____ us important lessons.   /s/ /z/ /iz/

g) A difficult experience _____ us to reflect and learn from it.   /s/ /z/ /iz/

h) A negative experience also _____ our resilience.   /s/ /z/ /iz/

i) A negative experience also _____ energy for us to change.   /s/ /z/ /iz/

j) A positive attitude _____ in most situations.   /s/ /z/ /iz/

WRITING

> ## Writing Strategy
>
> ### Writing a Paragraph
>
> Each paragraph you write must have
>
> - **one main idea**. For example, you could write a paragraph about how emotions help us appreciate life.
> - **one clear topic sentence**. Usually the first sentence of the paragraph tells your reader what the paragraph will be about. A topic sentence contains a topic and a point of view about that topic (a controlling idea).
>
>   <u>Emotions</u> add colour to our lives.
>   (topic)   (point of view)
>
> - **facts, details, and other information** to support your topic sentence. These can include statistics, examples, citations, research, personal experiences, and more.

 For tips on how to write a well-structured paragraph, see Writing Strategies page 117.

Choose one of the following topics and write a paragraph (75–100 words).

1. Think about a time when your positive attitude in a difficult situation helped you. Describe the situation and how your approach enabled you to resolve it satisfactorily.

2. Everyone makes mistakes. Think of a specific occasion when you made a mistake but were able to learn from it. Describe the situation and explain how you turned it into a positive experience.

WATCHING

Pre-Watching Activity

In "Personality Traits" on page 4, the writer asks: "If a child is hurt and alone, what would you do?" Imagine you saw a small child of about five years old in the park, alone and crying. What would you do and why? Write your answer below.

_____

_____

_____

_____

_____

Share your answer with a partner or a small group. Did you have similar responses? Earlier in the unit, you heard an interview about emotional intelligence. Consider all the different possible reactions to the crying child. Which reaction does your group think demonstrates the highest emotional intelligence? Why?

Vocabulary

Before watching the video, familiarize yourself with the following words and expressions that you will hear.

awareness (n)	knowledge of something's existence
tune in (phr v)	to notice or be aware of something
skill (n)	ability to do something through practice or training
get ahead (phr v)	make progress
deal with (phr v)	manage
mindfulness (n)	being aware of and focused on the present and accepting how you are feeling

Now complete the following sentences with the vocabulary above.

1. Being emotionally intelligent can help you __*get ahead*__ in life.

2. You can improve your relationships if you __*tune in*__ to other people's feelings.

3. Emotional intelligence is a __*skill*__ you can develop.

4. __*Mindfulness*__ means focusing on the moment and paying attention to your thoughts.

5. We need to __*deal with*__ our emotions to manage conflict.

6. __*Awareness*__ of your feelings is the key to emotional intelligence.

Emotional Intelligence (6:01) ▶

Let's Talk Live

Emotional intelligence (EI) can be defined as the ability to understand and manage your emotions and other people's emotions. We can't stop ourselves from feeling emotions but when we are aware of how we feel, we can choose how to respond to those feelings. That sensitivity is important to developing positive relationships. In this video, you will learn about the different elements of emotional intelligence and the important role EI plays in our lives.

Before watching the video, read the questions and highlight the key words as shown in the first question. This will help prepare you to answer the comprehension questions.

Comprehension

Answer the following questions in your own words. If the answer to a True/False question is False, rewrite the sentence to make it true.

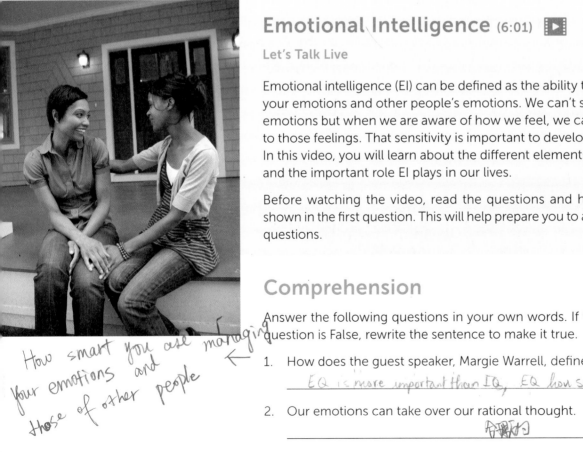

How smart you are managing your emotions and those of other people

1. How does the guest speaker, Margie Warrell, define emotional intelligence?
   *EQ is more important than IQ, EQ how smart you are how to deal with other relationships*

2. Our emotions can take over our rational thought. ☐ True ☐ False
   _____

3. Fill in the blank. Our emotional intelligence _Get better_ as we get older.

4. In which decade did Daniel Goleman pioneer research into emotional intelligence and develop the EI matrix?

   ☐ the 1960s   ☐ the 1980s   ☑ the 1990s

5. What does Warrell say is at the core of emotional intelligence?

   awareness

6. Which of the following ideas are mentioned in the video? Check all that apply.

   ☐ We can choose which emotions we experience.

   ☑ We can develop our emotional intelligence by becoming more aware of how people relate to us.

   ☑ Trying to understand others' reactions can help us better understand them.

   ☐ Your emotional intelligence depends on your personality.

   ☑ Recognizing negative patterns in our lives can motivate us to make changes.

7. What two questions can people ask themselves to become more aware of their feelings in the moment?

   what am I feeling
   what am I thinking

8. Complete the sentence. Being more emotionally intelligent can help people...

   understand each other / relationship

   work together better

9. Name two situations mentioned that could motivate people to examine their reactions and behaviour.

   _____

   _____

   _____

10. Think of a situation in which you experienced conflict. What was the problem? How could you or the other person have reacted differently? Write two to three sentences explaining the situation and a possible solution to the problem.

    understanding, respect

    _____

    _____

Emotional Intelligence Matrix

Self-Awareness	Social Awareness
Emotional Intelligence (EI)	
Self-Management	Relationship Management

SPEAKING

Choose one of the following activities.

Option 1

In a small group, develop three different responses for each of the following situations. Only one of the options should demonstrate a highly emotionally intelligent response. Individually, interview five students from other groups, asking them which of your three options they prefer and record their responses. Return to your original group and discuss the responses.

1. Two of your good friends have had an argument and are not speaking to each other. How can you help resolve the situation?

2. You have a team project that is worth 25 percent of your grade. One team member is not doing his or her share of the work. How can you resolve the problem?

3. Your best friend just broke up with his or her partner. How can you help your friend feel better?

4. You worked hard on an assignment but got a bad grade. What do you do?

Option 2

1. Complete the emotional intelligence quiz below on your own.

2. Then interview a partner. Make note of your partner's overall score in the quiz, then ask your partner to explain his or her ratings by giving examples. You might ask questions such as "Why did you circle '5' for question 1? Can you give me an example?" Summarize the answers in the chart below.

	Rating	Partner's answer and explanation
Awareness		
Identification		
Acceptance		
Expression		
Release		
Replace		
Rejoice		

3. Introduce your partner to a small group. As you describe your partner, refer to the quiz results and your partner's explanations.

Test Your Emotional Intelligence

How well do you deal with your feelings and emotions? Rate yourself between 1 and 5 in each of the following seven areas.

```
1                         3                         5
├────────────┼────────────┼────────────┼────────────┤
not at all              so-so            totally and completely
```

1. Awareness 5   1   2   ③   4   5
When your body feels something (fear, anger, sadness, shame, guilt, etc.), how much do you notice and affirm your feelings?

2. Identification 4   1   2   3   ④   5
When you notice that you're feeling something, how well can you identify or name the feeling you are having? How well can you separate them (for example, fear and anger)?

3. Acceptance 2   1   2   3   ④   5
How okay are you with feeling mad, or sad, or afraid?

4. Expression 3   1   2   3   ④   5
How well do you express your feelings and let them out, as opposed to bottling them up inside?

5. Release 2   1   2   3   ④   5
When your body experiences a negative feeling, how well can you let go of that feeling and let it dissipate?

6. Replace ~~5~~

How skilled are you at replacing negative feelings (anger, sadness, grief) with more positive ones (love, joy, peace)?

1 2 3 4 (5)

7. Rejoice! 4

How well do you encourage and respect your feelings, complimenting yourself for your awareness and expression?

1 2 3 4 (5)

Scoring

Add up your seven answers to this emotional intelligence test. If your score was between

25–35 Excellent You are fully aware of what's happening inside you. Congratulations! My guess is that you are pretty darned happy, in general.

15–25 So-So There's still plenty to learn. There's a whole world inside you that you may not be fully aware of or have access to. Do some work in this area and you will find more colour, life, and depth to your life!

0–15 Yikes! You're clueless, and probably in pain! Get help, fast.

REVISING AND EDITING

1. Underline and correct eight errors in the present tense.

    My best friend think<u>s</u> that I am more sociable than she is. When I <u>be</u> with new *am* people, I want to <u>learn</u> about them and discover who they <u>is</u>, but she <u>don't</u> like *are* to be in large groups of people and doesn't feel comfortable when she <u>talks</u> to strangers. She doesn't <u>feels</u> at ease. My mother <u>say</u> that I am too exuberant *says* and I <u>not</u> always listen well to others.   *do*

2. Underline and correct six errors in possessive adjectives.

    <u>Ours</u> actions and attitudes reveal a lot about our personality. For example, when my brother, Thomas, talks to <u>her</u> girlfriend, Maria, after a bad day at college, she doesn't listen to <u>her</u> stories—she is too busy on <u>his</u> phone texting <u>hers</u> friends *his* *her* about <u>theirs</u> plans for the weekend. I think that <u>she</u> is very disrespectful.

CONSOLIDATING

Writing

Write a short paragraph (100–125 words) to answer one of the following questions.

1. Describe your best friend or someone who is close to you. Include information about that person's personality, life, routines, likes, and dislikes. Pay attention to your use of possessive adjectives, adjectives, and the simple present tense.

2. Find a short personality test online and complete it. Is its description of your personality accurate? Are there any surprising results? Compare the results with your perception of your personality and summarize your conclusions.

    EXAMPLE The test says that I'm confident, but it depends on the situation. When I know people well or know the subject I'm talking about, I am confident, but if I don't, I am unsure of myself.

3. Choose your own answers to one or more of the quiz questions you've seen in this unit and give details of a personal experience that illustrates your answer.

> **EXAMPLE** When I feel angry or frustrated, I always do some physical activity like going for a run. This helps calm me down so I can work through the situation rationally.

Watching

Search online for a short video showing a scene from a movie that demonstrates either high or low emotional intelligence.

a) Write down the URL and the date you retrieved the video.

b) Write a brief summary of the clip and explain how the characters demonstrated either high or low emotional intelligence.

Vocabulary

Complete one of the following activities.

1. Choose five vocabulary words from the unit that you consider important. For each, write a definition in your own words. Then, use each word in a sentence that clearly demonstrates the meaning. You may also include a translation of each word.

2. Complete the following sentences using these vocabulary words from the unit.

    self-centred (adj)   mood (n)   aware (adj)   skill (n)   get along (v)

    a) It is important to be ____aware____ of your emotions.

    b) You can control your ____mood____ and not let it affect you.

    c) If you are ____self-centred____ you will not take others into consideration.

    d) Emotional intelligence will enable you to ____get long____ with others.

    e) Understanding your emotions is an important ____skill____ to develop.

Speaking

Choose one of the following activities and prepare a short oral presentation (3-4 minutes). Pay attention to your use of the simple present and present progressive.

1. Self-awareness is an important element of emotional intelligence. We can't help how we feel, but we can choose how to manage our emotions. Think of a typical situation that triggers a strong emotional reaction in you. Explain the context where you experience this reaction, how you feel at that moment, and what you do in these circumstances. Does the way you handle your reaction demonstrate high emotional intelligence? Would you like to behave differently next time you are in this situation?

2. How does your personality affect others? Are there aspects of your personality that you would like to improve, develop, or change? Why do you want to address this? How would changing this help you in your life? Explain which personality trait you believe requires development and describe the positive effect this could have.

UNIT 2
Express Yourself

Imagination is more important than knowledge. Knowledge is limited. Imagination encircles the world.

—Albert Einstein

What is the importance of the arts? What role does music play in contributing to our well-being? Is everyone creative in some way? Is it important to be able to express yourself in a creative way? How can music and art help us deal with difficult emotions? In this unit, you will learn about the many ways in which the arts enrich our lives.

Speaking

A. Complete the chart with your own answers. Give details to explain your responses. Then interview two other students and note their answers.

Question	You	Student 1	Student 2
How did you feel about studying art or music in school? What did you enjoy?	I have good feel about art because I am interested in learning art design/painting and singer	sueing /painting my emotional	Riko Technology /art painting
Why do you think it is considered important to have arts education in schools?	good job/good oportunely learning academik	motivation and creative.	actor, actoris painting /profosore
What creative activities do you like doing?	painting /cooking		painting landscape
What benefits do you get from your favourite creative activity?	good feeling		peaceful/pay attention

Share the results from your interviews with a small group or with the class.

B. Complete the following exercise with a partner. First, add the missing word (*do*, *don't*, *does*, *is*, or *are*) to form questions. Then use the questions to interview your partner and write his or her answers in the space provided. The first question is done as an example.

1. What kind of music ____do____ you like best? _____

2. _____ there any styles of music you don't like? Why _____ you like them?

   _____

   _____

3. _____ music help you study? Why or why not?

   _____

   _____

4. _____ there a specific song that evokes strong memories? What _____ the song? What memories _____ it bring back for you?

   _____

   _____

5. How _do____ you think music can help us in our lives?

   _____

   _____

Introduce your partner to another pair of students. Use your partner's interview responses to prepare your introduction. Remember to pronounce the final -s or -es.

EXAMPLE   Laurence love**s** hip-hop music and she listen**s** to it all the time.

READING

Reading Strategy

Using Context

Often you can determine the meaning of a word just from the context. Use these tips to help you.

Identify the part of speech: is the word a noun, a verb, or an adjective?

> It was a complicated <u>process</u>.
>
> The word *process* is a noun.

Does the word have a prefix, a suffix, or a root that can help you understand?

> Many people <u>under</u>estimate their creative abilities.
>
> The prefix *under* means *below* or *not enough*.

Is the word a cognate?

> Most artists have a unique and personal approach to creativity.
>
> This sentence has five cognates: *artists*, *unique*, *personal*, *approach*, and *creativity*.

Analyze the whole sentence in which the word appears. That will give you clues about what the word means.

Read the following paragraph with a partner. Use context to determine the meanings of the words in bold.

> Artists find inspiration everywhere, yet all have suffered through that **dreaded** moment when they have no inspiration, when their creative spirit **eludes** them. At the beginning of a project, writers fear the **blank** page when they sit down at their desks, while painters stare at the **blank canvas**. Songwriters listen **intently** to conversations to help them find the missing word for their **lyrics**, and photographers explore countless options before they find the perfect approach to capturing their subject. Sooner or later, they will **overcome** the obstacles to their artistic expression and get back into the creative flow.

dreaded _____	intently _____
eludes _____	lyrics _____
blank _____	overcome _____

Vocabulary in Action

To Listen To

In English, the verb *to listen* is followed by the preposition *to*.

> We all listen **to** music.

Try using word association: just remember that you have **two** ears!

S   For tips on how to read more effectively, see Reading Strategies page 134.

Vocabulary

With a partner, use context clues to help you determine the meaning of these words in the reading below.

boost (para. 2) _____

soothe (para. 8) _____

deal with (para. 8) _____

get (something) (para. 10) _____

engage (para. 10) _____

Whatever your personal taste in music, it is a language we all understand. Music expresses what we cannot say, fires our imagination, soothes our bodies, and feeds our souls. Read the following text to learn how music does all of this and why it is a universal art.

enhanced (v) improved

shiver (n) shaking or trembling movement

Seven Incredible Ways Music Helps You Process Emotions

By Bill Protzmann

1   Music is medicine.

2   Scientists call it "anecdotal evidence," but you hear the stories all the time: classical music makes you smarter; distance runners use music for **enhanced** endurance; some songs boost your happiness. Others just put you in the mood.

3   We know music is powerful, but let's leave the "why" aside for a moment. Here are seven ways music rocks your world.

1. It Makes You Fall in Love

4   Admit it—some music reaches right into your heart and unlocks all the beauty of being in love whenever you hear it. Scientists talk about dopamine and neurotransmitters, but let's keep it simple: don't you really enjoy the hope you feel in your heart and the **shivers** you feel down your spine when you hear a favourite love song?

5   These tremors are actually very health-giving in ways science is just beginning to understand (for things like releasing traumatic memory, etc.). You experience them when you listen to your favourite love song, use them to light up your heart and possibly heal it, too.

2. It Makes You Work Harder and Push Further

6   There's a reason that your endurance improves when you work out to music— and you already know that. Runners find their second wind when just the right song comes on. Adding music to your workout helps keep the part of you that wants to stop from being quite so persistent. When a great song boosts your motivation, you can go farther with less effort.

3. It Helps You Grieve

7 It's not self-indulgent to use sad music to help you let a few tears out. Just like the soundtrack you use for exercise, the songs you play to support your grief help you navigate the intensity of your sadness. Rather than holding it all inside, it's better to let it out and feel it fully.

4. It Reduces Physical Pain

8 Sometimes it seems **counterintuitive** to play music when you're in pain, but we still do it. My daughter had a number of reconstructive surgeries when she was very young, and she started asking for a CD player and headphones during recovery. Science understands that music soothes the mind and helps the body deal with pain better. But you probably already knew that on an intuitive level.

5. It Fuels (or Calms) Your Anger

9 There's a lot of angry music in the world. Why? Because, like sadness, music is a safe way for us to feel that emotion and let go of it! It's unsafe to rage on the road or with a loaded weapon, but music can enhance and then release feelings of anger in a safe way so you can work your way through it.

6. It Energizes Your Brain

10 If you like listening to a new genre of music that's not your usual choice—like classical music—you already get this. Taking time to explore something new is a great way to engage the part of your brain that science says we don't use much.

7. It Just Makes You Feel Happy

11 Whether it's a football fight song or your private feel-good playlist, you know how it feels to turn your joy music on, right? Like a movie without a soundtrack, turn off the music and life falls flat. Our human systems—especially the happy ones!—really love to punctuate great life moments with great music.

Now, Here's WHY Music Does All of That

12 We humans are vibratory beings. Atoms, cells, molecules, organs—everything about us and about our universe—vibrates. We hear and make vibrations when we listen and speak. We see vibration as colour. With every beat, our hearts make individual rhythms for us. Here's the **juicy** part: humans have a natural inclination to synchronize our music to what our body, brain, and heart need, and when we do, things can really feel better—fast!

13 So, what's the best music for you to use? You already know this—your best music is the music you already love. Play around with it. Pay attention and start to notice how each of "your" songs makes you feel. Do you speed up? Become thoughtful? Feel happy? Cry? Relax? It's good to know exactly which of your tunes works best for each activity in your day, and then queue them up accordingly to support that activity. (Even if it's an unpleasant one!)

14 Be gentle with yourself. We all have feelings that don't feel good. You'll find that music resonates with each feeling uniquely, allowing those feelings to move through you and leave you. But sometimes, those feelings and emotions need a little help. So **curate** your soundtrack to lead you through the entire emotional journey. Not just the feeling you have now, but the one you want to end up feeling.

Grammar in Context
Homophones

Homophones are words that sound the same but have different meanings. An example—*your* and *you're*—is highlighted in the text.

Your is a possessive adjective. *You're* is a contraction of *you are.*

> Music reaches right into **your** heart.

> The music you listen to can affect how **you're** (you are) feeling.

Underline the correct option in the following sentences.

1. Music has the ability to accentuate you're/your feelings.
2. When you're/your feeling down, your/you're favourite track can lift your spirits.

GG For more information about possessive adjectives, see Grammar Guide page 172.

GG For more examples of contractions see Grammar Guide, pages 162, 176, 207.

counterintuitive (adj) against what seems to be common sense

juicy (adj) interesting

curate (v) to choose and organize items for a collection

Comprehension

Answer the following questions. If the answer to a True/False question is False, rewrite the sentence to make it true.

1. What is the main idea of this reading?
   - ✓ a) Listening to music has several physical and emotional benefits.
   - b) Scientists have done a number of important studies on music therapy.
   - c) There is a type of music for every feeling.

2. How does music contribute to well-being in each of the following areas? Summarize the information from the text in your own words.

Love	it brings a new shiver in your spine that beggining when you hear the love song. There are dopamine and neurotrasmitters.
Exercise	when you do the workout same as running, you use to hear a song that boosks your motivation
Grief	when you hear a song, you can navigate your sadness and let it out for having good feel
Pain	The song sbothes you body, and you can have better feeling about your pain in your body
Negative emotions	when you hear anger musice, you can reach to clam and helps you have better feeling.
Brain activity	when you hear new music that doesn't your usual choice, you use the part of your brain that don't our
Happiness	our Human systems work with great musice to make happy.

3. Which one of these effects do you find the most interesting? Why? Explain your answer.

   I interested in brain activity because it can us to be young and make new idea about anything that don't think about it before.

4. According to the article, why does music help us?

   Because music is same as a medicine, and it can help on our Human systems. There are dopamine and neurotrasmitter to help us.

5. According to the reading, different types of music can enhance our feelings but cannot change our mood. ☐ True ☑ False

   They can change our mood with their effortion, neurotrasmitters.

6. Do you agree that music contributes to our well-being in different ways? Do you think that music can change your mood? For each question, give two specific examples from your personal experience to support your opinion.

   yes, when I'm sad and angry, the music helps me have better feeling and sometime the music helps me to remmeber especific old memories, so I can soothe my to solve my problems in here.

DISCOVER GRAMMAR

Simple Past and Past Progressive

 To learn more about the simple past and past progressive, see Grammar Guide pages 157–161.

Simple Past

Use the simple past to talk about something that happened in the past and is now finished.

> I **went** to a fantastic concert last summer at Osheaga. My boyfriend and I **arrived** early and **met** our friends. We then **waited** patiently until our favourite group **came** on.

Read the following paragraph and underline all simple past tense verbs.

> Last summer, I went to New York with my family to see *Hamilton* on Broadway. I'm not crazy about musicals, but I heard that the show was totally unique, so I agreed to go. I'm so glad I did because it was incredible! It's the story of Alexander Hamilton, an immigrant who became one of the Founding Fathers of the United States. I learned a lot about American history and loved the hip-hop–inspired music so much that I bought the soundtrack. It was the best show I've ever seen.

Past Progressive

use before

Use the past progressive to explain that the action was in progress at a specific moment or time in the past.

> During the break, some students **were chatting** while others **were checking** their phones when the fire alarm went off.

Use the past progressive tense to answer these questions.

1. What were you doing at 9:00 last night?

    _____

2. What was your family doing when you got home yesterday?

    _____

3. What were you doing when the teacher arrived in class today?

    _____

4. What was the weather like when you woke up this morning?

    _____

PRONUNCIATION

Endings: -ed

Regular past tense verbs end in -ed, but not all are pronounced the same way.

When verbs end in -p, -s, -k, -f, -x, -ch, or -sh, the -ed is pronounced /t/.

> fixed, kissed

When verbs end in a -t or -d, the -ed is pronounced /id/.

> tweeted, depended

For all other verbs, the -ed is pronounced /d/.

> smiled, danced

Listen to the recorded words and write the verb you hear in the correct column.

/d/	/t/	/id/

WATCHING

Pre-Watching Activity

In the previous reading, you learned about the ways in which music influences our emotions and well-being. Have you heard of music therapy? Who do you think could benefit from music therapy? In what ways might it help? With a partner, brainstorm some ideas below. Then share your ideas with the class.

People: _____

_____

Benefits: _____

_____

Henry Responds to Music from His Era (6:29)

Alive Inside

What if there was a way to help you connect and communicate with others when you seemed to have lost that ability? In fact, music does have that kind of power. Watch this video to learn about the transformational effect that music has on elderly patients living with Alzheimer's, helping them to interact with others and rediscover themselves.

Before watching the video, read the questions and highlight the key words. This will help prepare you to answer the comprehension questions.

Comprehension

Answer the following questions. If the answer to a True/False question is False, rewrite the sentence to make it true.

1. What is the main idea of this video?
   - ✓ a) Music helps people with Alzheimer's to reconnect with their emotions and to express themselves.
   - b) Elderly patients with Alzheimer's remember their younger days when they listen to their favourite music.
   - c) Music is a powerful tool that evokes strong emotions.

2. Yvonne Russell, the therapist, explains what happened when an elderly woman was given an iPod. What effect did listening to music have on her?
   shaking her head, hands

3. How does Henry's daughter describe her father when he was younger?
   He was amazing person

4. What is one specific memory she has of her father?
   He always listen music, dance, slumming, jumping, He and her brother sing together, falling in love with her every ___ singing in rainging/ walking on street

5. Give three adjectives that Dr. Sacks uses to describe Henry without music.
   make ① depress and ② n alive. ① under live ③ unresponsive

6. Name four physical effects that music has on Henry.
   eyes waid / animaitioned, move his arms / open aid

7. The positive effects only last while Henry is listening to music.
   ☐ True ☑ False
   He has good reaction when he listen music

8. Henry says he is __crazy__ about music.

9. What does Henry say music does to him?
   I don't have long mean. beautiful music and sorand like music and danc Cat Cale wy. you can brand   *falling in love*

10. In what way does Dr. Sacks believe music can help people like Henry?
    remmer who is, he is identity power music helping organazi /brain idcntity, interut story

11. Why do you think that many people suffering from Alzheimer's connect so strongly to music?
    because they remmebre their younge days and when I listen to favorinet music they can connect with their past and they find good feeling about themselves.

Prince performs during half-time at the Super Bowl in Miami

S For tips on how to generate ideas, formulate a clear topic sentence, and find supporting details, see Writing Strategies on page 116.

Writing

Think of a particular song that evokes strong memories for you. Write a paragraph (75 words) to explain what the song is and describe the memories you have when you hear that music. Where were you? What were you doing? Who were you with? How did you feel?

Start with a clear topic sentence and provide at least two supporting details in your paragraph.

SPEAKING

Work with a partner or small group to answer the following questions.

- How do you define *creative*?
- Are artists the only creative people?
- Give at least two examples of well-known people you consider creative. Why do you consider them creative?
- Can anyone be creative? Why or why not?
- Do you think you are creative? Why or why not?

Share your ideas with the class.

READING

Pre-Reading Activity

Working on your own, complete the following tasks in five minutes.

1. Describe five unusual uses for a paperclip?

   _____

   _____

   _____

   _____

   _____

   _____

   _____

2. Incorporate this shape into a few different drawings.

3. Write down a series of words, each one associated with the one before it.

   EXAMPLE   concert–music–summer–park–picnics

   blue - _____ - _____ - _____ - _____ - _____

Share your ideas for each task in a small group. Were any of your ideas similar?

Vocabulary

Use context clues to help you find the following:

1. A word that means *prove wrong* ~~assume~~ (para. 5) debunk
2. A two-word synonym for *writes* jot down (para. 6)
3. A word that means *difficult or unpleasant work* grind (para. 7) (a)
4. A word that means *effort or project* endeavour (para. 8)
5. A word that means *place and time* setting (para. 9)
6. A word that means to have made something seem more important than it really is _____ (para. 10)

It is true that some people have a natural talent for art, music, or other creative pursuits, but all of us have a creative side to our personalities that can be developed if we wish. You can learn to nurture your creativity and express yourself more fully.

Yes, Creativity Can Be Taught

By Neil Wadhwa
FreshGigs.ca

1. Creativity is a curious thing. It's a quality that some people just seem to have, while others **sigh** in discontent and express out loud, "I wish I were more creative." But those who do appear creative, and who work in creative fields, don't wish—they *do*. Every artist, every photographer, every chef, every writer had (and has) to put in thousands of hours of hard work to make a living out of their creative passions. Working in a creative field doesn't happen out of nowhere—like any other job or hobby, it requires training, education, application, and, of course, <u>deep-rooted</u> interest.

2. If you've ever wished to become more creative, here's what you need to know: creativity isn't in a <u>safe</u> that only a select few people know the <u>combination</u> to. Yes, creativity can be taught.

3. "Creativity isn't <u>elitist</u>. It's not just for 'special people.' Creativity is a <u>learnable</u> skill, and something that anyone who is willing to invest the time can achieve. You can learn to speak French. You can learn to drive a car," says David Usher, musician and author of *Let the Elephants Run*.

4. "You can also learn the steps of the creative process and creative thinking. It really is no different. Some will be more naturally <u>talented</u> at specific creative disciplines than others, but determination and **grit** mean as much, if not more, than natural talent."

sigh (v) let out a long breath to show you are tired, disappointed, or sad

grit (n) willingness to persevere or to work hard at something

struck with an idea (exp) suddenly have an idea

flash (n) sudden moment

divine anointment (n phr) a gift from God

Grammar in Context

Gerund as Subject

The gerund (-ing) form of a verb can be used as a subject to begin a sentence.

Painting can be a very rewarding pastime.
Not ~~To paint~~ can be . . .

Practising every day will help develop your creative skills.
Not ~~To practice~~ every day . . .

1. Find and highlight an example of a gerund used as a subject in the reading.
2. Write three sentences beginning with a gerund about activities that you enjoy.

Dancing is my favourite way to reduce stress.

GG For more information about gerunds, see Grammar Guide page 210.

main idea = Being creative doesn't depend on having a special envirment to work clogn in.

5 A lot of the confusion surrounding creativity has to do with myths that people (those who don't consider themselves to be creative) assume are true. Let's debunk a few myths here:

Prove that something isn't true

something that isn't true maybe people belive it

take something as the truth without questioning or checing first

Creative People Work Only When Inspiration Strikes

6 While creative people do get **struck with an idea** that can turn into something meaningful, the fact is that if everybody were to wait for a moment of inspiration to strike before working on something, nothing would ever get done. The writer puts pen to paper and jots down 5000 words a day (for example) even if feeling uninspired because that's what a writer does. It's work, just like any other job or profession.

7 The idea that creative people are creative simply because they get these **flashes** of inspiration—and that separates creative people from everyone else—is simply not true. You don't have to wait for anything, and if you have a willingness to learn about a particular subject or interest, you can take a class, view online tutorials, and simply teach yourself, and then get in the habit of practise, practise, practise. "It's easier to believe in **divine anointment** than in the endless grind. It's easier to believe in talent than in work and discipline," says David. "Want to be really good at playing the piano? Try practising every day, for four hours a day, and then do that for four years."

Creative People Have the Time to Be Creative

8 Being creative isn't an exclusive trait. If you're an accountant and work at a desk all day, it doesn't mean that you can't use your evenings and weekends to learn and practise your creative endeavours. Like everybody else, those working in creative fields have their own friends, family, commitments, obligations, client expectations, and more. Creatives experience days full of interruptions and days where nothing seems to be working. In short, creative people don't have empty schedules and endless amounts of time to simply be creative. Creativity can be taught, and if you want to learn, you can use the time you have available—even if it's just 10 minutes a day—to get started.

Creative People Work in Isolation

9 Somewhere along the line, people got the idea that writers live in cabins in the woods, isolated in the middle of nowhere, working away with a bottle of scotch nearby. It sounds idyllic, but the truth is that creative people can't wait for the perfect settings to appear before getting work done. If you want to paint, you need paint, a paintbrush, and a canvas—everything else is secondary.

10 If you think you can't be taught creativity, maybe it's because you've built up an idea of where creativity should take place in your mind—knock that down, the perfect settings for you to learn creative skills are all around you.

Comprehension

Answer the following questions. If the answer to a True/False question is False, rewrite the sentence to make it true.

1. What is the main idea of this reading?
   a) Anyone can be creative if they can find their inspiration.
   b) There are many biased myths about creative people.
   ✓c) Developing your creativity requires hard work and dedication.

2. What is the major difference between people who are creative and those who wish they were?

Work on it!, They were creative people "don't wish -they do: they put in a lot of hard work to get the job done.

3. According to the text, which of the following do you need to be creative? Check all answers that apply.

☐ natural talent ☑ interest ☐ the right place

☑ hard work ☑ inspiration ☑ willingness to learn

☐ lots of time ☑ dedication ☐ lots of money

4. Natural talent alone determines your creativity. ☐ True ☑ False

Hard work, dedication, and interest are more important.

5. What can someone do to improve their creative spirit?

Practise

6. Why is practice important in the creative process?

Practice helps improve us. You will only get better with practice.

7. Creative people have more time to be creative than other people. ☐ True ☑ False

They make the time for what they need to do.

8. Do you agree that anyone can learn to be creative? Why or why not? Explain your answer by making explicit reference to your own experience.

Yes, anyone can learn to be creative. The ~~more you~~ only way to become a better writer, for example, is to write a lot.

9. In another interview, David Usher says that you never see an elementary school class where two children are drawing and 22 others are just watching them and asking themselves why they are not creative. Most children embrace being creative while many adults say that they are not creative. What do you think happens between childhood and adulthood? Why do you think people lose that creative spark?

Children are more creative than adults because they don't place any limits on themselves.

Writing

Write a paragraph (100–125 words) about one of the following:

- your own creative activities. Perhaps you compose or play music, draw or paint, make videos, write, or do crafts. Explain what inspires you and what doing this brings to you personally.
- a well-known creative person. Explain where this person finds inspiration, what medium he or she uses to express a message, and describe his or her contribution to our world.

Remember to include a clear topic sentence and at least two supporting details.

LISTENING

Pre-Listening Activity

What are some sources of stress for students? What effects does stress have on people?

With a partner, brainstorm ideas below.

Sources of stress	Negative effects
Studying in diffrent language	you are understanding. you might fail – can't communicate
tution	you can't go throw your study program
Grade	you can't pass the level and go to next one.

Write a few sentences describing what you do to reduce or manage feelings of stress.

EXAMPLE   Whenever things get too much—school, work, whatever—I just go down to the basement, take out the drum kit and play until my arms hurt. It always works!

I get stressed about exams, so the best solution for me is to put on my favourite music and go for a run. It really clears my mind and I always feel calm after.

Share your ideas in a small group or with the class.

Vocabulary

You will hear each of the following words in bold in the listening.

Before listening, use the sentence context to determine the meaning of each word or phrase in bold.

1. Kallie Berens offers art therapy to provide an **outlet** for students dealing with stress.
   escape / release

2. Students have many **commitments**: they have to study, work, organize their time, and pay for school.
   Obligation / things you have to do

3. When people are stressed, they should **take a step back** and try to work through what they are feeling.
   Stop what they are doing and relax

4. When you are stressed, it's hard to get any work done as your concentration can be **shot**.

destroyed, ruined

5. Art therapy can help students **let out** their negative feelings.

release / express

Laurentian Students Check Out Art Therapy (5:29) 🔊

Jason Turnbull

CBC Points North

All students experience stress, but one student from Laurentian University in Sudbury, Ontario, decided to take action and develop an arts workshop to help students deal with stress in a positive way.

Before you listen to the clip, read the comprehension questions and highlight key words. This will help you anticipate the content of the listening and improve your comprehension.

Comprehension

Answer the following questions. If the answer to a True/False question is False, rewrite the sentence to make it true.

1. What is the main idea of this listening?
    a) Even if they are not creative, students can reduce their stress by doing art therapy.
    b) Students face a great deal of stress for different reasons, and art therapy can help them.
    c) Art therapy is a fun and effective way to reduce stress.

2. What does Kallie Berens ask the students to paint?

good dream / great dream

3. Why did she choose to offer art therapy sessions for students? Give three reasons.

relax (leave stress)   connect to yourself
anxious / anxiety —   She lives art

4. Studies show that students are more stressed these days than in the past.

☑ True ☐ False

5. What role does art play in reducing stress? _distraction_

6. Students have a feeling of _accomplishment_ when they have finished a creation.

Don't sweat the small stuff

7. Kallie Berens has difficulty dealing with _____anxiety_____, which affects her concentration.

8. How does painting help her? Name two ways. _____
   Concentrate
   put things in perspective (3次)

9. According to Lara Gardner, creating something has several benefits. Name two.
   Connect with each other
   express themselves

10. What do you believe are the benefits of creating something?

   _____

   _____

   _____

   _____

Speaking

In a small group, brainstorm some fun, simple, and practical ideas your college could adopt to help students combat stress at exam time.

Select your best idea and develop an oral presentation you could give to your college administration, student association, or program director.

Include the following information:

- the proposed activity
- the benefits for students
- equipment required (venue, supplies, etc.)
- financial resources required

Share your idea with the class.

REVISING AND EDITING

Underline and correct 10 errors in the simple past and past progressive tenses.

Tom Thomson (1877–1917)

Tom Thomson's landscape oil paintings reflect iconic images of Northern Ontario. When Thomson taked his first visit to Algonquin Park in 1912, he felt in love with the beauty around him. He beginned to paint scenes from the park, and often disappear for days to paint a beautiful scene. He was sketching mostly in the spring or summer, then return to Toronto where he worked his sketches into larger paintings. After late 1915, Thomson paint landscapes from memory in his Toronto studio. The National Gallery of Canada owns many of Thomson's sketches, as well as the larger paintings he maked from them. Thomson was drowning in Canoe Lake in 1917. At the time, many people were believing he was murdered, but the official report said that it was an accidental death while he canoed.

CONSOLIDATING

Reading

Find an article about a visual artist you consider to be particularly creative. It can be a painter, architect, photographer, designer, or anyone involved in the creative sphere in some way.

a) Print or photocopy the article. Write down the source and date you retrieved the article.

b) Copy or print an image, or images, of the artist's work to show the class or a small group. You could also bring a book or magazine.

c) Highlight 10 key words and write your own English definition of each word.

d) Prepare a short oral presentation (3–4 minutes) about the artist and his or her work for the class or your small group.

Speaking

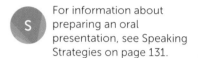

For information about preparing an oral presentation, see Speaking Strategies on page 131.

Choose one of the following.

1. Search online for a short video about using art or music as therapy.
    a) Write down the URL and the date you retrieved the video.
    b) Prepare a short oral presentation (3–4 minutes) about the video. Remember to answer the wh- questions and to explain why you found the video interesting.

2. Have you ever made a video, developed a game, or written and recorded music? Where did your idea come from? Prepare a short oral presentation (3–4 minutes) describing your project and what inspired you. If you are comfortable doing so, show your project to the class.

Writing

Choose one of these writing activities.

1. Look up the phrase "six-word memoirs" online. The challenge is to write a story, or to describe your life or a significant experience, in just six words.

    EXAMPLES   Thank you for taking my hand.

    What a difference a year makes.

    I believed I could do it.

    Then do one of the following:
    a) Using one of the six-word memoirs you found online as inspiration, write a paragraph (100–125 words) describing the full story you imagine the memoir tells.
    b) Write your own six-word memoir.

2. Reread the article about teaching creativity and summarize it in in a short paragraph (75–100 words). Remember to ask yourself the wh- questions (Who? What? Where? When? Why? How?). Ensure that you do not include your opinion in your summary.

Vocabulary

Complete one of the following activities.

1. Choose five vocabulary words from the unit that you consider important. For each, write a definition in your own words. Then use each word in a sentence that clearly demonstrates the meaning. You may also include a translation of each word.

2. Complete the following sentences using these vocabulary words from the unit.

   boost (v)   lyrics (n)   take a step back (exp)   outlet (n)   overcome (v)

   a) It is important to find an _____ for your negative feelings.

   b) The _____ of my favourite song evoke strong emotions.

   c) When you are stressed or anxious, it is good to _____ to evaluate the situation.

   d) There are many ways to _____ a creative block.

   e) You can _____ your creativity in many ways.

UNIT 3
Future Food

We need to start thinking about the future of food
if we are going to feed nine billion people in a
way that does not destroy our environment. —Bill Gates

In developed countries food is often wasted while all around the world—in
developed and underdeveloped countries—people struggle to feed their families.
Innovative solutions have been proposed to address local food needs and ensure
global food security. In this unit, you will learn about new practices that may be part
of the solution at home and around the world.

Speaking

There are many challenges facing our world that result in food insecurity. With a partner or in a small group, discuss the nature of the challenges, provide examples, and suggest solutions.

Establish a priority rating for each challenge.

★ = important   ★★ = very important   ★★★ = urgent

Challenges	Potential problems	Possible solutions	Rank
climate change			
reduced living space			
limited natural resources			
over-consumption			

Share your ideas with another group or with the class. How difficult was it for your group to agree on the urgency of each challenge? Which items did you agree or disagree on?

READING

Vocabulary

Find the following words in the paragraphs indicated and use the context to match each word with the correct definition.

Word	Definition
1. unsustainable (adj) (paras. 1,2) _d_	a) unfit, ruined
2. showcase (v) (para. 1) _e_	b) give special attention to
3. highlight (v) (para. 1) _b_	c) develop well
4. spoiled (adj) (para. 3) _a_	d) unable to continue for long
5. thrive (v) (para. 8) _c_	e) present in a positive way

Use the words above to complete the following sentences.

1. Without adequate nutrition, the world's population cannot _____.

2. Too much food is wasted because it is ___4___.

3. We should try to move away from ___unsustainable___ agricultural practices.

4. The conference will ___3___ innovative developments in the food industry.

5. It is essential to ___3___ alternatives to mass food production.

Pre-Reading Activity

When writing an article, an author often depends on the reader having some prior knowledge of the subject. Before reading the text, answer the following questions with a partner or a small group, in order to activate your existing knowledge.

cattle food = cow food

1. Why is cattle farming not good for the environment?

   big carbon footprint.

2. How can reducing food waste help the environment?

   Use less food, smaller garbage dumps

3. How could urban farming increase cities' resistance to climate change?

   _____

Share your ideas with the class.

THE
ARTIFICIAL
MEAT
BALL
—
*Tomorrow's
Meatball*

Tomorrow's Meatball: What We All Could Be Eating 20 Years from Now

SPACE 10

1   The future-living lab, Space10, has set out to explore creative ways of thinking about food in light of our current, unsustainable food practices. *Tomorrow's Meatball* aims to do more with less, showcasing alternative food sources like insects, algae, and foods that otherwise go to waste or are underutilized. underused It also highlights alternative production processes like powdered and 3D printed foods, taking the possibility of future food customization and personalized nutrition to the next level.

The Artificial Meatball

2   Artificial meat is an animal-flesh product, grown inside a laboratory. The first lab-grown beef burger was presented in 2013 and cost $325 000. Today, that very same burger costs only $10. Artificial meat is a viable near-future *able to be done* alternative to the increasingly unsustainable practice of **cattle farming**.

The Wonderful Waste Ball

3   Up to one-third of all food is spoiled or **squandered** before it is consumed by people according to UN's Food and Agriculture Organization. Dealing with food waste is prominent in the efforts to combat hunger, improve food *it's important*   *fight* security in the world's poorest countries, and preserve the environment. Reducing this loss is a critical step toward securing enough food for a fast-growing world population.

The Urban Farmer's Ball

4   Urban farming is booming. More and more people are growing food as locally as possible. Local food represents a serious alternative to the global food model. It reduces "food miles," offers fresh products year-round, generates employment, creates **greenbelts**, and strengthens cities' resilience to climate *ability to withstand* change.

Grammar in Context

Plural Nouns

The plural of most nouns is formed by adding -s or -es.

There are exceptions to this rule. An example is highlighted in paragraph 3.

Nouns ending in -y, change -y to -ies.

   baby → babies

Nouns ending in -f, change -f to -v and add -es.

   half → halves

Find and highlight three examples of irregular plural nouns in the reading.

 GG   For more information about plural nouns, see Grammar Guide page 142.

cattle farming (n) raising cows for food or milk

squandered (adj) wasted

greenbelt (n) conservation area where construction is not permitted

The Mighty Powder Ball

5   Powdered food has been **gathering traction** lately. The meal replacement is available in both liquid and powdered forms and includes all the elements of a healthy diet: protein, carbs, and unsaturated fats, alongside all the necessary vitamins and minerals. Today nutrient-dense products have become game-changers for treating severe malnutrition in developing countries.

The Lean Green Algae Ball

6   Algae are the fastest growing plant organisms in nature and are a great alternative source of vitamins, protein, and minerals. The **mean** and green aquatic plant has a lot of potential as a **scalable** food source because it can be grown anywhere—often in vertical fermentation tanks—without using large amounts of land or water.

The 3D Printed Ball

7   3D food printing has the potential to save the environment, while revolutionizing food production—converting alternative ingredients such as proteins from algae, **beet** leaves, or insects into delicious meals. In addition, 3D food printing opens the door to food customization and personalized nutrition.

The Nutty Ball

8   Grains, legumes, and nuts continue to gain in health reputation for providing abundant protein and micronutrients. In the near future, more and more local farmers will breed new varieties of grains to thrive in their regions, marrying classic seed selection with modern technology.

The Crispy Bug Ball

9   Insect eating is common to cultures in most parts of the world. More than 1000 different insect species are eaten in 80 percent of the world's nations. Insects generally contain more protein and are lower in fat than traditional meats and have about 20 times higher **food conversion efficiency**—making them a viable addition to our current menu.

10 These are just some of the innovative ways that we could address the world's food problem, whether by adopting new techniques or by changing our food consumption habits. Time will tell which practices will become common and which ones will not appeal to the general public.

---

gather traction (exp) gain increased support or interest

mean (adj) efficient; requiring few resources

scalable (adj) easy to expand or increase

beet (n) a dark red root vegetable

food conversion efficiency (n phr) how much food an animal consumes versus how much it produces

Vocabulary in Action

Security or *Safety*?

Security refers to the control, protection, or integrity of something, or to the freedom from danger or fear. *Food security* means reasonable (affordable) access to healthy food.

> Security at the airport has increased over the last two decades.

> Food security is an issue in poor communities in developed countries.

Safety refers to the avoidance of harm or injury.

> The crossing guard ensures students' safety on the busy street.

THE URBAN FARMER'S BALL
—
Tomorrow's Meatball

THE MIGHTY POWDER BALL
—
Tomorrow's Meatball

THE LEAN GREEN ALGAE BALL
—
Tomorrow's Meatball

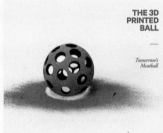

THE 3D PRINTED BALL
—
Tomorrow's Meatball

Comprehension

Answer the following questions. If the answer to a True/False question is False, rewrite the sentence to make it true.

1. What is the main idea of this reading?
   a) There are many innovative solutions to the current food crisis.
   b) Scientific innovation can help us resolve the problems of food production and supply.
   (c) Scientific developments and alternative food sources may help solve the world's food problems.

2. Take notes based on the reading to complete the following table. Use your own words when possible.

Proposed solution	Advantages
reduction of food waste	-Improve food security in to the poorest nations. - Good for enviroment.
urban farming	(Offer fresh food year round) -Offer fresh food year - round - generates employment -health food -reduces greenhose gases by eliminating need for transport.
powdered food	-help people with food problems get proper nutrition - contains all necessary natrients, vitamins, and minerals.
3D printed food	- Saveing the enviroment by converting waste to useful food. - Can hlp people personalize their diets for what they need.

Compare your answers with a partner or small group.

3. Why do you think the price of an artificial burger has dropped so dramatically in just a few years?

   The technology has improved and costs have gone down.

4. In paragraph 4, what do you think the term "food miles" means?

   The distance food has to travel from the source to your plate. distance

5. Why do you think powdered food is so important to combatting malnutrition in developing countries?

   because there are a lot of nutrition included in powdered food

6. What is the major advantage of using algae in food production?
   a) it is a great alternative source of protein and nutrients
   b) it can be cultivated in small spaces
   c) cultivation requires little water
   d) all of the above

7. How can 3D printed food help personalize nutrition?

   If you print food yourself, It's easy to change the ingredients.

8. The increasing interest in the health benefits of grains, legumes, and nuts will lead to
   a) trying to convince people to eat more grains, legumes, and nuts
   b) designing crops that are specifically adapted to the local environment
   c) working to improve the nutritional value of grains, legumes, and nuts

9. Insects are not a common food source around the world.   ☐ True   ☑ False

10. Review your answers to the three questions in the pre-reading activity. How did your prior knowledge of the subject contribute to your understanding of the text?

Speaking

1. Which of the food production solutions discussed in the reading do you think would be the most and the least successful in solving the world's food problem? Why do you think this? Write down at least two ideas to support your opinion.

   Most successful _____

   Reasons _____

   Least successful _____

   Reasons _____

2. In a small group, discuss your answers. Try to convince your partners that your point of view is valid by providing strong arguments. What did you agree or disagree on?

Writing

For more information on developing a coherent paragraph, see Writing Strategies page 117.

Review your answers to the Speaking activity you just completed. What do you think the future of food will be? Write two paragraphs (75–100 words each), developing your ideas. Begin each paragraph with a clear topic sentence and support your ideas with at least two facts or examples from the reading or from your own experience and knowledge.

Pre-Watching Activity

Urban farming, also known as urban agriculture, is a fast-growing trend. Why do you think this is the case? What are the specific benefits of urban agriculture? Are there any disadvantages? What potential problems could an urban farm face? Are there limits to what can be grown or raised in an urban location?

Work with a partner or small group to brainstorm some ideas below, and then share them with the class.

Urban Agriculture		
Benefits	**Disadvantages**	**Potential problems**

Vocabulary

You will hear each of the following words in bold in the video.

1. The **soil** is enriched by compost made from food waste.

2. City Farm uses a **vacant lot** to grow vegetables.

3. The total area of land used to raise all the **livestock** in the world is about the size of Africa.

4. Corn is an important **crop** in the US.

5. Most of the agriculture in developing countries is **subsistence farming**.

6. Urban farms are an **asset** to the community.

Using the context provided in the sentences above, match each word with the correct definition.

Word	Definition
1. crop (n) ___e___	a) earth
2. livestock (n) ___b___	b) animals raised for food purposes
3. vacant lot (n) ___d___	c) something that is useful
4. soil (n) ___a___	d) unused land in a city
5. subsistence farming (n) ___f___	e) plant or product grown by farmers
6. asset (n) ___c___	f) providing just enough to live

Crop growth depend on the weather.

Why We Should Be Urban Farming (7:33 min)

The Good Stuff

More and more people are discovering the pleasures of growing their own food in their backyards and even on balconies. In this video, you will learn about people participating in an initiative to transform the urban environment and to reconnect to their food supply.

Comprehension

Answer the following questions. If the answer to a True/False question is False, rewrite the sentence to make it true.

1. Watch the introduction (0:00–0:56) and complete the following sentences with the missing word or number.

    a) The cities of the world contain over **half** of the population of this world.

    b) The global population is supposed to hit **9 billion** in the next **40** years.

    c) **57%** of earth's land is uninhabitable.

    d) Roughly **¼₃** of the food we produce is wasted.

2. Where does City Farm get food waste from to make its compost? Check all answers that were mentioned.

    ☑ restaurants   ☐ hotels   ☑ other places

    ☐ supermarkets   ☐ individuals   ☑ grocery stores

3. City Farm receives a delivery of food waste every day.   ☑ True   ☐ False

    _____

4. Why do grocery stores throw out fruits and vegetables that are still edible?
    ~~It doesn't look nice~~. Can't sell it because of appearance and quality

5. Having an urban farm improves our food supply system in a number of ways. Name two of them.
    more **Freshness, less use of fossil fuels.**

    _____

6. Both rich and poor soil produce the same quality of tomato.
                                                    ☐ True   ☑ False
    The soil with nutritions grows food with better quality

7. Urban climate can be both an advantage and a disadvantage to urban farming.
                                                    ☑ True   ☐ False

    _____

8. What are three advantages of a local farm community mentioned in the video?

- to solve pollution.

- use vacant land.

- Produces healthy food.

9. Name three approaches to solving the food problems facing our local community and the world.

~ eat less processed food.   - Farm up instead of farm wide.

- waste less food.   - keep things local & fresh

~ focus on nutrition, not calories. - eat lower on the food chain.

~ employ new farming ~~technology~~ techniques & return to old one

10. In your opinion, what are the main challenges facing the development of urban farms?

Cost of water, employees, availability of land. /Space

in some cases sunshine.

11. How could local governments assist in the development of urban farms?

Provide land, encourage the development of urban farming culture, teach people how to farm, establish markets.

WRITING

Writing Strategy

Working from a Thesis Statement

An effective introduction presents the subject in an interesting way to capture the reader's attention.

The thesis statement is a sentence that identifies the main idea of an essay. The thesis statement is developed and explained in the body of the essay and is generally placed at the end of the introduction.

Read this sample introduction and thesis statement and then complete the activity.

How can we feed the growing population of our planet? Our world is facing a global food crisis that requires creative solutions to ensure food security. One possible solution may be exploring alternative food sources such as insects or artificial meat. The answer could also lie in developing new production processes, including 3D printed food or powdered substitutes. Or the solution may involve reducing food waste and maximizing use of space in urban areas. **Solving the global food problem will require both innovation and better utilization of current resources.**

Using information from the reading and the video, develop an outline for an essay based on the thesis statement above.

Body paragraph 1 (Topic: innovative techniques)

Topic sentence: _Technology could help improve global food security._

Support 1: _3D Printed food_

Support 2: _powdered food_

Support 3: _artificial meat_

Body paragraph 2 (Topic: efficient use of resources)

Topic sentence: _Using current resourced more Efficien._

Support 1: _____

Support 2: _____

Support 3: _____

S For information about developing effective topic sentences and support, see Writing Strategies page 118.

Using the following thesis statement, write two paragraphs (approximately 100 words each) explaining your point of view. Start each paragraph with a clear topic sentence and support your opinion with information from the video.

Urban farms have tangible value to local populations, but they also have environmental benefits.

SPEAKING

Work in a small group.

a) Brainstorm ideas to solve the food challenges around the world.

b) Individually, do online research to learn about programs or initiatives dedicated to reducing food waste and solving the global food crisis.

c) Share your information with your partners.

d) As a group, using PowerPoint or another presentation program, prepare a five-minute presentation for the class about the most interesting information your group discovered.

READING

Vocabulary

Many words have more than one definition, so it is necessary to use context or a dictionary to determine the correct meaning.

1. Look at the two different meanings of the word *argue* below. Find the word *argue* in paragraph 4 of the reading on page 50 and decide which meaning is the most appropriate in that context.

    argue
    verb

    1. [intransitive] to speak angrily to somebody because you disagree. *My sisters are always arguing.*

    argue (with somebody) (about/over something) *They're always arguing with each other about money.*

    2. [intransitive, transitive] to give reasons why you think that something is right or wrong, true or not true, to persuade people that you are right. *She argued that she was old enough to stay out later than midnight.*

    Correct definition (from para. 4): _____

2. Look at the two different meanings of the word *address* below. Find the word *address* in paragraph 6 of the reading on page 51 and decide which meaning is the most appropriate in that context.

    address
    verb [transitive]

    1. to give a formal speech to a group of people. *The Prime Minister addressed the House of Commons.*
    2. (formal): to think about an issue and decide how to deal with it. *We will have to address the problem of climate change.*

    Correct definition (from para. 6): _____

3. Look at the three different meanings of the word *foreign* below. Find the word *foreign* in paragraph 9 of the reading on page 51 and decide which meaning is the most appropriate in that context.

    foreign
    adjective

    1. in or from a country that is not your own. *She speaks with a foreign accent.*
    2. [only before noun] dealing with or involving other countries. *The government's foreign policy is controversial.*
    3. foreign to somebody/something (formal) not known to somebody and therefore strange. *Cheating is foreign to his nature.*

    Correct definition (from para. 9): _____

Pre-Reading Activity

Some people believe that 3D printing could radically change the food production process. What do you know about 3D printing? Work in a small group and answer the following questions.

1. What kind of things can be 3D printed? Name as many items as possible.

2. How does 3D printing work? Do you know? Can you explain the process?

3. What are the benefits of 3D printing?

4. How do you think 3D printing will change the world?

Share your ideas with another small group or the class.

Would you be surprised to learn that 3D printed food already exists? Is it realistic to believe that one day everyone will have a 3D printer in their kitchen, beside the stove? Will someone create an app to order personalized 3D meals from local restaurants? Read the following text to learn more about this intriguing new technology.

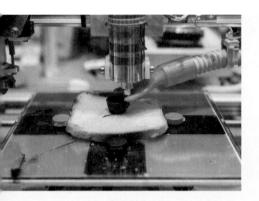

compounded (adj) made up of many parts

leftovers (n) food that remains after a meal is finished

Vocabulary in Action

Compound Adjectives

Compound adjectives are adjectives made up of two or more words with hyphens (-) between them.

> three-dimensional meals, technology-based solutions.

Find five more examples of compound adjectives in the reading.

Is 3D Printing the Future of Global Food?

By Sylvain Charlebois

The Globe and Mail

1   A few weeks ago, Londoners were able to eat at the world's first 3D-printed pop-up restaurant. In early June, a German-based company introduced the word's first plug-and-play food printer, which may be ready for shipping as early as next year. With the cost to produce this technology dropping, making it increasingly accessible, 3D printing could fundamentally change our relationship with food.

2   Simply put, the process uses ingredients to generate three-dimensional meals by placing layers of **compounded** food on top of each other. Since 2012, the food industry has used this technology to produce products, including candy, chocolate, pizza, noodles and even crackers. Despite its relative novelty, many companies are recognizing its potential—and recognizing how 3D food printing can revolutionize our global food systems.

3   In particular, 3D printing could radically alter food production practices by enabling companies to manage resources more responsibly and reduce waste across the food continuum—whether you are a processor, a distributor or a consumer with **leftovers**. Indeed, many well-known agribusiness corporations have already dedicated a great deal of time and research on 3D systems. There is a potential benefit to consumer health, as well. For example, PepsiCo recently announced that it is using 3D printing to develop a healthier potato chip.

4   Beyond manufacturing, 3D printing could also boost culinary creativity by allowing renowned chefs to create shapes and forms that were previously thought impossible. Some have argued that it can give the food-service industry the ability to customize products based on individual nutritional needs.

5 Given the demographic challenges we face in coming decades, this can become a key benefit. In Germany, many **nursing homes** already produce a pureed 3D-printed food product called smoothfoods for residents who have difficulty ingesting food, or chewing it. Regular smoothies have been on the menu, but haven't proved as popular. Elderly residents eating smoothfoods can receive all the nutrients they require while enjoying an aesthetically pleasing meal. As a result, they can live healthier, higher quality lives.

6 More significantly, some experts believe 3D printing could effectively address global food security problems. Ingredients such as algae, **duckweed** and grass could be **embedded** into familiar dishes. A recent study in Holland added **milled mealworm** to a shortbread cookie recipe through 3D printing—most would agree that a cookie-shaped food product is much more appetizing than the look and feel of a worm. By using insects and other protein sources, the growing need for protein the globe is currently experiencing, which adds increased pressure to beef and pork prices, could be **mitigated**.

7 3D food printing still faces major obstacles. The technology is expensive and complex. The engineering required to produce food is much more sophisticated than producing objects with metal and plastic. Food scientists acknowledge how difficult it is to effectively make edible meals in 3D food printing—ingredients in food interact in many complex ways, particularly with meats. At this point, 3D food printers do not produce great tasting food, and still do not have the overwhelming endorsement of the culinary world.

8 However, the technology is improving at an incredible pace, so that very soon, anything might be possible.

9 The concept of 3D printed food is foreign to many of us, and may challenge our collective appreciation of where food comes from, and how it is produced. Let's face it—when it comes to food, we are all traditionalists to some extent, protective of our food heritage. Printing food is a drastic departure from the art of cooking as a way of celebrating nature's **bounty**.

10 But the reality is that in just a few years, we will have more than nine billion people to feed. One way to responsibly address global food security issues is to consider technology as a primary source for sustainable solutions. Treating alternatives to established food production systems as **mere fads** may not be the best approach. After all, the future of the dinner table may be as different, and as simple as "Press print and eat."

Grammar in Context
Preposition + Gerund

Prepositions such as *by, for, after, before,* or *without* are followed by a gerund. An example is highlighted in paragraph 3.

> 3D printing could boost creativity **by allowing** chefs to create impossible shapes.

> **Before rejecting** the idea of 3D printed food, you should try it. **After tasting** it, you might change your mind.

Find and highlight three examples of a preposition followed by the gerund in the reading.

 For more about gerunds, see Grammar Guide page 210.

nursing home (n) place where elderly people live and are cared for

duckweed (n) small plant that grows on the surface of water

embedded (v) included in

milled mealworm (n) powdered insect larvae

mitigated (adj) reduced

bounty (n) generous gift

mere (adj) simple

fad (n) something people are interested in for a short time

Comprehension

Answer the following questions. If the answer to a True/False question is False, rewrite the sentence to make it true.

1. 3D food is not yet available on the market.   ☐ True   ☑ False

_____

_____

_____

2. How might 3D food benefit each of the following groups? Summarize the information from the text and complete the table below.

food industry	
consumers	*health*
chefs	*help chefs to creat shapes and forms*
elderly people	*healthier*
world population	

3. What are the two major obstacles facing 3D-printed food?

   expensive. complexe.

4. What do you think this sentence in Paragraph 9 of the text means?

   ". . .when it comes to food, we are all traditionalists to some extent, protective of our food heritage."

5. Do you believe that the future of the dinner table could be "press, print and eat"? Why or why not? Explain your answer in 4–5 sentences and provide facts and examples to support your point of view.

   Share your answer with a small group. What do you agree or disagree on?

DISCOVER GRAMMAR

Future

The future tense is most commonly expressed with *will* or *be going to*.

   In just a few years, we **will have** more than nine billion people to feed.

   By 2050, the population of the world **is going to be** over nine billion people.

Use *be going to* to express planned actions.

   The government **is going to** address the food crisis in Africa.

Use *will* for spontaneous decisions.

   I'll do the cooking tonight; you sit down and relax.

Both forms are used for predictions.

   We **will** have to find solutions if we want to feed the whole planet.

   We**'re going to** need investment in technology to solve the food problem.

[handwritten: I am going to do it]

Select *will* or *be going to* for the following sentences. Be prepared to explain your choices.

GG For more information about the future tense, see Grammar Guide page 162.

1. We (will/are going to) have a big family dinner at Thanksgiving.

2. The doorbell rang. It must be the pizza delivery. I (will/am going to) get it!

3. This summer, my parents (are going to/will) start a vegetable garden.

4. Let me help you with dinner. I (will/am going to) light the barbecue.

5. What (will/is going to) happen if we don't stop wasting so much food? *[handwritten: both]*

PRONUNCIATION

Can and Can't

Can and *can't* look very similar, but they are pronounced very differently. Understanding this will help your comprehension and speaking skills.

Can: When *can* is placed before a main verb, the vowel is **not** stressed and sounds like /kin/. The stress is placed on the subject and main verb in the sentence.

> We can solve the world food crisis.

Can't: When *can't* is placed before a main verb, the vowel sound **is** stressed. It sounds like /kant/.

> We can't continue to waste food as we do now.

1. Listen to each sentence and write the word you hear: *can* or *can't*.

    a) Urban farming techniques __Can__ help our environment.

    b) Food __can__ now be printed using a 3D printer.

    c) Many people __can't__ imagine eating insects.

    d) Artificial meat __Can__ be grown in a laboratory.

    e) Powdered food __Can__ reduce malnutrition in developing countries.

    f) In Canada's climate, you __Can't__ grow vegetables outside throughout the entire year.

    g) Some people just __Can't__ stop eating chips once they start.

    h) Everyone __Can__ help reduce food waste.

    i) Many families __Can't__ afford healthy, nutritious food.

    j) Urban farming __Can__ reduce fossil fuel consumption.

2. With a partner, practise saying the following sentences out loud. Listen to each sentence being read, repeat it, and then listen again to check your pronunciation.
    a) 3D food can change the global food system.
    b) Some people can't imagine eating insects.
    c) We can't produce enough food for everyone in the world.
    d) The consumer can benefit from personalized nutrition.
    e) Elderly people can live healthier lives if they eat well.

[handwritten: World War III is going to broke out]

Pre-Listening Activity

Taste is a very personal matter. Everyone has a favourite food, or a food that they strongly dislike. What foods do you like and dislike? Why? Is it the taste? The texture or appearance? Or do you associate positive or negative emotions or experiences with that food?

How willing are you to try new culinary experiences? What is the most unusual thing you have ever eaten?

Complete the chart with your answers and then interview two classmates to learn about their likes and dislikes.

	You	Partner 1	Partner 2
Favourite food (give reasons/ associations)	My favourite food is Korean BBQ. Actually I like meats like rib, Pork belly or steak, and like the smell from the grill. Also the taste is so dillcious		
Least favourite food (give reasons/ associations)	Fish is my least favourite food because It doesn't a point for me appearing.		
Most unusual food you've tried	Indian food that it unusual food I've tried. It has long white rice with something spicy. Thats so strange and I don't like It.		
Food you refuse to try (give reasons/ associations)			

Share your results with the class or a small group.

Sustainable, Efficient, and Slightly Nutty—
What It's Like to Eat Insect Burgers (7:37) 🔊

Nora Young

CBC Spark

There are more than 1900 types of edible insects in the world, and more than two billion people eat insects on a regular basis. Katharina Unger is an industrial designer, originally from Austria, who has invented a kitchen countertop container used to raise mealworms as a food source. She would like to see it in your kitchen so you can harvest insects yourself. Are you up for the challenge?

Comprehension

Answer the following questions. If the answer to a True/False question is False, rewrite the sentence to make it true.

1. What is the main idea of this listening?
   a) Insects are a nutritious food that can easily be harvested domestically.
   b) People around the world eat insects regularly.
   c) Eating insects could solve some of the world's food problems.

2. What was Katharina's reaction before she ate an insect for the first time?
   She was shaking and it tooks a day to be ok.

3. People eat approximately 500 grams of insects every year without realizing it. Name three products that may contain insects.
   Chocolate , Juice / Soup /

4. Katharina says that once a Hive (the countertop insect farm) is fully operational, each week it will produce
   a) 100–400 grams of worms
   b) 200–400 grams of worms
   c) 200–500 grams of worms

5. Mealworms contain approximately the same amount of __protein__ as beef, have the essential amino acid profile of __tofu__, and require only __10%__ of the land required to raise cattle.

6. Name three ways in which mealworms can be prepared for eating.
   for burger / Crispy / sweet with chocolate / fry as snack

7. Why is Katharina interested in understanding where her food comes from?
   She grew up in a samll farm in Astria.

8. Education can help change people's perception of insects as a food source.
   ☑ True ☐ False

   _____

9. Name two foods that were considered unfit for human consumption in the past.
   Potato, lobster / lobser potato / lobster vegetable

Glossary

grasshopper (n) a plant-eating insect with long legs used for jumping

raise (v) to grow something (plants or animals)

hive (n) container, usually for bees

mealworm (n) larva of a beetle

beetle (n) insect whose hard outer wings protect the inner wings when at rest

pupa (n) insect in the stage of development between larva and adult

tray (n) an open container with low sides that is used to hold or carry something

harvest (v) to collect something, generally used to refer to food

self-sufficiency (n) the ability to live without outside help or support

10. Why do you think insect-eating is taboo in many Western countries, yet normal for more than two billion people around the world?

_____

_____

_____

_____

REVISING AND EDITING

An essay should always begin with an interesting introduction that captures the reader's attention. Read the body and conclusion of the essay below and complete the following steps.

1. Revise and improve the topic sentences for each development paragraph. (The topic sentences are shown in italics.)

2. Write a short introduction. Begin with a general description, historical background, or an anecdote. End your introduction with a thesis statement that expresses the main idea of the essay.

Introduction _____

_____

_____

_____

_____

_____

_____

> For more information about developing effective topic sentences, see Writing Strategies page 118.

> For more information about writing an effective introduction, see Writing Strategies page 123.

Firstly, urban agriculture is good. Growing food locally reduces the carbon footprint and "food miles" associated with long distance transportation. Vegetable gardeners can use grey water for their crops, thereby reducing the need for waste water treatment. Similarly, urban farms can use compost from local households, food scraps that would otherwise end up in landfills. Finally, spaces devoted to urban farms create small oases of greenery that reduce the heat-island effect, as well as harmful air pollution.

Secondly, urban farming is fun. Research has found that community gardens can strengthen social bonds and networks among neighbours and people who participate in such programs. In addition to creating job opportunities, urban agriculture can teach people important life skills, such as self-sufficiency. Schools that are involved in community garden initiatives use urban agriculture to teach young people about science, the environment, and healthy eating.

In conclusion, urban agriculture has both environmental and social benefits for communities involved in these initiatives. In the future, vegetable gardens grown in vacant lots or unused spaces will become a more common sight in our cities.

Grey water is relatively clean waste water that can be reused. It is typically generated by household uses such as baths or washing machines. Grey water does not contain excrement.

Speaking

1. Search online for an article about the future of food. You could do further research on something from this unit that interested you, or you could look for other solutions being proposed to solve the global food crisis.
   a) Write down the URL and the date you retrieved the article.
   b) Choose five key words in the article that are unfamiliar to you and try to figure out the definitions, using a dictionary if necessary.
   c) Write a summary of the main idea of the text.
   d) Share the information with a small group in a short presentation (3–4 minutes).

2. Work with a small group of students and brainstorm ideas you could develop to combat food waste.
   a) Individually, research online to learn about programs or initiatives dedicated to reducing food waste.
   b) Share your information with the group.
   c) As a group, decide which waste-reduction idea is the most interesting opportunity.
   c) As a group, prepare a PowerPoint presentation for the class about the most interesting solution you discovered on how to combat food waste.

Watching

Search online for a short video about a successful urban agriculture project or about opposition to such a project (e.g., urban beekeeping or backyard farming). Write down the URL and the date you retrieved the video. Then complete one of these activities.

1. Write a summary of the video clip (75–100 words).

2. Explain what you found to be most interesting about the video (100–150 words).

3. Explain one thing that you learned from the video and what related areas you would now like to explore (100–150 words).

4. Watch the video with a small group. Prepare at least five discussion questions for the group to debate after watching the video.

Vocabulary

Complete one of the following activities.

1. Choose five vocabulary words from the unit that you consider important. For each, write a definition in your own words. Then use each word in a sentence that clearly demonstrates the meaning. You may also include a translation of each word.

2. Complete the following sentences using these vocabulary words from the unit.

   harvest (v)   crops (n)   unsustainable (adj)   raise (v)   spoiled (adj)

   a) More than 80 percent of _____ grown in the US are transformed into processed food.

   b) It is becoming increasingly popular to _____ chickens in urban areas.

   c) Food that is imperfect, but not _____ is often thrown out by supermarkets, although it is still edible.

   d) We cannot continue to rely on _____ agricultural practices if we want to feed nine billion people.

   e) Fall is a time to _____ many fruits and vegetables.

UNIT 4
Bright Ideas

Every person can make a difference and every person should try.

—John Fitzgerald Kennedy

Around the world, organizations, associations, and individual citizens participate in activities and projects that help to make the world a better place for all. In this unit, you will learn about some of these initiatives and have the opportunity to reflect on how you could contribute to changing the world.

Speaking

1. In a small group, discuss these questions. What does *making a difference* mean to you? How would you like to make a difference? Give some examples to explain your answers.

2. In a small group, make a list of well-known individuals who are making a positive difference in the world. They might be political figures, artists, entrepreneurs, inventors, social activists, or others. Who are they? What have they done? How have they affected people's lives? Share your ideas with the class.

3. Individually, choose one person from your group's list and explain to a student from another group why you chose this person and why his or her contribution is important by making a connection to your own life and interests.

READING

Vocabulary

Using a dictionary, match each word in the column on the left with the correct definition.

Word	Definition
1. random (adj) (para. 2) _C_	a) dependable
2. prevalent (adj) (para. 3) _D_	b) make possible
3. tear apart (v) (past tense: torn apart) (para. 4) _E_	c) without pattern or reason
4. reliable (adj) (para. 7) _A_	d) common
5. shortcoming (n) (para. 14) _F_	e) destroy violently
6. enable (v) (para. 18) _B_	f) fault, defect

For this team reading activity, your teacher will assign you to a team: A, B, C, or D. Read the article you have been assigned and then complete the comprehension activities.

At the age of 17, Malala Yousafzai was a co-winner of the 2014 Nobel Peace Prize for her campaign supporting female education in Pakistan. Because of her activism, she was shot and wounded by the Taliban in 2012. She made a full recovery and has continued her advocacy for girls' educational rights. Malala is just one example of a young person whose ideas have changed the world. In the following readings, you will learn about four other young people, from very different backgrounds and with very different interests, who are all making a difference in their own way.

Beyond Malala: Teenagers Changing the World

The Guardian

RaSia Khepra

Reading A: RaSia Khepra

1   College freshman RaSia Khepra had always wanted to address the rampant violence **plaguing** his home city of Chicago—where more than 500 people were killed by guns in 2012—but the death of his close friend is what motivated him to act.

2   Hadiya Pendleton, 15, was killed at random by a gunman on Chicago's South Side, a week after she performed at Barack Obama's inauguration celebration in January. Khepra was familiar with the sounds of gunfire in his neighbourhood and knows several people who have been shot, but Pendleton's death inspired him to take action. "I don't think having somebody that close to you [get killed] can ever leave your mind if they've been taken in such a way," Khepra told the Huffington Post. "I do, definitely, think about her every day because I'm used to seeing her every day."

3   Khepra and other Chicago teenagers created the anti-violence awareness campaign Project Orange Tree. The group helps coordinate community activities to stimulate a conversation about the causes of gun violence and is supported by the rapper Lupe Fiasco. Khepra said gun violence was often **written off** as a gang problem, but the issue also affected members of the community not affiliated with gangs. "I don't think a lot of the violence that's being labelled gang-related violence is as prevalent as it's being **hyped up** to be," he said.

Reading B: Kelvin Doe

4   Kelvin Doe was born to a single mother when Sierra Leone was being torn apart by civil war. "Her resilience and self-belief made it possible for me to be alive today," he once said.

5   He is the personification of how the west African country is trying to rebuild and look forward. A short film about him has been viewed more than five million times on YouTube.

6   Doe is a self-taught engineer of astonishing precocity. At the age of 11, he **rummaged** in garbage cans for scrap electronics parts that could fix local problems. At 13, he made his own battery by throwing together acid, soda, and metal in a tin cup, waiting for the mixture to dry and wrapping tape around it. This proved a big financial saving on batteries.

7   Frustrated by the lack of a reliable electricity supply in his neighbourhood, Doe built a generator using parts that were homemade or "rescued" from the garbage. The generator also powered a community radio station that he built from recycled materials. He plays music under the name DJ Focus and employs his friends as journalists and station managers.

8   "They call me DJ Focus because I believe if you focus, you can create an invention perfectly," Doe said in the video that became a worldwide hit on the Thnkr YouTube channel.

9   He had never been more than 10 miles from his home in Freetown until he won a national schools innovation competition and was picked for a trip to

---

plague (v) to cause pain or trouble to somebody or something over a long period

written off (phr v) dismissed as unimportant

hyped up (exp) exaggerated

rummage (v) to move things around carelessly while searching for something

Grammar in Context

Present Perfect

The words highlighted in yellow in Readings A and B are present perfect verbs.

The present perfect tense is used to

1. describe actions that started in the past and continue in the present (duration)

    Kelvin Doe **has lived** in Sierra Leone all his life.

2. describe actions that happened at unspecified past times (indefinite)

    The inspirational effects of Kelvin's YouTube video **have been** remarkable.

Highlight three present perfect examples in Reading C and two examples in Reading D.

Kelvin Doe

 To learn more about the present perfect, see Grammar Guide page 167.

favela (n) a poor area in or near a Brazilian city, with many small houses that are close together and in bad condition. Also: **shantytown**

mainstream (adj) generally accepted

scold (v) to speak angrily to somebody, especially a child, who has done something wrong

crossfire (n) a situation where guns are fired from different directions

tiresome (adj) boring

Rene Silva

America, where he spoke at the Meet the Young Makers panel at the World Maker Faire in New York.

10 His mentor David Sengeh, a PhD student at the MIT media lab, said "The inspirational effects of the original Thnkr YouTube video have been remarkable. It has had a tremendous impact on Kelvin's life, on my life and on millions of people all over the world. Everywhere. In Sierra Leone, other young people suddenly feel they can be like Kelvin."

Reading C: Rene Silva

11 While most Brazilian teenagers are interested in computer games, homework, football, or baile funk, Rene Silva has dedicated himself to fighting negative stereotypes about his **favela** community. He set up his first newspaper at the age of 11, live tweeted a police raid on his neighbourhood at 17, and has just completed his first book at the age of 19.

12 The **shantytowns** of Rio de Janeiro were long seen as violent no-go zones run by armed drug gangs. But Silva has used social media to show a more sympathetic, complex, and hopeful side.

13 "The important thing about being young and doing what I do in the favelas is to create new points of reference," he said. "In the past, it was drug trafficking. Today, there is more recognition of the people who are trying to do good and change the reality of the place where they live."

14 Conscious of the shortcomings of the **mainstream** media, one of his teachers asked him to set up a community newspaper in 2005. At first, his family was doubtful about what he could achieve. His mother would **scold** him for getting home late from school because he had spent so long reporting and writing for *Voz das Comunidades* (*Voice of the Community*).

15 But he became the focus of every media organization in the country five years later when he live tweeted a huge military and police operation to "pacify" the Alemão favela where he lived. Silva's microblog corrected mistakes made by TV reporters and raised warnings about a young boy who was caught in the **crossfire** between the police and gangsters. His followers jumped from a few hundred to tens of thousands and his newspaper—now largely online—secured sponsorship.

16 Silva published a book, *A Voz do Alemão*, about the residents of his favela, which he hopes will further change perceptions of Rio's shantytown communities and expose the problems they continue to face after pacification.

Reading D: Zea Tongeman

17 Zea Tongeman, a 14-year-old from south London, was not a self-proclaimed tech geek. "I used to think technology was just fixing computers and saying things like "have you tried turning it on and off again?" she says. But when she realized, after a Little Miss Geek workshop in her school, that tech could be fun and a force for good, she changed her mind. With a friend, Jordan Stirbu, she designed an app called Jazzy Recycling that aims to get people recycling by turning the sometimes **tiresome** task into a game. "As Mary Poppins says: 'You find the fun and it becomes a game,' and that is exactly what our app does," she says.

18 Jazzy Recycling helps users find places to recycle, tells them what they can recycle, and then enables them to scan, share, and get rewards for their efforts.

19 Tapping into the teen mania for sharing even the most **mundane tidbits** of daily life on social media, the game is then shared among friends.

mundane (adj) ordinary

tidbit (n) detail

20 Now Zea has some celebrity backing. Raj Dhonota, business consultant and an angel investor, who appeared on *The Apprentice*, is helping the pair build the app and they hope to launch in 2014.

21 She says: "To have people actually using our app and to know we have made a difference would be incredible, so fingers crossed it all goes to plan."

Comprehension

1. Read the article you were assigned and complete the table below with information from the article. Check your answers with those students who read the same article. Then form a group with students who read each of the other three articles. Take turns sharing with the group the details about the article each of you read. Group members should take notes in the appropriate column as they listen to the speaker.

	Reading A	Reading B	Reading C	Reading D
Name	Rasia Khopra	Kelvin Doe	Rene Silva.	Zea Ton Jenman
Country/City	chicago	west Africa	Brazil, Rio de Janeiro	South London
Motivation to act	his Friend killed by gun (randomly)	lack of reliable elct supply	his community, live tweeted a police raid.	workshop in school
Achievement	create a Orange Tree compain against violence	recycling - buil genarator - local radio station	writing for Voz das Communidades	an app Jazzy Recycling
Mentor/Support	Lube hiasco (rapper)	David Sengah	Alemão favela	Jordan stirbu
In their own words	" 61 "			63
Other interesting information				They want to launch the app in 2014

Answer the following questions. If the answer to a True/False question is False, rewrite the sentence to make it true.

2. RaSia Khepra believes that gun violence is only a gang issue.

    ☐ True   ☐ False

    _____

3. How did Kelvin Doe's mother influence his development?

    _____

4. Why do you think that young people in Sierra Leone have been inspired by Kelvin Doe?

    _____

    _____

5. Rene Silva has . . .

    Check all answers that apply.

    ☐ played football professionally   ☐ used Twitter to inform people of events

    ☐ run a newspaper   ☑ written a book

6. Why do you think Rene Silva was motivated to fight negative stereotypes about his community?

     He wants to bring a sympathetic to society

7. Has Zea Tongeman always liked technology? Explain your answer.

    _____

    _____

8. Which one of the four young people do you find the most inspiring? Explain your answer.

    _____

    _____

DISCOVER GRAMMAR

GG To learn more about the present perfect, see Grammar Guide page 167.

Present Perfect

The present perfect refers to an action that started in the past and continues to the present.

The present perfect is formed using *has/have* + the past participle.

> I **have been** to Brazil three times.

> She **has changed** the way people think about girls' education.

Which of the following sentences are in the present perfect? Underline the verbs in the sentences that contain the present perfect.

1. RaSia created an anti-violence campaign with friends.

2. He has known several people who were victims of violence.

3. Kelvin built a generator using old parts he found in the garbage.

4. Rene has reported on many different events in his favela.

5. Rene live tweeted a police raid when he was 17.

6. Rene published a book called *A Voz do Alemão* in 2013.

7. Rene has published a book called *A Voz do Alemão*.

8. Zea has designed an app to make recycling fun.

9. She didn't think of herself as a geek.

Question Formation

Working with a group of students who read the same text as you, write five questions you would like to ask the young activist profiled in your reading. Use the present perfect and simple past tenses. For example, you might ask Kelvin:

How **did** you **learn** to repair and make electronic products?

What **was** it like to travel to America?

How **has** your life **changed** in the past few years?

VOCABULARY

Word Families

A simple and effective way to develop your vocabulary is to learn the different forms of a word.

For example, you know the verb *to symbolize*. Do you know the adjective *symbolic*, and the noun *symbol*? As you learn the word forms (noun, verb, adjective, adverb) within word families, you will discover typical suffixes for different parts of speech, and enrich your vocabulary.

1. Complete the table below with word families, using a dictionary if necessary.

Noun	Verb	Adjective	Adverb
inspiration	inspire	inspirative	inspiratively
finance	finance	financial	financially
benefit	benefit	beneficial	beneficially
development	develop	developmental	developmentally
innovation	innovate	innovative	innovatively
power	power	powerful	powerfully
dedication	dedicate	dedicated	dedicatedly
recognization	recognize	recognizable	recognizably
creation	create	creative	creatively

2. Read each sentence below and decide which form of the word given is required to complete the sentence (verb, noun, adjective, or adverb). Then, using the table you completed above, find the appropriate word to complete each sentence. The first sentence has been completed as an example.

a) **inspire**   Malala Yousafzai has been an __inspiration (n)__ for young people around the world.

b) **finance**   An investor has promised ___financial___ support for Zea Tongeman's recycling app.

c) **innovate**   Kelvin Doe had an ___innovative___ idea to build generators for his community.

d) **power**   Collaboration between countries is a _____ development tool.

e) **dedicate**   RaSia Khepra is _____ to eliminating gun violence in his community.

f) **recognize**   These young people have received ___recognization___ for their work helping others.

g) **create**   All these people have shown great ___creativity___ in finding solutions to help others.

PRONUNCIATION

Words Beginning with *h*

Hair or *air*? The pronunciation of *h* at the beginning of a word can be challenging for students learning English. They often omit the *h* sound or add it unnecessarily.

To practise pronouncing the *h*, place your hand a few inches from your mouth and feel your breath as you pronounce *hair*. Now practise saying the word *air*. You should not feel your breath on your hand.

1. Listen to the recording and repeat each word after the speaker.

hair	air	high	eye
had	add	hold	old
heart	art	his	is
heat	eat	hate	eight
hedge	edge	heal	eel

To avoid adding the *h* sound before certain words, native speakers link them to the previous word (i.e., the words run together and sound like one word instead of two). Listen to a recording of the following sentence: *There are eight students who are taking art courses.*

Notice how the words *are eight* and *taking art* are linked—or run together—when the speaker says the words.

2. Listen to the recording of the following sentences. With a partner, practise saying each sentence out loud.
    a) I love to eat outdoors in the summer.
    b) Could you keep an eye on my things for a moment?
    c) How old is your brother?
    d) More details will be added as necessary.
    e) The air here is so pure and fresh.

WRITING

Choose one of the quotations below and write a paragraph (125–150 words) that explains why you believe this quote is true. Use examples from your own experience to support your point of view. Remember to start with a clear topic sentence and provide adequate support.

S For information about writing paragraphs, see Writing Strategies page 117.

a) "Alone we can do so little. Together we can do so much." (Helen Keller)

b) "Nobody can do everything, but everyone can do something." (Anonymous)

c) "If you light a lamp for somebody, it will also brighten your path." (Buddhist saying)

READING

Reading Strategy

Scanning

To *scan* means to read a text quickly, looking for specific information that you need. You look quickly and carefully for a name, date, fact, or answer.

Scan the reading below to find answers to the following questions. Find the information as quickly as possible.

1. About how many years ago did Cirque du Soleil start making money?

    _____

2. In how many countries has Cirque du Monde done workshops?

    _____

3. One person dies every _____ from not having access to clean water.

4. If we don't act now, when will we run out of water resources for more than two-thirds of the world's population?

    _____

S For more information about scanning, see Reading Strategies page 135.

Vocabulary

Find each word in the reading. Use the context to help you match each word with the correct meaning.

	Option 1	Option 2
aim (v) (paras. 1 & 5)	to have an objective	to see a result
workshop (n) (para. 1)	short training program for people to learn something	place where things are made
sustainable (adj) (paras. 3 & 4)	temporary	long lasting, durable
follow suit (exp) (para. 3)	to practise	to do the same
loan (n) (para. 4)	money someone gives you with the understanding that it must be paid back	prize

Guy Laliberté is known for his work as creator and founder of Cirque du Soleil. Did you know that he also created the One Drop Foundation whose aim is to improve access to clean water for millions of people around the world? Read the text to learn more.

The One Drop Foundation: An Interview with Guy Laliberté

By Bret Love and Mary Gabbett

Green Global Travel

1 Can you tell me a little about the origins of One Drop?

Ever since we created Cirque du Soleil, part of our fundamental values was also "to make a better world." As soon as Cirque du Soleil started making a bit of money, about 25 years ago, we started giving back. Staying true to our origins, being from the street, we created a social program called Cirque du Monde. This program was designed for at-risk youth, using circus skills in workshops aimed at giving them some sort of self-esteem. Cirque du Monde still runs today, and has done workshops in more than 50 countries. As we approached our 25th anniversary, I started reflecting on how I wanted to approach this important **milestone**: Either we celebrate our successes, or look forward and imagine how we could make a new difference for the next 25 years. I chose the **latter**. I wanted to create a new foundation that could make a difference in many people's lives. I chose water because, as an artist, it is an important source of inspiration. But I also learned a very significant statistic: One person dies every 20 seconds from not having access to clean water. That is how and why One Drop was born.

milestone (n) an important moment or event in the development of something

latter (n) the second one mentioned

2 **Of all the causes in the world you could have dedicated yourself and your company to, why were water preservation and access so important?**

Water is the 21st century's greatest challenge. If we don't address lack of access, pollution and over-consumption now, more than five billion of us—that's two-thirds of the planet—will run out of this life-sustaining resource in 10 years. That is why One Drop **strives** to ensure that water is accessible to all, today and forever. Water is also at the source of every major issue facing the world today: education, the situation of women, pollution, health . . . it is key to our survival as a species.

3 **What are some of the more important initiatives the organization has been working on?**

Since the beginning of One Drop, I wanted the team to create programs that would be innovative and sustainable. That is true for our field projects, where we try to mix technical and financial solutions, but we also have social arts activities within the communities, to touch people while delivering an important conservation message. I call it our "soft medicine" approach. When it comes to fundraising, I believe that we have an original approach there as well. I've always tried to do things that can have many benefits—a sort of **"kill three birds with one stone"** type of thing. That is why the *Big One for One Drop* and *All In For One Drop* projects were successful, I believe. It was creating something original and exciting and, at the same time, **raising awareness** and funds. I believe *One Night for One Drop* will follow suit.

4 **What do you hope the organization will accomplish through events such as this?**

From its beginnings, One Drop has directly contributed to improve the lives of 300 000 people forever through its integrated water-access projects. To achieve lasting and significant positive impacts in Nicaragua, Honduras, Haiti, El Salvador, India and Burkina Faso, One Drop has designed a unique "tripod approach," based on three complementary components: a technical component aimed at improving access to water and promoting responsible water management and preservation principles; a microfinance component for granting loans to populations who already have better access to water so they may start productive revenue-generating activities; and a social arts and popular education component designed to raise collective awareness as well as educate and mobilize the population on water-related issues. One Drop strives to create sustainable change.

5 **Where would you like to see the world's water situation 10 years from now? And how do you envision us, as a global community, getting there?**

By 2017, with the aid of committed and action-driven partners and donors, One Drop aims to significantly and durably improve the living conditions of more than 1 000 000 human beings. In 10 years, we would like to see that water, this vital resource, is available to all. We think that in order to achieve this great challenge, we need to work together—to collaborate. Everyone has the capacity to act and to make a difference, and One Drop intends to motivate and to convince people to join and act.

Grammar in Context
The Possessive Form

The word highlighted in yellow in paragraph 2 is an example of the possessive form.

Most singular nouns are made possessive by adding apostrophe -s ('s).

> Water is the 21st century's greatest challenge.

> 21st century's greatest challenge = the greatest challenge of the 21st century

If a noun is plural and ends in -s, it is made possessive by adding only an apostrophe *after* the -s.

> Developing **countries'** health depends on clean water.

> countries' health = the health of developing countries

Highlight two examples of the possessive apostrophe in the reading.

 For more about the possessive form, see Grammar Guide page 207.

strive (v) to try very hard

kill two birds with one stone (exp) to achieve two things with one action. Here, Laliberté implies that One Drop is achieving several things at the same time.

raise awareness (exp) help people know about and understand an issue or problem

Comprehension

Answer the following questions. If the answer to a True/False question is False, rewrite the sentence to make it true.

1. What is the main idea of this text? Answer in 2 to 3 sentences.

   the organization protect water

2. What was the first social program created by Cirque du Soleil?

   This program was designed for at-risk youth.

3. What prompted Guy Laliberté to create One Drop?

   water
   As they approached the cirque du soleils 5th anniversary

4. One Drop has sponsored programs in Latin America and India.

   ☐ True ☑ False

5. What are the three elements of the "tripod approach" favoured by One Drop?

   Technical component, micro finance component Social arts and popula.

6. What is required for One Drop to achieve its objective of improving the lives of one million people?

   The aid committal and action driven po

7. Scan the paragraphs indicated and find a word that matches each definition. Circle the appropriate word in the reading.
   a) basic/important (para. 1) *fundamental*
   b) use up (para. 2)
   c) parts (para. 4) *componente*
   d) essential/crucial (para. 5) *vital*
   e) persuade/convert (para. 5) *convence*

8. Why do you think One Drop is so successful? Give at least two reasons.

9. Find five words in the reading from the word family table you completed on page 65. List the words and identify the parts of speech as used in the reading.

Writing

Summarize the article in your own words. Ensure that in the summary you answer the Wh- questions: Who? What? Where? When? Why? How? Remember that you must not include your opinion in a summary. Begin your summary with the sentence "In an interview with Guy Laliberté, founder of *Cirque du Soleil*, . . . "

Speaking

Prepare a presentation (3–4 minutes) about someone who has inspired you. It can be someone well known or someone you know personally. Who is this person? What has he or she done to inspire you? What are the qualities you admire? What impact has he or she had, locally or globally? Describe exactly how this person has positively affected your life.

Vocabulary in Action

Make or *Do*?

Rene Silva says that people are trying to *do good* and Zea Tongeman says that she has *made a difference*. When do you use *make* and when do you use *do*?

Generally, **make** is used when the activity involves creating or producing something, whereas **do** is used for accomplishing or performing a task.

> I **did** the shopping and then **made** dinner for friends.

However, some common expressions, including those below, do not follow this rule, and simply have to be memorized.

Make	Do
make a mistake	do your part
make a decision	do your best
make a promise	do nothing
make a difference	do well
make an effort	do something

1. Complete these sentences with expressions that include *do* from the box above. The words in parentheses are clues.

   a) Small actions can _____ (act) to help our planet.

   b) If we _____ (don't act), the world will have no more water in 10 years.

   c) Nobody expects miracles! Just _____ (contribute) by volunteering for a cause that you care about.

   d) Many people _____ (try hard) to help others in need.

   e) Guy Laliberté said that as soon as Cirque du Soleil started _____ and making money, the company started giving back and helping people.

2. Complete these sentences, using expressions that include *make* from the boxes above. Conjugate *make* as necessary.

a) Everyone can _____ (change in a positive way) in this world by becoming involved.

b) We should all _____ (try) to change the world for the better.

c) After the death of his friend, RaSia _____ (vowed) to change things in his community.

d) When you _____ (decide) to become involved, you will find there are many others who think as you do.

e) It's easy to _____ (do something wrong). What is important is to learn from it.

WATCHING

Watching Strategy

Predicting

Predicting means making an "educated guess" about the content of a reading, or an audio or video clip. Thinking ahead and using your experience to predict will help you to connect ideas and information and will improve your comprehension.

1. Watch a short video clip. Your teacher will stop the video at certain points and ask you to make predictions about the subject.

2. What is the video about? Were you able to predict accurately? Is the video effective? Why or why not?

Pre-Watching Activity

Freewriting is a fun, easy way to get your ideas down on paper. You write non-stop about a topic for a set period of time without worrying about spelling, punctuation, or grammar.

Take 4–5 minutes to freewrite about the ocean using any or all of the following questions as prompts:

1. What memories do you have of the sea or the ocean?

2. What do you associate with the sea or the ocean?

3. What challenges do the oceans face today? Which ones would you like to help solve?

Ocean Cleanup Project (7:20) ▶️

PBS

Boyan Slat is a young Dutchman who has devised an ingenious method of *(clever)* cleaning up ocean pollution. In the following interview, you will learn why he developed the Ocean Cleanup project and how his invention could help to resolve the problem.

Comprehension

Answer the following questions. If the answer to a True/False question is False, rewrite the sentence to make it true.

1. Listen to Boyan Slat's comments and fill in the blanks.

   Within ___10___ years from now, we would already be really close to getting clean oceans again and perhaps in ___20___ [to] ___30___ years, I think the oceans can be like they were in perhaps the ___1950___, before we were using plastic [on] this scale.

2. Why is it important to remove large pieces of plastic from the ocean?
   Because don't let large pieces break down and dispersed. the animal eat it. goes to food (intercept the big plastic) chain

3. Ocean garbage patches are created by ocean currents.   ☑ True   ☐ False
   ___170,000___

4. What motivated Boyan Slat's concern about the quantity of plastic in the ocean?
   6 years ago when having a vacation with his family. diving in Greece, diving, more plastic than fish

5. After coming up with the idea for the barrier, Boyan quit college and did each of the following. Put the steps in order from 1–5.

   raised money through crowdfunding **1**   co-authored a report on the project **4**
   tested a scale model of the barrier **4**   tested the model at sea **3 5**
   hired a staff of specialists **2**

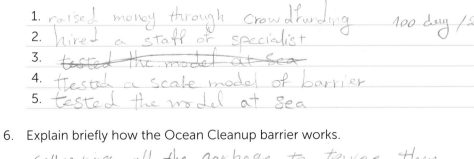

   1. raised money through crowdfunding   100 day / 2.2 million $
   2. hired a staff of specialist
   3. ~~tested the model at sea~~
   4. tested a scale model of barrier
   5. tested the model at sea

6. Explain briefly how the Ocean Cleanup barrier works.
   Collecting all the garbage to towee then move it to the shore to recycle.

7. How does engineer Allard Van Hoeken describe the testing process that will be used for the barrier?

put corn garbage to barrier to see it works or not (keep and collect)

8. What is the length of the final barrier that will be placed in the Pacific Ocean and when will it be in position?

62 miles / 2020

9. All the funding for the prototype comes from private investors.

☐ True   ☑ False

most investores and dutch government

10. Nick Mallos is sceptical about the project. Why? What alternative does he suggest?

dynamic sy dangerous eco system machine and change

11. What do you think of the project? Discuss the advantages and disadvantages of such an initiative with a small group.

LISTENING

Pre-Listening Activity

Work with a partner or small group to answer these questions.

When someone mentions a homeless person, what images come to mind? How do you see the person? What does this person do every day? What difficulties does he or she face? Have you ever wondered how the person ended up living on the streets? What resources or organizations are available for the homeless and what kind of help do they provide?

Share your answers with the class.

Paying It Forward (6:11) 🔊

David Gray and Jennifer Lee
CBC Calgary Eyeopener

You don't need to be a bright young teenager or a billionaire to help others. Listen to the story of a homeless man from Calgary named Gaston who, despite having very little, wanted to contribute to society. Learn how his initiative inspired others to make a difference.

Comprehension

Answer the following questions. If the answer to a True/False question is False, rewrite the sentence to make it true.

HIV (abbr) Human Immunodeficiency Virus—the virus that causes AIDS

COPD (abbr) a lung disease that makes it hard to breathe

Inn from the Cold (n) Calgary's original and largest emergency family shelter

1. What is the main idea of this listening? Answer in 2 to 3 sentences. *few*
   homeless addictive didn't have family and friends

2. How did Jacqueline help Gaston? *him*
   fixed the place to live, support (settle a place to live)

3. Why did she like him?
   He's such a funny guy, sterne, oppinion, doesn't like people mess with him.

4. What did Gaston do with the money he received for the bottles he collected?
   bottle picking (buy tricycle)

5. Why does the director of Inn from the Cold think that Gaston left his possessions to the association?
   he like to help women and children who need a help

6. What happened to Gaston's bike?
   a) It was given to a child.
   b) It was sold in a garage sale.
   c) Another homeless person took it.
   d) Someone bought it at a silent auction. *(d circled)*

7. Cole, a 10 year-old boy, bought Gaston's bike. ☐ True ☑ False

8. Give two reasons why Cole wants to continue Gaston's work.
   Want to donate, raise money for food and shelter for children

9. Why does the director say that Gaston's story is "perfect"?
   the child who steps inward and help others (children)

10. What do you find most interesting about this story? Why? Share your answer with a partner or a small group.
   has a such obstacles that face will carry on

Speaking

Discuss these questions with a partner, then share your answers with the class.

1. Has this story changed your opinion of homeless people? Why or why not?

2. Provide an example of a time when you changed your opinion of someone and explain why you changed your mind.

3. Do you think we are too quick to judge others? Can you give examples?

4. Do you agree with the quote at the end of the interview: "You've never truly lived until you've done something for someone who can never repay you"? Why or why not? Explain your answer.

Writing

For information about writing a well-structured essay, see Writing Strategies page 120.

Choose one of the Speaking activity questions above and write a four-paragraph essay explaining your answer and point of view. Start with an interesting introduction. Include two development paragraphs with appropriate support and end with a brief conclusion.

REVISING AND EDITING

Read the following text and correct the eight past tense errors and two word choice errors.

Malala Yousafzai of Pakistan jointly win the Nobel Peace Prize in 2014 for risking her life to fight for young women's right to education. The decision make Malala the youngest Nobel winner ever. Raised in Pakistan's beautiful Swat Valley, Malala had just 11 years old when she begun speaking out in TV interviews, determined to do a difference for girls who aspired to education. She were critically injured in 2012, when a Taliban gunman boarded her school bus and shotted her in the head. She survived through luck (the bullet did not entered her brain) and underwent several operations in Britain. She continues her activism and her studies. She learn of her Nobel win while she was in chemistry class at Edgbaston High School for Girls in Birmingham, a city in England where she now lives with her family. Her father, Ziauddin Yousafzai, sayed that Malala winning the Nobel Peace Prize will be beneficial for the rights of girls around the world.

Indonesian activists celebrate Malala Yousafzai's Nobel Peace Prize award.

Writing

Choose one of the following activities and write a short essay (four paragraphs). Remember to start your essay with an interesting introduction and cite your source. Include two development paragraphs with support from your video or report. End your essay with a brief conclusion.

GG For more information about verb tenses, see Grammar Guide page 215.

1. Go online and search using the term "One Drop Foundation featuring In-Q." Watch the short video and write a response to a phrase or image that you found interesting or surprising.

2. Find and watch a short report online about a person or a group making a difference. Identify the main idea of the report. (Ask yourself: Who? What? Where? When? Why? How?) Explain what you found most interesting about the report and write two questions you would like to ask the people involved.

Reading

Find an article online about a person or a group making a difference. Read the article and then do the following:

a) Write down the URL and the date you retrieved the article.

b) Write down the main idea of the article. (Ask yourself: Who? What? Where? When? Why? and How?)

c) Highlight five different verb tenses in the article and explain why each tense is used.

Speaking

Choose one of the following activities and prepare a short oral presentation (3–4 minutes) summarizing the results of your research.

S For information about preparing an effective oral presentation, see Speaking Skills page 131.

1. Research online to learn about a young person who is making a difference in the local community or in the world.

2. Interview someone you know who is making a significant contribution to his or her community.

Vocabulary

DONATIONS

1. Complete a word family table, like the one on page 65, for five important new words you learned in this unit. Remember that not all word families contain all four parts of speech.

Noun	Verb	Adjective	Adverb

2. Complete the crossword using words you have learned in this unit.

Across

2   durable or long-lasting

4   generally accepted

5   common

6   an important moment or event

7   dependable

8   make possible

9   without pattern or reason

10 try hard to do your best

Down

1   move things around carelessly while searching for something

2   a poor area with many small houses in bad condition

3   knowledge of a situation or problem

UNIT 5
The Sharing Economy

The more we share, the more we have.

—Leonard Nimoy

Consumer behaviour is undergoing radical change with the growth of an economy in which the focus is less on ownership and more on the collective sharing of resources. Is this new business model truly more equitable and beneficial for all? In this unit, you will explore how the sharing economy is changing our lives.

Speaking

Complete the chart, thinking about items that you own.

	Do you own this?	On average, how many hours per day do you use it?	Would you be willing to share it with a stranger when you are not using it?
car	☐ Yes ☑ No	never	☐ Yes ☑ No
bike	☐ Yes ☑ No	no	☐ Yes ☑ No
cellphone	☑ Yes ☐ No	4 hours	☐ Yes ☑ No
computer/laptop/tablet	☑ Yes ☐ No	2 hours	☐ Yes ☑ No
video game console	☐ Yes ☑ No	No	☐ Yes ☑ No
skis/snowboard/skates	☑ Yes ☐ No	No	☑ Yes ☐ No

For each of the items you said you would be willing to share (in column 3), would you charge money to the person for sharing it? Explain why or why not.

Are there other items you would or would not share with others? What are they?

Would your answers be any different if you were being asked to share with a friend rather than a stranger?

Vocabulary in Action

Lend or Borrow?

Lend: to give something (money or an article) to someone temporarily with the understanding that it will be returned

> Imran often **lends** his car to Laura.

> Imran often **lends** Laura his car.

Note You "lend something **to** somebody" or you "lend someone something." Notice the absence of *to* in the second example.

Borrow: to have someone give you something (money or an article) for temporary use with the understanding that it will be returned

> Laura often **borrows** the car from Imran.

> Laura often **borrows** Imran's car.

Note You "borrow something **from** somebody" or you "borrow somebody's something." Note the absence of *from* in the second example.

Which of the following sentences indicates that you are *not* the owner of the car?

☐ I lent him my car.　　　　　　☐ I borrowed his car.

☐ I exchanged my car with his car.　　☐ I returned his car.

READING

The Sharing Economy

By Terry O'Reilly

Under the Influence, CBC.ca

1   The Sharing Economy has two main elements: either the sharing of goods, or the sharing of services. That's why it's also called the P2P market, or Peer-To-Peer, because it eliminates the need for traditional, big corporations. It's a person-to-person transaction. In a nutshell, it's the sharing, bartering, lending, trading or swapping of goods without having to own them.

2   Rachel Botsman, who wrote an excellent book on the subject entitled *What's Mine Is Yours*, explains it this way: Sharing products without owning them is based primarily on products with a **"high-idling capacity."** For example, there are over 80 million power drills in North American homes. Do you know the total time an average power drill will be used in its lifetime? 13 minutes. In its lifetime. Do you own a car? Chances are your car will sit in your driveway 23 hours a day. That's the definition of "idling capacity"—many of the products in our lives simply sit idle and unused. The average car costs about $8000 a year to run. So the sharing economy asks: Why own a car when you can just share a car with someone else?

3   From this thinking, new companies have been born. For example, if you want to borrow that drill, you could log on to Neighborgoods.net. It's a website that connects people with items to people who need items. The best part is the Neighborgoods website facilitates the transaction by connecting you with someone in or near your neighbourhood and charges nothing. Its mission is to help people conserve resources and live more connected lives. You also have the option of swapping goods. There are many websites like SwapItShop.com or SwapSity.ca that connect you to people who have goods they want to trade.

4   Let's talk car ownership. For decades, you only had a few choices. You could buy a car. Lease a car. Or rent a car. Then along came companies like ZipCar. Suddenly, you could rent cars by the hour, or even for an hour, instead of by the day—a concept that revolutionized the car rental industry. While ZipCar is not a "sharing site," it did begin to alter the mindset around car ownership. Many people now had the option to rent a car for occasional **errands**, instead of owning a car that sat idle for most of the day.

5   Rachel Botsman tells of a fascinating study ZipCar did in 2009. ZipCar took 250 self-confessed car addicts from 13 cities and convinced them to surrender their keys for a month. If they wanted to go somewhere, they had to walk, bike, or take transit. After one month:

- participants collectively lost 413 pounds (187 kilograms)
- distances biked increased 132 percent
- distances walked increased 93 percent

But here was the amazing statistic: 100 of the 250 participants did not want their keys back.

Grammar in Context

Passive Voice

An example of the passive voice is highlighted in paragraph 1.

The passive voice is used to place the focus on the object of an action, rather than the person doing that action.

> The sharing economy is called the P2P market.

The emphasis is on the sharing economy. (It doesn't matter who is calling it the P2P market).

Compare with an active sentence:

> People also call the sharing economy the P2P market.

In an active sentence the emphasis is on the person who performed the action.

The passive voice is formed by the verb *to be* + the past participle.

Find five examples of the passive voice in the reading.

 For more information on the passive voice, see Grammar Guide page 212.

high-idling capacity (n phr) spending a long time not in use

errand (n) short trip to do or get something

6 Remember, these were car addicts. And they had lost their urge to own. That wasn't just an interesting statistic; it was a revelation. Suddenly, new online companies launched to serve the growing segment of the population that no longer wanted to own a car. One is Uber, which involves using an app to hire private cabs and car services.

7 A site called Shared Earth.com matches people with land to share, with people who want to grow things. Gardeners get free access to backyards by sharing what they grow with the owners. Within three months of its launch, 29 million square feet of land had been shared.

trump (v) to be more important than

currency (n) something valued like money

8 There are two fundamental building blocks of the sharing economy: One is the belief that access **trumps** ownership. The other is trust among strangers. All sharing sites use reputations as **currency**. Borrowers rate lenders, lenders rate borrowers, and you can flag another member's account if something goes wrong.

recalibrated (v) changed

9 Those two concepts had their roots in two things: a generational attitude shift, and an economic downturn. When the Great Recession hit in 2008, many people lost their jobs, some lost their homes, and the way most people lived was completely **recalibrated**. Job insecurity and fear of making big, expensive purchases changed people's behaviour.

empowerment (n) a sense of influence or power

burden (n) something difficult to accept or deal with

10 Then there is the demographic impact. The Millennial generation, born between the early 1980s and the early 2000s, are a larger group than the Baby Boomers. And by 2030, they will make up 75 percent of the buying public globally. They don't see ownership as **empowerment**; they see it as a **burden**. Not only do they not want ownership, they don't want the responsibility of ownership. As the *New York Times* recently said, the only thing they want to own is their reputation. A good reputation is like having a giant key that will open multiple doors. Young people just don't want to own the door.

11 Many Millennials watched their parents struggle through the recession, and they, themselves, are still having a difficult time finding stable jobs in a post-recession economy. As a result, they have been culturally programmed to rent, borrow, and share. And the sharing economy is giving them options.

Comprehension

Answer the following questions. If the answer to a True/False question is False, rewrite the sentence to make it true.

1. What is the main idea of this reading? Answer in 2–3 sentences.

    Sharing economy

2. Explain how the sharing economy threatens traditional big businesses.

    People don't own as many things because they are sharing them, which results in a loss of profits for businesses that selling these things.

3. According to the text, what is the main advantage of sharing certain items?

    We are reducing the times that things are sitting idle. People pay only for what they need. It helps people connect with each other and saves resources.

4. How does Neighborgoods help people conserve resources and live more connected lives?

3 It conserves resources because less things are being purchased, so we don't have to produce as many items. It connects people because it lets them meet their neighbors and borrow things from them.

5. How did Zipcar revolutionize the car rental industry?

4 It lets people rent cars by the hour instead of by the day.

6. Borrowers and lenders rate each other online.   ☑ True   ☐ False

8

7. What role did the recession play in the development of the sharing economy?

9 People lost their jobs and had less money, so they couldn't afford to own as many things as before and didn't want to make expensive purchases.

8. The reading mentions car-sharing, land-sharing, and goods-sharing. Name some networks you know of that offer other items or services for sharing.

5 Bike-sharing; reusing building materials; buying used textbooks; Sharing phone chargers; AirBnB; times sharing.

Car-Sharing: Uber, ZipCar.

7. land - sharing: shared Earth. com.

good-sharing: swapltshop.com

9. After the Zipcar study, 100 of the 250 participants decided that they no longer wanted to own a car. Give three reasons why you think they didn't want their car keys returned.

Their health was improved by the exercise they had to do. It was per to not own a car. Didn't have to car worry about Parking.
' Pollution.

10. Why do you think a good reputation is so important to Millennials? (Use your own ideas to develop your answer).

A good reputation can help you get a job, or get a loan or mortgage; People will lead you things; you can rent an apartment; people trust you. to do things that not everyone gets to do.

Vocabulary

Use context clues to help you find the following:

1. Two words that are synonyms for *exchanging* trading, swapping (para. 1)

2. Two words that mean *pay to use something for a period of time* rent, lease (para. 4)

3. A word that means *strong desire* urge (para. 6)

4. A word that means *evaluate how good something is* rate (para. 8)

5. A word that means *identify as a problem* flag (para. 8)

Writing

The effects of the sharing economy are regularly debated in the news. One point of view is that the sharing economy is taking income away from people such as taxi drivers or hotel employees. Others argue that it creates healthy competition in these industries. How do you feel about the sharing economy? Is it generally a positive or a negative phenomenon? Write a paragraph (about 100 words) explaining your opinion. Remember to start with a clear topic sentence and to provide adequate support.

DISCOVER GRAMMAR

Modals

GG For more information on modals, see Grammar Guide page 177.

Modals include *can, could, may, might, must, have to,* and *should*. They are used with verbs to express ability, possibility, obligation, prohibition, and advice or to request permission. Below is a list of common modals and their meanings.

Modal	To express	Example
can	ability	**Can** you explain the idea of the sharing economy to me?
could	past ability	I **could** have bought a snowboard, but I preferred to borrow one from a friend.
may/might/ could	possibility	I **may** use a bike-sharing service this summer. They **might** stay in an apartment rather than a hotel. You **could** go on a student exchange.
must/have to*	obligation	You **must** follow the rules when participating in the sharing economy. When I was younger, I **had to** share my toys with my brother.
don't have to	no obligation	You **don't have to** own a car nowadays; you can share one.
must not	prohibition	You **must not** damage an object you have borrowed.
should	advice, recommendation	She **should** swap her clothes with friends.
can may (formal)	asking permission	**Can** I join the group? **May** I borrow your bike?

***Note** *Have to* means the same as *must* but *have to* is more commonly used.

1. Read each sentence and circle the correct modal form.
    a) possibility → People (may/must) trade items they no longer want.
    b) ability → Consumers (can/should) save money by borrowing goods.
    c) obligation → You (must/don't have to) be respectful when you rate someone online.
    d) possibility → The sharing economy (might/can) change over the next decade.
    e) advice → Everyone (should/must) contribute to the reduction of waste.

2. Find and highlight two modals along with the verbs that they accompany in paragraph 6 of the reading on page 89.

Speaking

Complete the following chart with your own answers, and then interview two other students and record their answers.

	Your answer	Student 1	Student 2
When on vacation, would you stay in a room in someone's home rather than a hotel? Why or why not? What are the advantages and disadvantages of staying in someone's home?			
Have you ever used a ride-sharing service? Why or why not? What are the advantages and disadvantages of ride-sharing services?			

Share the results of your interviews with a small group or with the class.

WATCHING

Vocabulary

Read the introduction to the video and note the words in bold.

> Taxis and hotels are some of the oldest business models around. Now they're being **disrupted** by an even older idea: sharing. Whether it's your unused room or a ride in your car, there are **networks** to help you rent what you have to **willing** customers. No **middle man**, no regulations. So you can imagine established businesses around the world are trying to stop it because this new sharing economy is **worth** billions of dollars and is still growing.

Using the context provided in the paragraph above, match each word with the correct meaning.

	Option 1	Option 2
disrupted (adj) _1_	prevented from continuing as usual	stopped completely
network (n) _1_	groups that are connected for a specific purpose	a computer system
willing (adj) _2_	interested	ready to do something without persuasion
middle man (n) _2_	person in charge	an agent who is the link between supplier and consumer
worth (adj) _2_	sold	equal in value to

How the Sharing Economy Is Catching On (10:50) ▶

Chris Brown

CBC News

The people of British Columbia are known for being among the first to adopt new ideas. One trend that is now popular everywhere, sharing things rather than owning them, appeals to people who want to do more with less. Opinions differ about the impact of the sharing economy but there's no doubt that this new approach is disrupting old ways of doing business. See what people on both sides of the issue have to say.

Comprehension

Answer the following questions. If the answer to a True/False question is False, rewrite the sentence to make it true.

1. a) Why does Alisha Damani share her dog?

   _____

   _____

   b) Why do some people borrow her dog?

   _____

2. Sharing is a smart way to do more with less for people who . . .

   Check all answers that are mentioned.

   ☐ have busy lives   ☐ have tight budgets

   ☐ don't really need something   ☐ like the social aspect of sharing

3. In just six years, Airbnb has grown to a business worth _____

4. Airbnb makes its money by taking commission only from people who rent out their homes.   ☐ True   ☐ False

   _____

5. How many Canadians have their properties registered with Airbnb?

   ☐ 2000   ☐ 10 000   ☐ 20 000   ☐ 200 000

6. What advantages of the Uber service does the Uber driver mention in the report?

   _____

   _____

   _____

7. What is Calvin Welch's main criticism of Airbnb?

   _____

   _____

8. Airbnb and Uber have inspired other community initiatives. Name two of them.

   _____

9. The video presents both sides of the argument about the sharing economy. What are they? What additional arguments for each side can you find?

Pros
— cheap, convenient, | _Cons_ _— hurting big bussinesses_
Individuals can earn their | _— Can hurt poor people too_
own money and control their | _— People have to worry about their_
shedules. | _reputations_

10. In 3–4 sentences, summarize the main idea of the report.

_____

_____

_____

_____

PRONUNCIATION

Silent Letters

In English, some letters are silent. This is often because pronunciation has changed over the years, but spelling has not.

1. Listen to the audio recording of the following pairs of words, and circle the silent letters for each group. An example has been done for you.

		Silent letter	
listen	often	(t)	e
bomb	thumb	m	(b)
foreign	sign	(g)	n
debt	doubt	(b)	t
knife	knee	n	(k)
could	should	(l)	d
write	wrap	(w)	r
hour	honest	o	(h)
island	aisle	(s)	l
psychology	psychiatry	s	(p)
daughter	thought	(gh)	t

2. Listen to the following words. With a partner, take turns practising the correction pronunciation.

crumb _b_   whistle _t_
doubtful _b_   wrist _w_
handsome _d_   muscle _c_
calm _l_   island _s_
pneumonia _p_   guest _w_

Vocabulary in Action

Slang

It is natural to use informal English in casual conversation, but avoid slang and overly familiar vocabulary in written assignments for college.

I met my ~~buddies~~ <u>friends</u> when we were all ~~kids~~ <u>children</u> at elementary school.

Use standard verb forms.

I'm gonna → I'm going to

I wanna → I want to

Find five examples of informal English in the reading on pages 88–90.

BYOB= bring your own booze

pixie haircut (n) a short hairstyle cut in layers

bust (n) failure

READING

Pre-Reading Activity

In a small group, discuss the following questions.

1. Have you ever created or participated in a public or private Facebook group?
2. Why did you create or join this group?
3. What was the objective of the group?
4. How many members were involved?
5. Was it successful? Explain.
6. What are the advantages of participating in a Facebook group?

Share your answers with another group or with the class.

Vocabulary

Scan the paragraphs indicated and, using context clues, determine the meaning of these words.

dawn on (v)   (para. 1)   <u>to have an idea occur to you, to realize something that you didn't before.</u>

flourish (v)   (para. 2)   <u>to grow and become successful</u>

copycat (adj)   (para. 2)   <u>similar, duplicate</u>

vet (v)   (para. 5)   <u>to get more info about someone to see if they are a good person.</u>

appeal (n)   (para. 6)   _____

Facebook Flea Market Has Just One Rule: No Cash Allowed

By Geoffrey Vendeville

Toronto Star

*From vintage bike saddles to **pixie haircuts**, almost anything can turn up in the Bunz Trading Zone.*

1   It all started because Emily Bitze needed a can of tomatoes. The artist and musician planned noodles for dinner, but didn't have the ingredients for a sauce, or the money to pay for it. That's when it dawned on her to invite her friends to form a private Facebook trading group called Bunz Trading Zone. "I didn't get what I wanted, but I was offered a can of hearts of palm. It was something," she recalled on a mid-summer Tuesday, in an interview at a bar on College St.

2   Her first trade was a **bust**: She turned down the hearts of palm because she finds them "gross," she said. But, to her surprise, the group flourished.

Two years later, it has surpassed 12 000 members, and copycat groups have emerged in other Canadian cities. The Montreal version of Bunz, a public group, has more than 700 members, while Peterborough has more than 500 and Edmonton has just over 100.

3   Toronto "bunz," as members call one another, trade anything and everything. The only rule is no money allowed. **TTC** tokens and booze *[alcohol]* are the most common substitute. One man posted an ad trying to exchange a Bee Gees booklet for a "solid **lead** on a reasonably priced place for my cat and me to live." Another wanted to swap a sky blue, vintage bike saddle from her grandmother's tricycle for a sewing lesson, beeswax candles, or other **knickknacks**.

4   Bitze, 31, says she acquired her most prized possession, a German eight-track player and radio, through the group for a bottle of whisky and another of gin. It's equipped with a flashing party light and doubles as a bar, she said. "I use it every day. It's my favourite thing."

5   The administrator of the group, **a.k.a**. Mother Bunz or Queen Bunz, she mediates between members, kicking out troublemakers. She also works in a vintage clothing store on Queen St. W. and plays guitar and sings in the band Milk Lines. In Bunz's early days, she screened each person who applied to join. The criteria were: Do you live in Toronto? Do we have mutual friends? She also wanted to know if you looked like a creep. Now, she gets hundreds of applicants a week, more than she can possibly vet, and simply approves everyone.

6   Jonathan Hall, an assistant professor of economics at the University of Toronto, says it's puzzling that the group has become so popular. Since transit tokens and booze are almost like money, he says he doesn't quite understand the appeal. "This is more psychology than economics, but some people dislike markets," he said. "Sometimes when you just call it something different, people are OK with it." He speculated that it may be the social aspect of the group—the fact that many members share friends and can see one another's profile—that distinguishes it from classifieds sites like Craigslist, which has a free stuff section. "Whenever I sell something on Craigslist or Kijiji, I always call my brother and say, 'By the way, someone's coming by my house; if you don't hear from me in an hour, I was murdered.'" People may think Bunz is a little safer and more reliable when they know they are trading with a friend-of-a-friend, he said.

7   For Bitze, the secret to the group's popularity is that its members have developed a strong sense of community built around the idea that one person's junk is another's treasure. "It's not just this corporate blah, blah, blah," she said. "People have made friends. They've found jobs. They like to support and help each other." Her only worry, she says, is that the group will soon grow so large that it stops working. Already, it's become so big that posts are quickly overtaken by others and buried at the bottom of a pile. It's inevitable that the group will come to an end one day, she says. "That special thing will be gone, and maybe some of those people won't be there anymore, or people will get bored with it," she said. "It would be such a bummer. But it started with just a bunch of my friends, so I could just do it again."

Grammar in Context
Comparative and Superlative Adjectives

Use the comparative form of adjectives to compare two things or people.

For one-syllable adjectives, add -er.

> On vacation, it is usually **cheaper** to stay in an apartment than in a hotel.

For adjectives of two or more syllables, add *more* + adjective.

> It is **more interesting** to stay in someone's home and get to know the local culture.

Use the superlative form of adjectives to compare three or more people or things.

For one-syllable adjectives, add *the* + adjective + -est.

> Car-sharing is **the cheapest** way to use a car without owning one.

For adjectives of two or more syllables, add *the* + *most* + adjective.

> The sharing economy is **the most interesting** social initiative of the past 15 years.

Find two examples of comparative adjectives and two examples of superlative adjectives in the text.

 For more information on comparative and superlative forms, see Grammar Guide page 189.

TTC (n) Toronto Transit Commission (public transportation system)

lead (n) information

knickknack (n) small object or ornament

a.k.a. (abbr) also known as

Comprehension

Answer the following questions. If the answer to a True/False question is False, rewrite the sentence to make it true.

1. What is the main idea of this reading?
   a) Facebook groups are a great way to connect with people who share common interests.
   b) Facebook groups connect communities and enable them to share goods and services.
   c) Facebook groups created to share goods and services are popular because they connect communities who appreciate the social aspect of the site.

2. Why did Emily Bitze first create the Facebook group?
   She needs a con of tomatoes, but didn't have money

3. Emily didn't expect the group to be as successful as it was. ☑ True ☐ False
   _____

4. Give three examples of trades that were offered through the site.
   Trading a Bee Gee album for information on an apartment
   Trading a vintage bicycle seat for sewing lesson
   Trading a German eight-track player for alcohol.

5. What is Emily's role with Bunz Trading Zone?
   She is the administrator. She is also known as Mother Bunz
   or queen Bunz.

6. To what does Professor Jonathan Hall attribute the appeal of the site?
   some people don't like markets or corporations
   some people like the social aspect of the site
   Bunz might be safer and more reliable than other sites
   _____

7. Does Emily Bitze agree with Professor Hall's analysis? Explain your answer.
   She agrees with his analysis because she says people have turned
   it into a community, and it's appealing because it's not corporate.
   _____

8. Would you participate in a group like this? Why or why not?
   No, because it's too consuming and there aren't any items in my area
   that I interested it.

9. This reading provides several examples of familiar language. With a partner, come up with a synonym for each of the following informal words or expressions in the reading.

   gross (adj) _disgusting_ (para. 2)
   booze (n) _Alcohol_ (para. 3)
   stuff (n) _things_ (para. 6)
   bummer (n) _disappointment_ (para. 7)
   a bunch of (exp) (para. 7)
       a group of

Writing

Professor Hall and Emily Bitze each express an opinion on why Bunz Trading Zone and similar sites are so successful. Why do you think people participate in them? Write a paragraph (about 100 words) giving your opinion. Remember to start with a clear topic sentence and to provide pertinent support.

SPEAKING

Create an in-class trading zone. The objective is to exchange two items you have at home for something new that interests you more.

1. Write each item you are willing to trade on a separate card. Write your name on each card.

2. Move around the class to find items you want and people who want your items.

3. If you find someone to trade with, exchange cards. Remember, you can keep trading and exchanging items as you negotiate for something that you want.

4. Continue trading until you have two new items that you want.

LISTENING

Vocabulary

You will hear each of the following words in bold in the listening.

1. The municipality passed a **bylaw** prohibiting parking on the main street.

2. Despite rumours of wrongdoing, the company does all its business **above board**.

3. There is no point in having regulations unless the city is able to **enforce** them.

4. People can determine whether guests are **trustworthy** by checking their online reputation.

5. One **pitfall** of renting out a room in your home is finding that your activities are illegal.

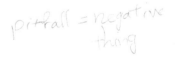

pitfall = negative thing

Using the context provided in the sentences above, match each word with the correct definition.

Word or expression	Definition
✓1. pitfall (n) __b__	a) legitimately, legally
✓2. trustworthy (adj) __c__	b) hidden danger or difficulty not easily recognized
✓3. bylaw (n) __d__	c) dependable, reliable
✓4. above board (adv) __a__	d) regulation made by local government
✓5. enforce (v) __e__	e) to ensure that the rules are followed

The Pitfalls of Collaborative Consumption (6:57) 🔊

working together

Nora Young *buy sth*

CBC Spark

So far in this unit you have explored different aspects of the sharing economy: the individual, community, and social benefits. But what role does the law play in this changing market and should the law change to reflect new situations and changing social realities?

Comprehension

Answer the following questions. If the answer to a True/False question is False, rewrite the sentence to make it true.

1. What is the main idea of this listening?
    a) People like to use short-term rental services like Airbnb because of the social aspect.
    b) Short-term rental services are illegal in many places, but most municipalities do not enforce the law.
    c) Although they are breaking the law, many hosts and guests use short-term rental services like Airbnb.

2. Most people who rent Lily's apartment are tourists who stay for a couple of days.   ☐ True   ☑ False

    some of them rent for month

3. Lily checks that potential guests are reliable. Name two methods she uses.

    facebook check
    communication directly
    Airlab profile and rate

4. Name three benefits that Lily gains from renting out her apartment.

    Source of income
    make lots of friend
    feel part of culture
    city

5. In Vancouver, renting out an apartment for less than 30 days is illegal.   ☑ True   ☐ False

6. Why is there a bylaw regulating short-term rentals?

changing the character

7. When will the city of Vancouver intervene to enforce the bylaw?

Do sth

if there is complain

8. Name two other cities where short-term rentals have caused problems.

San-fransisco – newyork – Amesterdam

9. Name two conflicting "legitimate interests" that are mentioned in the report.

tradition business – powerful business – neighbours

10. Do you think the rental bylaws should change to reflect the realities of the shared economy? Why or why not? Provide two examples or reasons to support your opinion.

Speaking

Now that you have read, watched, and listened to various points of view on the sharing economy, what is your opinion of the issue?

1. Individually, write down the two best arguments in favour of the sharing economy and the two best arguments against the further development of it. Support each of your arguments with examples from the material in this unit as well as your own experience.

2. Form a small group of four to six students and share your ideas.

3. As a group, select the three most compelling arguments for and against the issue.

4. Share your ideas with the class.

WRITING

Using the arguments developed in the previous activity—in support of or against the sharing economy—take a position on the issue. Write a well-structured essay (300–350 words) on the subject.

REVISING AND EDITING

For more information about developing an effective thesis statement and topic sentences, see Writing Strategies page 117.

For more information about writing an effective conclusion, see Writing Strategies page 124.

Read the essay below and complete the following steps.

1. Write a thesis statement for the essay.

2. Write a topic sentence for each development paragraph.

3. Write a short conclusion. Summarize the main points of the essay and finish with a suggestion or prediction.

4. The essay contains eight modal errors. Underline the errors and make the corrections.

An Old Idea Comes Back into Vogue

The barter system, or trading, has been used around the world for centuries, even after the invention of money. For example, in the Middle Ages, Europeans travelled the globe to trade goods in exchange for silks and spices. Later, British and French explorers in Canada exchanged simple commodities with First Nations peoples for furs. More recently, bartering has regained popularity and become more organized through the use of technology.

Thesis statement: _____

_____

Topic sentence: _The barter system has been used again._

Connecting with a Facebook group or through another online site or app must help you trade items you no longer want for something you need, but should afford. For example, you can be able to swap that bike you loved as a child for something more useful to you now, like a printer. When was the last time you wore that T-shirt? Using social media, why not organize a clothes-swapping party with friends, to renew your wardrobe and have fun at the same time? Finally, you have to even find sites for exchanging apartments with other travellers. All you need to do is find someone from a city you've always wanted to visit, and you must trade homes and save money at the same time.

Topic sentence: _____

_____

Sites such as JOATU connect people who offer one service in exchange for another. For example, you would like to practise your English with a native speaker. Visit a sharing site, search for someone in your neighbourhood, and offer to exchange language lessons. You will improve your language skills, and you will might make new friends too! Maybe you are a yoga enthusiast who would love to learn how to snowboard. You are able to find a way to share your interest with someone and learn a new sport at the same time. Finally, you could get your bike fixed, but have no expertise? Why not offer to paint a room in exchange for the repair service? Exchanging services with someone is limited only by your skills and abilities.

Conclusion: _____

_____

_____

_____

CONSOLIDATING

Reading

Find an article expressing an opinion about a company involved in the sharing economy. The article can be in favour of or against this new business model.

1. Print or photocopy the article. Write down the source and the date you retrieved the article.

2. Highlight five key words and write your own definition of each.

3. Summarize the arguments presented in the article in approximately 100 words.

Writing

Search online for a video or article about how the sharing economy is changing areas of our lives such as office spaces, restaurants, and cafés. Try using search terms such as "we work," "anti-café" or "sharing economy + office."

1. Write down the URL and the date you retrieved the video or article.

2. Write a four-paragraph essay summarizing the video or article. Start with an interesting introduction and cite your source. Include two development paragraphs with support from your video or article. End your essay with a brief conclusion.

> **S** For more information about writing a well-structured essay, see Writing Strategies page 120.

Speaking

Do some research online about The Little Free Library, Neighborgoods, Cohealo, Skillshare, WeWork, tool libraries, or any another collaborative consumption project.

Prepare a short oral presentation (3—4 minutes) summarizing the services offered.

> **S** For information about preparing an oral presentation, see Speaking Strategies page 131.

Vocabulary

Complete one of the following activities.

1. Choose five vocabulary words from the unit that you consider important. For each, write a definition in your own words. Then use each word in a sentence that clearly demonstrates the meaning. You may also include a translation of each word.

2. Complete the following sentences using these vocabulary words from the unit.

     trade (v)   network (n)   willing (adj)   enforce (v)   flag (v)

a) Many people are ___willing___ to share their goods with others free of charge.

b) It is sometimes difficult to ___enforce___ the law.

c) Facebook is just one example of a social ___network.___

d) It is essential to ___flag___ _(rude, racist)_ inappropriate comments on the Internet.

e) If you have an item you no longer use, you could ___trade___ it for something more useful.

UNIT 6
The Volunteer Dilemma

You make a living by what you get, but you make a life by what you give.

—Anonymous

Volunteering is about giving: giving your time, skills, and energy to help others. Volunteering can help you learn new skills, bring you into contact with a diverse range of people and cultures, and expand your perspectives on life. In this unit, you'll discover the many sides of volunteering and how it can change lives for the better.

Speaking

Have you ever done volunteer work or do you know someone who has? What exactly do volunteers do and what kinds of organizations do they work with? What are the benefits of volunteering?

1. Interview three students and complete the following table.

	Student 1	Student 2	Student 3
1. Have you (or has anyone you know) ever done any volunteer work? If the person answers No, skip to question 5.			
2. What exactly did you (or the person you know) do?			
3. What did you (or the person you know) enjoy about the experience?			
4. What did you (or the person you know) learn?			
5. Would you like to volunteer? Why or why not?			
6. Why do you think people volunteer?			
7. What are the benefits for the volunteer and for the organization?			
8. On a scale of 1–5, how important do you think it is to give your time for volunteering? Explain your answer. (1 = not important; 5 = essential)			

2. Your teacher will now assign you to a small group that includes at least one person who has volunteer experience. The experienced volunteer will be the presenter.

Presenter: Give a brief oral presentation (2–3 minutes) about your volunteer experience. Explain where and why you volunteered, what you did, and what you learned. Be prepared to respond to questions from your group.

Audience: As you listen to the presentation, make a note of what you learn or information that surprises you. Ask the presenter questions to find out more details about the experience.

As a group, discuss your findings with the class.

READING

Pre-Reading Activity

Many people choose to do volunteer work abroad. Why do so many people want to help others? What motivates them? What advice do you think would be useful to someone wishing to volunteer in another country? What are some of the challenges of working in a different culture and environment? Brainstorm your answers to these questions with a partner or small group.

_____

_____

_____

_____

Share your ideas with the class.

Vocabulary

You will see each of the following words in bold in the reading.

1. Many people **buy into** the idea of volunteer travel without questioning the motives of trip organizers.

2. Young people can **be shaped by** a positive volunteer experience.

3. The wish to contribute to the well-being of society **fuels** many people's desire to volunteer.

4. Some people are motivated by a strong **impulse** to help a worthy cause.

5. Most reasons given for volunteering abroad are **sound**.

Using the context provided in the sentences above, match each word with the correct meaning.

	Option 1	Option 2
buy into (v) _2_	purchase	accept or believe
be shaped by (v) _1_	to be influenced	to be given form
fuel (v) _1_	support	supply
impulse (n) _1_	strong desire	movement
sound (adj) _2_	loud and noisy	showing good sense or judgment

Before volunteering in another country there are some simple things to think about to ensure that the experience truly benefits everyone involved. The following text offers advice about issues to consider before embarking on such an experience.

voluntourism (n) tourism that involves doing volunteer work in a local community while on vacation

clamour (n) strong demand for something by many people

scope (n) space or opportunity given

[handwritten: range]

Grammar in Context

Much or Many?

Many is used with plural countable nouns such as people or organizations.

> There are **many ways** to support a community.

Much is used with uncountable nouns such as information, money, or time.

> Many developing countries don't have **much money** to devote to projects.

Underline the correct word in the following sentences.

1. (Many/Much) effort is put into creating good relationships with the volunteers.
2. (Many/Much) people are interested in helping out.
3. Get as (many/much) information as possible before you volunteer abroad.

The Voluntourist Dilemma: Why We Still Volunteer Abroad

By Pippa Biddle

Go Overseas

1   Despite criticism of **voluntourism**, travel companies continue to rationalize why volunteering abroad makes sense. The volunteer travel industry presents its trip packages as meaningful, life-changing, and affordable. Especially for young and unskilled people, the trips look attractive. And when there is a **clamour** for a service and the chance to make money, the market responds by offering opportunity.

2   There must be a root cause, beyond the vague desire to do good, that causes well-meaning people to buy into the voluntourism experience. There must be a reason that, despite all the evidence that it isn't efficient or in the best interest of communities, people are doing it anyway.

3   In exploring voluntourism, we need to take into account the opinions of locals and industry professionals who know the field.

Remember Who We're Supposed to Be Helping

4   In a series of articles published in 2007 as part of the Brookings Institution's Brookings Policy Brief Series, David L. Caprara et al. identified some of the benefits of volunteer travel. They emphasized the positive impact that service work has on those taking part and write that international volunteers "tend to develop enduring habits of civic engagement." This improves both the lives of communities abroad and the volunteers' communities back home.

5   I will never argue that volunteer trips, both domestic and abroad, aren't positive learning and growth opportunities for participants. I believe that who I am today was shaped by the travel I've been able to do, some of it voluntourism. From packing vegetables for underprivileged families in Connecticut to working with HIV-positive children in the Dominican Republic, I am who I am because of the perspective and **scope** I acquired through volunteer work. Even my ill-fated trip to Tanzania made me more socially and globally aware, fueling what has become a passion for sustainable, community-focused development.

6   Let's ignore who I've become, and how every person who volunteers is changed, because that isn't supposed to be the purpose of volunteer travel. Most articles I write are met with the same criticism: "But it changes my life, so isn't it worth it?" No, that's not a good enough reason. Volunteer abroad, but *do so with others in mind*. Make sure your motives are truly unselfish and that you have something valuable to give.

Adjusting Our Methods and Marketing

7   Rather than trying to measure the benefit to the volunteer, look at evaluating the benefit to the community. That process leads to more sustainable development work without killing opportunities for travel and adventure

altogether. We must continue to encourage volunteering. The impulse that inspires a young person to volunteer is the *right* impulse and the reasons that they want to go are *good* reasons.

Here reason why you want to do something

8   Intent is not the problem. Execution is. We have to take that impulse to help and direct it toward the *most morally sound* and productive response. We must travel in a way that **empowers** and invests in local communities rather than presuming what's right for them and deciding that our unskilled young people are the solution.

why you feel something is

empower (v) to encourage self-realization

to encourage you to do something for yourself

What Does This Mean for Me?

9   Wanting to travel isn't bad, and wanting to give back isn't bad either. But the combination of travelling to new places and doing development work is rarely as simple as travel organizations say it is. Think about these points before planning your next trip.

10   **1. Where do you want to go and why?** Travel is exciting, and you should do it as much as you can, but knowing why you want to go somewhere is important. It's okay to be a tourist in Tanzania, and a volunteer in your hometown. Ask yourself: Where do I want to go and why?

11   **2. Do you really have the skills to volunteer abroad?** Knowing English doesn't make you an English teacher. Think hard about what you're qualified to do and whether your dollars, spent locally, could actually do more. Ask yourself: Who am I really trying to help and do I have the skills to be effective?

12   **3. Is volunteering really the only way to support the community?** There are many ways to support a community without taking part in voluntourism initiatives. Consider staying in small, locally owned hotels or hostels instead of big, foreign-owned **resorts**, for example. Ask yourself: Is there a way to travel to the place I'd like to go that will support local communities directly without having to "volunteer"?

a hotel

resort (n) place providing recreation and entertainment for vacationers

13   **Maybe volunteering isn't for me?** If, after reading this, you're not sure if volunteering is a good fit for you, but you still want to help communities abroad, travel differently, or find a way to meet another travel goal, there are alternatives.

- Live with a host family. (It's not just for students!)
- Take a language course.
- Find an NGO, development organization, Peace Corps volunteer, or other initiative you want to support, then visit them or bring donations. (Note: Please do not bring "handouts for the kids" but go through a **vetted** organization to donate items or money.)
- Support local businesses, hotels, and shops while you're abroad.
- Wait. If you're not skilled yet, hold on to the dream for a little later in life.

something reputation is good

vetted (adj) approved; checked to ensure it is acceptable

14   **Do your answers still lead you to volunteering?** There are times when having a volunteer in a community abroad is a very positive thing. If you have specialized skills that cannot be found locally and you still want to volunteer, do it. Just volunteer responsibly.

15   Thoroughly investigate the program provider and the host organization you'll be volunteering with. Whenever possible, work directly with organizations and be honest with yourself about what you will accomplish while you are there. Also remember that training a local is like teaching a man to fish. By passing along your skills you'll have a much greater impact than you would otherwise.

Comprehension

Answer the following questions. If the answer to a True/False question is False, rewrite the sentence to make it true.

1. What is the main idea of this reading?
   a) Voluntourism seems beneficial, but prospective volunteers need to reflect on what motivates them and how they can best help others.
   b) Voluntourists can be helpful but volunteers must ask about the long-term benefits for the community.
   c) People should not participate in voluntourism because these initiatives do not help local communities.

2. What do you understand by the statement in paragraph 4 that volunteers "tend to develop enduring habits of civic engagement"?

   It means that people who volunteer in another country tend to come home and volunteer in some way for the rest of their lives. It benefits their community as well as the one they are living

3. Generally, the author believes that her character and personality have been positively influenced by her travel experience. ☑ True ☐ False

   _____

4. According to the author, why is the statement "but it changes my life, so isn't it worth it?" not a good enough reason to volunteer?

   Volunteering should be done to improve the lives of as many people as you can, not just your own life. The statement is a selfish one.

5. What are two major problems with the way many voluntourism projects are currently executed?

   2/ These voluntourism organizations don't consult local people about what they really need.
   2/ Sending unskilled volunteers isn't an effective way of making lasting change in a community.

6. In your own words, summarize the advice given by the author in paragraphs 10 to 12.

   10/ Examine why do you want to travel.
   11/ Evaluate whether you are qualified to do work.
   12/ Consider other ways to support the local communities.

   _____

7. Name four ways people can help communities abroad without becoming involved in voluntourism initiatives.

   Bring donation for local charities.
   Support local business by shopping there or paying to use their serv
   Stay in local hotels or pay a host family.
   sho

8. When can volunteering abroad be a positive act?

   It can be positive if you have special skills that can't be found in that community.

9. In your own words, explain the phrase "training a local is like teaching a man to fish."

   Sharing skill and knowledge will benefit people for the rest of their lives - teaching them will make them self-sufficient.

10. Overall, how convincing do you think the author is? What do you consider the best arguments put forward by Pippa Biddle to support her position? Make specific reference to the reading in your answer.

Speaking

What do you think this common expression means?

   Charity begins at home.

Your teacher will divide the class in half. Half the class will develop arguments for volunteering at a local or national level, while the other half develops arguments for volunteering abroad. After brainstorming your arguments in the two large groups, find a partner from the opposite group, and take turns trying to convince each other that your point of view is correct.

   Group A: develop arguments for volunteering in your community or country.
   Group B: develop arguments for working as a volunteer overseas.

PRONUNCIATION

Word Stress

Unlike French, English is a stress-timed language. All words in English with two or more syllables have one syllable that is accentuated more than the others. This means that the stressed syllable is pronounced with more emphasis. For example, in the word *knowledge*, the first syllable is pronounced slightly louder and slightly longer: **knowl**-edge.

Understanding word stress will help your pronunciation and build your confidence in speaking English.

Listen to the following words from "The Voluntourist Dilemma." Circle the stressed syllable in each word. Repeat each word out loud, paying attention to the stressed syllable. Check your answers with your teacher.

1. vol·un·teer
2. af·ford·able
3. or·gan·i·za·tion
4. op·por·tu·ni·ty
5. en·cour·age
6. com·mu·ni·ty
7. pro·fes·sion·al
8. in·ter·na·tion·al
9. sus·tain·able
10. de·vel·op·ment
11. ex·pe·ri·ence
12. i·ni·tia·tive
13. at·trac·tive
14. val·u·able
15. ev·i·dence

Working with a partner, say each of the following words out loud and circle the stressed syllable in each word.

1. impact
2. attitude
3. project (n)
4. connection
5. positive

Then listen to the recording and repeat each word out loud, paying attention to the stressed syllable.

LISTENING

Pre-Listening Activity

In a small group, discuss the following questions. Make a list of your ideas and answers.

1. What organizations do you know of that help people in developing countries?

2. What kinds of support and services do those organizations offer?

3. How is their contribution important to the communities and people they help?

Share your answers with the class.

Vocabulary

You will hear each of the following words in bold in the listening.

1. The result of the volunteer experience depends on your **mindset**.

2. Could you **walk me through** the process of finding a valuable project?

3. All good organizations **are aligned with** the community they serve.

4. The best volunteer projects are **grassroots** initiatives.

5. She has volunteered in various **shelters**.

Using the context provided in the example sentences, match each word with the correct definition.

Word	Definition
1. mindset (n) _____	a) community-based
2. walk someone through something (exp) _____	b) attitude
3. align with (phr v) _____	c) be in agreement with, relate to
4. shelter (n) _____	d) place that provides food or protection
5. grassroots (adj) _____	e) explain or demonstrate

Volunteer Tourism (7:38) 🔊

Jason Moore with Shannon O'Donnell

zerototravel.com

Shannon O'Donnell is an author and an experienced international volunteer. Her website, *A Little Adrift*, documents her travels and volunteer experiences around the world. In this interview she explains how her journey began and makes recommendations for people who want to become involved in socially responsible volunteering.

Comprehension

Answer the following questions. If the answer to a True/False question is False, rewrite the sentence to make it true.

1. Where is Shannon during the interview and what is she doing there?

   _____

2. What motivated Shannon to leave Los Angeles?

   _____

   _____

   _____

3. What volunteer or service experience did she have before she started her world travel? Check all the answers you hear.

   ❏ working in clinics   ❏ working with the homeless

   ❏ working with animals   ❏ working with children

   ❏ building schools   ❏ working on farms

4. When she decided to volunteer abroad, Shannon found it easy to find opportunities.   ❏ True   ❏ False

   _____

   _____

5. She initially intended to spend _____ year travelling, but has now been travelling for _____ years.

6. Shannon O'Donnell suggests that the voluntourism experience is for people who are more _____, while the grassroots experience is for those who are more _____.

7. Name two types of locally run initiatives where people can volunteer.

   _____

8. What are the three criteria Shannon O'Donnell uses to define ethical volunteering?

   _____
   _____
   _____
   _____

9. How does O'Donnell's example of building a school illustrate her point?

   _____
   _____

10. After reading and listening to advice about volunteering abroad, what are your conclusions? If you were to go on a trip, what kind would you choose, and why? What type of project would you like to contribute to and what skills could you share with others?

    _____
    _____
    _____
    _____

DISCOVER GRAMMAR

The Conditional

GG For more information about the conditional, see Grammar Guide page 198.

The conditional is used to describe possible or probable situations in the present and near future, situations that are unlikely to happen in the near future, and situations in the past that did not happen.

If we wish to refer to a situation that is unreal or unlikely, we use the structure: *If* + past tense + *would* + base verb

   If I had enough time, **I would volunteer** at the seniors' home. (but I don't have enough time)

Complete the following sentences.

1. If she spoke fluent English, she _____ (work) with an international organization.

2. If you had time to do some research, you _____ (find) a reliable volunteer association.

3. If we organized ourselves, we _____ (solve) the problem of poverty.

4. If all schools required community service, students _____ (become) involved citizens.

5. If the government gave more money to community associations, they _____ (be able to) help more people in need.

READING

Pre-Reading Activity

What are some possible effects of volunteering abroad, both for the volunteers and for the communities they try to help?

With a partner, brainstorm some ideas. Include both positive and negative effects.

Effects for volunteers		Effects for the community	
Positive	Negative	Positive	Negative

Share your ideas with the class.

There are many ways you can help a community and that may involve volunteering your time and energy. Opportunities can be found locally and around the world. Some volunteering opportunities come with a fee and others are free. Before becoming involved, research your options to find out the best way to contribute to a cause.

The Downside of Overseas Volunteering

By Bob Hepburn

Toronto Star

1   Repairing schools and working with orphans may make you feel great, but it can do more harm than good.

2   Each winter, friends of mine fly to Central America as part of a church group and spend two weeks digging **wells** and repairing schools in impoverished rural villages. When they return to Canada, the well-meaning couple email photos showing them banging in nails or laughing with smiling little children.

well (n) a source of drinking water

Vocabulary in Action

Assist or Attend?

Assist (v): to give support or help to someone

> The agency **assists** women and children who are victims of conflict.

Attend (v): to go to or be present at an event

> More than 400 people **attended** the meeting held in Toronto.

Choose the correct verb in each of the following sentences.

1. Do volunteers truly (assist/attend) the community when they work abroad?
2. She was the first Canadian to (assist/attend) the conference on international cooperation.
3. The president of the association was (assisted/attended) by other members.

booming (adj) prosperous

tradespeople (n pl) skilled workers

toddler (n) young child just learning to walk

outback (n) countryside far from towns

yearning (n) desire

gap year (n) a one-year break between high school and college or university

3 It's an experience that tens of thousands of Canadians share every year as overseas volunteers.

4 But these eager volunteers—church groups, high-school students and others—often are doing more harm than good, argues Samantha Nutt, one of Canada's top humanitarian activists. Canadians "believe that having good intentions will lead to a good outcome, and that is not always the case," says Nutt, co-founder of War Child Canada, an international agency that assists war-affected children and women.

5 In particular, Nutt is highly critical of the **booming** industry of volunteer tourism, dubbed "voluntours." These programs, run largely by for-profit entities, charge from $2000 to $12 000 for a two- or four-week "volunteer" experience somewhere in the world.

6 What's wrong with them?

7 These short-term, everyone-is-welcome ventures "make a spectacle out of poverty and expose overseas communities, especially children, to exploitation and abuse," she says.

8 Speaking recently to more than 400 people at the Toronto Reference Library, Nutt said this "make-work philanthropy" actually puts local carpenters and **tradespeople** out of jobs and robs local high school kids of the chance to be involved in rebuilding their own schools.

9 In addition, such short-term volunteerism creates hyper-affectionate **toddlers** who are psychologically harmed by having formed repeated attachments to total strangers. Imagine the trauma if your own 4-year-old child came to know and love somebody every two weeks and then they were gone, and then there'd be someone else and they'd leave too, and this occurs for most of their childhood.

10 Such outcomes are irresponsible, argues Nutt, a family physician who has worked in and out of war zones for nearly two decades. In her book, *Damned Nations: Greed, Guns, Armies and Aid*, Nutt attacks the mass marketing of volunteer tours, suggesting they have "replaced **outback** canoe trips as the character-building adventures of a lifetime."

11 "Ethical, responsible development programs serve the needs of communities first, not the **yearnings** of students in their **gap years**," she adds. "A revolving door of unskilled workers on the ground every two weeks is more of a burden than a benefit to any community."

12 Nutt doesn't fault Canadians for wanting to help because it often comes from a very good place. But she says it's critical for volunteers to fully understand the impact of their actions and to ask themselves hard questions about how they truly can help improve conditions overseas.

13 That's because good development projects require on-the-ground knowledge and experience, strong local leadership and consistent investments in and training for local residents much more than the feel-good efforts of a tourist digging a well.

14 So what should Canadians do?

15 First, don't waste money on for-profit volunteer ventures. Instead, if people want to visit Africa or Latin America, then go and be a tourist. Join an eco-

tour. Spend your money in local markets, buying products at women's cooperatives and bringing them home as gifts to friends.

16 For students concerned about global issues, Nutt suggests taking part in local campaigns and events organized by recognized organizations such as Amnesty International. While working at home lacks the allure of overseas trips, it's a great introduction to the work of such groups.

17 Clearly, Canadians want to roll up their sleeves, as Nutt says, and be at the centre of the action. Such desire is commendable. The key, though, is to ensure that the best of our intentions are best for the people we want to help.

Comprehension

Answer the following questions. If the answer to a True/False question is False, rewrite the sentence to make it true.

1. Read the paragraphs indicated and use context clues to find the appropriate words.

    a) A word that means *enthusiastic* _____ (para. 4)

    b) A word that means a *result* _____ (para. 4)

    c) A word that means *happens* _____ (para. 9)

    d) A word that means a *problem* _____ (para. 11)

    e) An expression that means *becoming involved* _____ (para. 16)

2. What is the main idea of this text? Remember, to find the main idea ask yourself: Who? What? Where? When? Why? How?

    _____

    _____

    _____

    _____

3. Samantha Nutt argues against volunteering overseas with a for-profit organization. How does she support her point of view? In your own words, list the reasons she gives.

    _____

    _____

    _____

    _____

    _____

4. Which of these arguments do you consider to be the most persuasive? Why?

    _____

    _____

5. According to the reading, what are the three most important elements of successful development projects?

    _____

    _____

Grammar in Context

Preposition *to* with Verbs of Movement

The preposition *to* is used with verbs of movement such as *go*, *drive*, *walk*, *travel*, and *fly* + a destination.

> Every year, friends of mine **fly to** Central America as part of a church group.

Find and highlight another example of the preposition *to* with a verb of movement in paragraph 2 of the reading.

6. Samantha Nutt argues that people can take action in different ways to truly help communities in developing countries. How does she support her argument? In your own words, list the actions she recommends.

_____

_____

_____

_____

7. Review your answers in the Pre-Reading activity on page 107. Which of your ideas were mentioned in the text? Which negative effect mentioned in the text do you find the most concerning? Explain your answer.

_____

_____

_____

SPEAKING

Form a group of 3–4 students and prepare a short volunteer-recruitment campaign to encourage your classmates to join your organization. Find a volunteer organization or charity working for a cause or a group that interests you. Make a note of the following information:

- What kind of volunteer activities do the volunteers do?
- Who benefits from the organization's services?
- In which communities or countries do volunteers work?
- How much time is a volunteer typically expected to devote to the organization?
- How can someone become involved?

Use visuals to make your presentation more attractive and dynamic. Your teacher will provide guidelines for how presentations will be organized.

Vocabulary in Action

Negative Prefixes

The text contains several words with common prefixes, including *irresponsible* and **un**skilled.

The prefixes ir- and un- both mean *not* or *opposite of*. Other prefixes that mean *not* are il-, in-, and im-.

Add the correct prefix (ir-, un-, il-, in-, or im-) to the following words to make them negative.

_____patient	_____happy	_____eventful	_____rational
_____equal	_____personal	_____mature	_____perfect
_____complete	_____legal	_____acceptable	_____relevant
_____responsible	_____practical	_____regular	_____possible
_____moral	_____likely	_____logical	_____justice

Vocabulary

You will hear each of the following words in bold in the listening.

1. Many people have a **genuine** wish to help others.

2. Voluntourism may **disturb** the local economy.

3. The children form a **bond** with their teachers.

4. Critics say that volunteer help from the developed world could be considered **patronizing**.

5. The voluntourism trend contributes to **spreading** clichés about poverty.

Using the context provided in the sentences above, match each word with the correct meaning.

	Option 1	Option 2
genuine (adj) _____	enthusiastic	sincere
disturb (v) _____	upset	help
bond (n) _____	strong connection	dependence
patronizing (adj) _____	condescending	supportive
spread (v) _____	to get bigger	circulate

The Voluntourist: Is Voluntourism Doing More Harm than Good? (4:36) ▶️

Chloé Sanguinetti

In the past few years, humanitarian trips have become increasingly popular, particularly for students. For many people, the idea of helping others who are less fortunate while experiencing another culture is very attractive. However, although many of these trips are positive, others do not have the positive effect that volunteers expect.

Comprehension

1. Fill in the blanks with the numbers you hear.

    Every year, an estimated _____ voluntourists will travel abroad, and

    spend between £_____ and £_____.

2. What reasons does Max give to explain the interest in volunteering abroad?

    _____

    _____

3. According to Amy and Sarah, why should unskilled young people **not** volunteer to teach children abroad?

    _____

    _____

NGO (abbr) Non-Governmental Organization

4. Fill in the blanks. It seems _____ and _____ the good intentions of volunteers is a profitable business.

5. What three harmful effects of voluntourism are mentioned by the narrator?

   _____

   _____

6. How do critics of voluntourism trips often describe them?

   _____

   _____

7. What does the narrator suggest people do before going on a voluntourism trip?

   _____

8. Instead of volunteering, people can help in other ways. Name three ways to help mentioned in the video.

   _____

   _____

9. What do you find the most interesting or surprising element of the video? Explain your answer using specific examples from the report to support your opinion.

   _____

   _____

WRITING

For more information about writing an essay, see Writing Strategies page 120.

In this unit, you explored some positive and negative aspects of volunteering abroad. What are your conclusions?

1. Prepare an outline for an essay (350 words) in which you explain your position on volunteering or voluntourism. Your outline must include an introduction, two development paragraphs (with two elements of support in each one), and a conclusion.

2. Write and revise your essay.

REVISING AND EDITING

1. Underline and correct the 10 verb tense errors and then write a topic sentence for the paragraph.

   _____

   _____

   We all lead busy lives, but if you would volunteer, you will meet many new people. Volunteering provided an opportunity to meet people who will have similar interests and who care about the same things you do. It can also helps your mental health because you give your time to do good work for your community, which made you feel more connected to others. People who volunteered did note that they discover more self-confidence when they learn a new skill or solved a problem. Volunteering also will mean that you think less about your own worries and focus on others who truly need your help. What are you waiting for?

2. Underline and correct 12 errors in spelling and word choice.

While many people critic volunteers who work abroad, saying it is a loss of time and ressources, my personnal experience was fantastic. With my school, I went on a travel to Ecuador to do humanitarian work in a small community. In total, we were twenty students involved in the projet. During two weeks, we worked on a farm, planting and harvesting crops like bananas, coffee, and chocolat, and working with childs. We stayed with local families and ate the local food, which was delicious. At the end of our working vacancy, we had created great relations with our hosts in Ecuador and improved our Spanish. It's an experience I'll always remember.

CONSOLIDATING

S For information about preparing an oral presentation, see Speaking Skills page 131.

Speaking

Choose one of the following activities.

1. Find an article about a volunteer organization providing services within a Canadian community.
   a) Print or photocopy the article. Write down the source and the date you retrieved the article.
   b) Highlight 10 key words and write your own definition of each.
   c) Take notes about the main idea and important details of the article. Remember to ask yourself questions: Who? What? Where? When? Why? How?
   d) Using your notes, prepare an outline with key words only for a short oral presentation (3–4 minutes) about the work accomplished by the organization.

2. Search online for a short video about a volunteer organization providing help to a community in Canada or abroad.
   a) Write down the URL and the date you retrieved the video.
   b) Write a main idea summary of the video. Remember to ask yourself questions: Who? What? Where? When? Why? How?
   c) Prepare a short oral presentation (3–4 minutes) about the organization's activities.

Writing

Choose one of these two topics to write about.

1. If you choose to research an organization that arranges volunteer trips overseas, refer to your research from the Speaking section. How does the organization attract people? How much does a trip cost? How long does a trip typically last? What age group is targeted? To which countries do people travel? What kinds of activities do volunteers do?

   Write a four-paragraph essay summarizing your findings. Start with an interesting introduction. Include two development paragraphs with adequate support. End with a brief conclusion.

2. Choose one of the following quotations and write a four-paragraph essay that explains why you believe this quote is true. Make specific reference to your personal experience to explain your opinion. Start with an interesting introduction. Include two development paragraphs with adequate support. End with a brief conclusion.

   a) Volunteers do not necessarily have the time; they just have the heart. (Elizabeth Andrew)

   b) If you want to touch the past, touch a rock. If you want to touch the present, touch a flower. If you want to touch the future, touch a life. (Anonymous)

   c) Kindness, like a boomerang, always returns. (Anonymous)

Vocabulary

Complete one of the following activities.

1. Choose five vocabulary words from this unit that you consider important. For each, write a definition in your own words. Then use each word in a sentence that clearly demonstrates the meaning. You may also include a translation of each word.

For more information about writing a well-structured essay, see Writing Strategies page 120.

2. Complete the following sentences using these vocabulary words from the unit.

   grassroots (adj)   shelter (n)   booming (adj)   outcome (n)   cater to (phr v)

   a) She worked as a volunteer at a _____ for homeless women and children.

   b) Voluntourism is a _____ sector of the travel industry.

   c) You can find volunteer opportunities with local _____ organizations.

   d) Many voluntourism companies _____ people's desire to travel while helping others.

   e) The ideal _____ is an experience that benefits everyone involved.

Learning Strategies

Writing Strategies

GENERATING IDEAS

When you receive a writing assignment, it is important to generate ideas *before* you begin to write. This preparation helps you focus and organize your thoughts.

Brainstorming is the most commonly used technique for generating ideas. Brainstorming before writing an essay helps you find and organize good content and ensures you do not forget anything important.

There are two essential steps to brainstorming: **generating ideas** and then **choosing which ideas are most useful and pertinent**. Mind Mapping and Association are two excellent ways to generate ideas.

Mind Mapping

A mind map is a graphic way of organizing your ideas and information. Like your brain, a mind map organizes information according to connections and associations. Highly visual people like this technique.

STEP 1: Place the subject of your writing assignment in the centre of your paper, then write down ideas related to the subject and connect them to the centre with a line. Each idea you write down might lead to related ideas, which can then be connected with more lines. Starting in the centre provides you with a clear focus on the topic, but gives your brain freedom to develop ideas in different directions. Using a line to connect subtopics to the central topic improves your memory of how ideas are connected.

To help generate ideas, ask yourself questions about the subject: Why? In what way? How?

STEP 2: Analyze your mind map and choose the most **useful and pertinent ideas** for your essay. Choose ideas that will help you to communicate about the subject in an organized and cohesive way.

Tip

You may discover that one brainstorming technique works better for you than the other. Select one of these ideas and use both brainstorming techniques—mind mapping and association—to generate ideas. See if you prefer one technique to the other.

My personality
My future goals
My inspiration

Essay Subject: Starting College Can Be Stressful

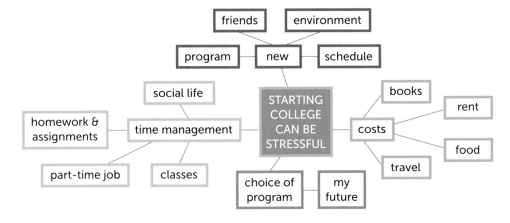

Association

The association technique frees your brain to think creatively and generate ideas. Ignore rules, logic, and methods of organization and write down thoughts as they occur, in any format you like (list, point form, single words, and so on).

STEP 1: Start with the essay subject (e.g., Starting College Can Be Stressful), and write down all the ideas that come to mind. To generate ideas, ask yourself questions: Why? In what way? How? Do not stop to evaluate your ideas or worry about grammar or spelling. Give yourself the freedom to be creative and generate as many ideas as possible. This step is about **quantity**, not quality.

STEP 2: Analyze your ideas and choose the most **useful and pertinent ideas** for your essay subject. Choose ideas that will help you to communicate about the subject in an organized and cohesive way. This step is about **quality**, not quantity.

Essay Subject: Starting College Can Be Stressful

Starting College Can Be Stressful

Money	Everything is new!	Right program?	Time Management
rent	friends	make the right choice?	classes
food	city	future job prospects?	homework/assignments
social life	schedule	motivation?	socializing
books	freedom/independence	number of courses?	part-time job?
need a part-time job?	school		

WRITING A PARAGRAPH

A well-structured paragraph develops **one main idea** and has **three elements**:

- a **topic sentence**, which states the main idea
- the body of the paragraph, which provides **supporting details** for the main idea
- a **concluding sentence**, which summarizes the information in the paragraph

Owning a car is not necessary for getting around in most big cities. —— Topic sentence

People should consider using a car-sharing network such as Communauto or Car2Go. Bike-sharing programs also exist. For example, in Montreal and Quebec City, for six months of the year, people can pick up and drop off Bixi bikes in areas throughout the city. Another alternative to owning a car is taking public transportation or walking when possible. —— Supporting details

All these options are viable alternatives to car ownership when you live in the city. —— Concluding sentence

Topic Sentences

A topic sentence states the main idea of a paragraph. It is generally the first sentence of the paragraph and is supported by every sentence in that paragraph.

The topic sentence contains words that **limit and control** the idea to be developed in the paragraph.

EXAMPLE   Music **can help you to relax after a stressful day**.

Advertising **can have a negative effect on children**.

The extreme cold in Quebec during winter **determines how we dress**.

Topic Sentence Checklist

A good topic sentence

❑ has a clear focus: it is not too general
❑ is a complete sentence
❑ is not personal (Do not write "I'm going to explain why . . ." or "My subject is . . .")
❑ can be developed and supported in a paragraph

TRY IT OUT

1. In each topic sentence below, <u>underline</u> the subject and highlight the words that limit and control what should be discussed in the paragraph.

    a) Many movies contain too much violence.

    b) For some, Christmas is a depressing holiday.

    c) A professional athlete's career is usually very short.

    d) Everyone could benefit from learning another language.

    e) Social media can contribute to intimidation.

2. Read the following topic sentences. Check *Yes* or *No* to indicate if each one is a good topic sentence. If you answer *No*, rewrite the sentence to make it a good topic sentence.

    a) Exercise is important   ❑ Yes   ☑ No

    Exerice _____

    b) I love to travel.   ☑ Yes   ☑ No

    _____

    c) Music can help you relax.   ☑ Yes   ❑ No

    _____

    d) Learning a new language can be a challenge.   ☑ Yes   ❑ No

    _____

    e) In this paragraph I'm going to explain why I prefer living in the country.

                                                          ❑ Yes   ☑ No

    _____

Supporting Details

When you have written your topic sentence, you must find supporting details to help you develop the paragraph. A topic sentence can be supported by facts, examples, anecdotes, or stastistics and research.

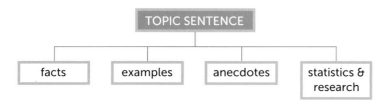

EXAMPLE

Topic sentence: Having a part-time job has several advantages.

Support

1. A part-time job can help you earn money to pay for part of your college expenses. (fact)

2. Working a part-time job during college can help you build strategies for time management and balancing responsibilities. (example)

3. According to Statistics Canada, 15-year-olds who work part-time hours during school earn more at age 23 than those without that experience. (statistic)

Note the four elements of support as outlined above.

TRY IT OUT

Choose one of these topic sentences and write three details to support it.

1. Learning a new language can be a challenge.

2. People travel to escape their routines.

3. Exercise can help reduce stress.

Topic sentence: _____

_____

_____

Support:

a) _____

b) _____

c) _____

> **Tip**
>
> To find supporting details or ideas, ask yourself questions: Why? In what way? How?

Paragraph Unity

A well-structured paragraph has **one main idea**, expressed in the topic sentence, that is developed and supported with facts and examples. Reread the paragraph on car ownership on page 117 and notice how every sentence (the supporting details) contributes to the development of the topic sentence.

Read the following paragraph and cross out any sentences that are not pertinent to the subject.

> Although it is cheap, fast food is not always a healthy choice. Many items on the menu contain too much fat, salt, and calories. A typical burger from a popular chain may have more than the daily recommended limit for salt. Also, fast food chains only pay their employees minimum wage. Nutritional information about the food is not always available so people don't know how much unhealthy fat they are eating. Employees sometimes have to wear ugly uniforms. There are not many healthy options of fruit and vegetables available in these restaurants. For health reasons, it is better to limit your consumption of fast food.

ESSAY WRITING

An essay has three elements: an **introduction**, **body paragraphs**, and a **conclusion**.

Read the following essay and note how these elements form a well-structured text.

The Benefits of Exercise

Introduction — In the past, people did not go to the gym or play sports to keep fit because they lived physically demanding lives. Times have changed and today, most people work in an office, spend too much time in their cars, and deal with stress on a daily basis; therefore, regular exercise is essential to living a long and healthy life. **Being active has both physical and mental benefits.**

Body paragraphs —

Firstly, regular exercise has a positive effect on physical health. People who exercise for at least 30 minutes, three to five times a week, can control their weight without dieting, lower their blood pressure and heart rate, and improve their cardiovascular health. Exercise also reduces the risk of developing diseases such as diabetes. In addition, people who are physically active have more energy during the day and sleep better at night. You don't have to be a professional athlete to experience positive changes in your health; even moderate physical activity is good for your body.

Furthermore, exercising regularly is good for your mental health. Physical activity releases "happy" hormones and neurotransmitters such as endorphins, serotonin, and dopamine into the brain. These contribute to feelings of happiness and help combat depression and reduce stress. Regular exercise also increases self-confidence and self-esteem, which leads to more satisfaction in life. Being active can also help your social life because you meet people who share similar interests. By exercising on a regular basis, you will boost your mental health.

Conclusion — In conclusion, everyone needs to make time for exercise to guarantee physical and mental well-being. Find an enjoyable activity, whether it is playing hockey, skiing, or yoga, and do it regularly. Your mind and body will thank you.

Thesis Statement

The **thesis statement** is a sentence that identifies the **main idea** of an essay.

> When people first fall in love, they often make several mistakes.

> Effective communication is the key to successful relationships.

The thesis statement is developed and explained in the body of the essay.

After writing the thesis statement, ask yourself these questions: Why? How? In what way? Your answers will help you develop the body paragraphs of the essay.

Thesis statement
When people first fall in love, they often make several mistakes.

Topic sentence 1	**Topic sentence 2**
They believe that their partner is perfect.	They may neglect their friendships.

Thesis Statement Checklist

A good thesis statement

- ❑ has a clear focus: it is not too general
- ❑ is a complete sentence
- ❑ is not personal: do not write "I'm going to explain why . . ." or "My subject is . . ."
- ❑ can be developed and supported in the essay

TRY IT OUT

1. Read the following sentences. Check *Yes* or *No* to indicate if the sentence is a good thesis statement. If you answer *No*, rewrite the sentence to make it an effective thesis statement that can be developed.

   a) A strong community helps create a good neighbourhood.

      ❑ Yes   ❑ No

      _____

   b) I never eat fast food.

      ❑ Yes   ❑ No

      _____

   c) Human activity contributes to climate change.

      ❑ Yes   ❑ No

      _____

   d) Generation Z has good values.

      ❑ Yes   ❑ No

      _____

   e) In this essay, I'm going to explain why technology isolates people.

      ❑ Yes   ❑ No

      _____

      _____

2. Using what you learned about thesis statements, write a thesis statement for two of the following subjects.

   Healthy eating   Part-time work   Hobbies   Living in the country/city

a) _____

b) _____

3. Now select one of the thesis statements above and brainstorm details you could use to develop this statement. Remember to ask yourself questions (Why? How? In what way?) to come up with your ideas.

Supporting details

1. _____

2. _____

3. _____

4. _____

Tip

To find ideas, ask yourself what you want to say about the subject.

Tip

What is the difference between a thesis statement and a topic sentence?

   A **thesis statement** expresses the focus of **the essay**.

   A **topic sentence** expresses the focus of **a paragraph**.

Look at the essay on page 120. The thesis statement is

   "Being active has both physical and mental benefits."
   —This is the focus of the essay.

The topic sentences are

   "Firstly, regular exercise has a positive effect on physical health."
   —This is the main idea of the first development paragraph.

and

   "Furthermore, exercising regularly is good for mental health."
   —This is the main idea of the second development paragraph.

Model Essay

Tip

To develop a good topic sentence, read the paragraph and identify supporting details *before* writing the topic sentence.

1. Read the essay and underline the thesis statement.

2. Read the development paragraphs in the body of the essay and write a topic sentence for each paragraph.

Cyberbullying

Unfortunately, bullying and intimidation have always existed in schools. In the past, many young people were afraid to go to school, knowing they could only survive the day by avoiding the person responsible for their bullying. Once school was over, however, they could escape to the safety of home. Now, with the existence of social media, there is no safe place for the victim. The Internet has added a disturbing new dimension to bullying and intimidation.

Topic sentence: _Cyberbul_____

_____

Before the explosion of social media, most bullying happened at school. While it was difficult and frightening to deal with the violence or verbal abuse during the day, once students returned home, they could relax and feel safe. Now, with everyone connected to social media, there is no escape. Every time people post a comment or a photo on a website, they expose themselves to potential intimidation at any time of the day, anywhere. This cyber-intimidation only adds to their sense of fear and insecurity.

Topic sentence: _____

_____

In the past, victims always knew who was bullying them, and therefore it was possible to avoid them. Now anyone can hide behind a screen and threaten or make fun of someone without revealing his or her identity. Furthermore, information is shared so quickly and so extensively on the Internet that victims can become a source of ridicule for many people. They may never even know who is responsible for the insults directed at them.

In conclusion, the Internet and, particularly, social media contribute to the nightmare of bullying experienced by too many young people. Now victims do not feel safe even in their own homes and probably do not know who is responsible for their terrible situation. Parents should ensure that their child or teenager knows what to do and how to react if they are victims of cyber-intimidation.

Introductions

An effective introduction presents the subject of an essay in an interesting way that captures the reader's attention. Remember that first impressions count!

Several ways you could develop the introductory paragraph of an essay are

- give a **general description**: write a few descriptive sentences related to the subject
- give **historical background**: write some historical information on the subject
- share an **anecdote**: write briefly about an event or experience related to the subject

The final sentence of the introduction is the thesis statement. It presents the focus of the essay.

Introduction = general statement(s) +thesis + list your supporting points.
Body paragraph = Topic sentense,
First example, explanation.
Second example. explanation,
Concluding sentence (1, Just a summary
a summary of what you wrote in this
paragraph, or 2. A restatement of
the thesis and how the paragraph
Prove it).

Conclusion = Restate (repeat in different
words) Your thesis and your support

TRY IT OUT

Read the following introductions, highlight the thesis statement, and decide which introductory style is used.

1. Before the Internet and cellphones existed, people communicated with each other in several different ways. They wrote long letters to family and friends regularly, and urgent news was often sent by telegram. When the telephone was invented, communication became faster and more effective, as long as you were at home or at work! Now email, text, and smartphones allow us to be in touch constantly, wherever we are. Technology has changed the way people communicate.

a) general description   b) historical background   c) anecdote

2. When I was a child, I was so shy that I couldn't speak in public or to strangers. For example, when I had to give a presentation in front of my class in elementary school, I was so afraid that the other children would laugh at me I couldn't say anything. Or when I was out with my parents and a stranger spoke to me, I would hide behind my mom. Then, when I was 13 years old, I had a small part in a theatre production and discovered that because I was playing a role, I was no longer paralyzed by my shyness. Since then, I've completely changed and now I love doing public performances. A hobby can contribute to the development of one's personality.

a) general description   b) historical background   c) anecdote

3. Look around any park on a hot summer day and watch people enjoying themselves. Children run around the playground, shouting with joy while their parents talk to friends and neighbours. Young couples lie on the grass, sharing quiet, intimate conversations while a group of friends gather around a picnic table to celebrate a birthday. An old couple is sitting on a bench and exchanging a few words with young parents pushing a newborn baby in a stroller. Green spaces are vital for a neighbourhood community.

a) general description   b) historical background   c) anecdote

Using the models above to help you, write an introductory paragraph for one of the following subjects or choose one of your own. End your introduction with a clear thesis statement.

Volunteer work   Friendship   Smartphones   Video games

Tip

Never introduce new information in the concluding paragraph.

Conclusions

The final paragraph of your essay rephrases your ideas and leaves your reader with something to think about.

A conclusion has these elements:

- a **summary** of the main points in the essay
- an interesting **closing statement** (This can be a prediction or a suggestion. Do not end your essay with a question.)

TRY IT OUT

Read this conclusion to an essay about first impressions. Underline the summary of the main points of the essay and highlight the closing statement.

To conclude, first impressions are very powerful but often incorrect. On average, we take only three seconds to make a judgment about someone based on physical appearance, clothes, and behaviour. If we take time to get to know the person, we often realize how wrong our initial impression was. So when you meet someone for the first time, don't be too quick to judge only what you see.

Model Essay

Read the following essay. Then work with a partner to

- decide what the subject of the essay is
- underline the topic sentence of each development paragraph
- write an interesting introduction (general description, historical background, or anecdote)
- place a clear and concise thesis statement at the end of the introduction
- write a short conclusion

Tip

To help you create your thesis statement, read the topic sentences carefully and ask yourself what idea they are supporting.

The Negative Influence of Advertising on Body Image

Introduction

_____

_____

_____

_____

_____

First of all, advertising presents an unrealistic image of women's bodies. Most of the women in beauty and cosmetic ads show an idealized version of feminine beauty. The models are all thin, perfectly made-up, and always photoshopped. All women, but particularly young women who are most vulnerable, compare themselves to these images and may feel dissatisfied with their own bodies. This can lead to a loss of self-confidence, lower self-esteem, and even eating disorders. The idealized images shown in magazines are impossible to achieve for most women.

In addition, young men are also increasingly exposed to unrealistic ideals of masculinity in advertising. Men in ads are generally strong, muscular, and athletic with a six-pack. This can encourage teenage boys to work out excessively and take steroids in the pursuit of the perfect physique. Additionally, young men are always shown as cool and confident, and often dominant. These physical and mental characteristics are presented as necessities for a young man's success. This one-dimensional presentation of masculinity does not represent the reality for most young men and can be harmful for their development.

Conclusion

_____

_____

_____

_____

_____

ESSAY OUTLINES

The final stage in the preparation process is to make a plan for your essay. A good outline will ensure that all the essential elements of the essay are present.

Look at this example of an outline for the model essay "The Benefits of Exercise" on page 120.

Introduction

Historical information

Thesis statement: Being active has both physical and mental benefits.

Development paragraph 1

Topic sentence: Regular exercise has a positive effect on physical health.

Support: weight control, lower blood pressure, stronger cardiovascular system, avoid disease, more energy, better sleep

Development paragraph 2

Topic sentence: Furthermore, exercising regularly is good for your mental health.

Support: release of hormones and neurotransmitters to brain, less depression, better able to manage stress, more self-confidence, better self-esteem

Conclusion

Restatement of main points

Concluding statement (suggestion): find a physical activity you enjoy

Tip

A blank outline template can also be downloaded from Compass Online.

TRY IT OUT

Using the model below, complete an outline for the subject assigned by your teacher.

Essay Outline

Introduction _____

_____

_____

Thesis statement: _____

_____

_____

_____

Development paragraph 1

Topic sentence: _____

_____

Support: _____

_____

Development paragraph 2

Topic sentence: _____

_____

Support: _____

_____

Conclusion _____

_____

_____

_____

Concluding statement: _____

_____

_____

_____

TRANSITION WORDS

Transition words connect ideas, sentences, and paragraphs. They guide the reader and help your writing flow. Used effectively, transition words contribute to the logic and coherence of your text.

Common transition words					
Chronology	**Example**	**Addition**	**Emphasis**	**Contrast**	**Conclusion**
first(ly)	for example	in addition	clearly	however	in conclusion
second(ly)	for instance	also	above all	but	to conclude
third(ly)		as well	in fact	on the other hand	lastly
next		and		although	finally
after that		furthermore			in summary
finally					

TRY IT OUT

Read the following paragraph and underline the correct transition words.

Time management can be a source of stress in college. **First/Next**, most students have more than 20 hours of class and also have to find time to study and do assignments. **Second/Finally**, some travel for more than two hours a day to get to college and home again. **In addition/Above all**, many students have a part-time job to help pay for their studies. Who has time for a social life? **However/Lastly**, keeping an organized schedule can help reduce stress and ensure that students do not fall behind in their work or feel overwhelmed by the multiple demands on their time. **In fact/Clearly**, making a weekly plan (and sticking to it!) can be a valuable habit for life. **In conclusion/Although**, organization and planning are the keys to a successful college session.

CONDUCTING EFFECTIVE INTERNET RESEARCH

Plan

Planning is essential to conducting an efficient Internet search. Follow these steps to make the best use of your time and energy.

1. Define the topic you want to research. What exactly are you looking for?

2. Make a list of key words associated with the subject or ask your teacher to provide search terms.

Use nouns, not articles, pronouns, or prepositions. Ensure your spelling is correct.

Search

Your teacher may recommend certain sources. If so, start with those sources.

Start your search by entering a combination of key words into a search engine such as Google.

> **EXAMPLE**   benefits art therapy

Google's Advanced Search function allows you to use an exact phrase, to include additional words, and to exclude certain terms. These features can help you search more efficiently.

File   Edit   View   Favorites   Tools   Help

Google

Advanced Search

Find pages with

all these words   benefits

this exact word or phrase   "art therapy"

any of these words

none of these words

numbers ranging from   to

To find exact words, put the words or phrase in quotes. The results will include only pages with those words in the same order. Use this only if you're looking for an exact word or phrase, otherwise you'll exclude many helpful results by mistake.

> **EXAMPLE**   "effect of music on the brain"

Using the Search Tools function also enables you to refine your search. For example, you can restrict your search for videos only, then refine by duration, date of posting, and source.

If your initial search does not provide interesting material, try a different combination of key words.

To exclude specific sites from your search, use a dash before a word or site. For example, if your college does not accept Wikipedia as a valid source, you can eliminate that site from your results.

> **EXAMPLE** urban agriculture-wikipedia.org

To find information from one specific site, use *site*: to identify the specific site.

> **EXAMPLE** sharing economy site:cbc.ca

To find pages that use different terms for something, use *or*.

> **EXAMPLE** urban agriculture OR farming

You will find more tips to refine web searches at Google Support (for example using symbols to search social media or hashtags, and more).

Scan and Skim

Quickly scan the results to find potentially interesting material. Skim through selected articles to determine whether they are appropriate. Don't try to read everything in detail during your research stage.

Save

Bookmark or save any sources that seem interesting to you. Online material can disappear, and there is nothing more frustrating than trying to locate lost material!

EVALUATING SOURCES

It is essential to evaluate your chosen sources for validity and reliability. Remember that anyone can post information online, so it is important to evaluate the quality of sources and information that you find.

Tips for Evaluating Sources

As you search for information from print or online sources, evaluate sources by using the CARS Checklist: Credibility-Accuracy-Reasonableness-Support

- **Credibility** Is the site trustworthy and respected? What are the author's credentials? Is this person qualified?
- **Accuracy** Is the information up-to-date? Is it factual? Who is the intended audience? What is the objective of the information provided? To inform? To persuade? To sell?
- **Reasonableness** Is the tone moderate? Are arguments presented in a balanced, objective manner? Is the tone neutral?
- **Support** Does the author cite other sources? Can the information be verified with reliable outside sources? Is contact information provided?

Always find two other sources that corroborate information you want to use. Taking the time to evaluate your sources will ensure that the information you find for an assignment is valid and reliable.

Tip

"Decoding" Internet addresses will help you understand a site's mission. The most common domains are

.org   a not-for-profit organization

.edu   a higher education institution

.com   a business or commerce

.gov   government

.ca   an organization in Canada

~   a personal page

Avoiding Plagiarism

Plagiarism is academic cheating and is a serious offence. Some plagiarism is deliberate fraud, but often plagiarism happens when students do not know or understand the rules related to using other people's work.

There are two ways to avoid plagiarism: quote directly or reformulate the information in your words. In both cases, you must credit the source.

1. **Direct Quotation** Taking the exact words from an original source is called *quoting*. You quote material when you believe the way the original author expresses an idea is the best way to communicate the point you want to make.

2. **Reformulation or Paraphrasing** If you want to borrow an idea from an author, but do not need his or her exact words, you can reformulate—or restate—the author's ideas in your own words.

EXAMPLE

Original text The following text is from "Changing Voices: An Introduction to English Language Change over Time" at www.bl.uk/british-accents-and-dialects/articles/changing-voices-an-introduction-to-english-language-change.

"All languages change over time, and vary from place to place. They may change as a result of social or political pressures, such as invasion, colonization and immigration." ("Changing Voices")

Direct quotation The writer introduces the topic in his or her own words, uses quotation marks to show which text was written by someone else, and credits the original source. When you are quoting directly, every word must be exactly as you saw it in the original. You cannot make changes to anything within the quotation marks.

All languages evolve. "They may change as a result of social or political pressures, such as invasion, colonization and immigration." ("Changing Voices")

Reformulation When you reformulate or paraphrase a sentence, it says basically the same thing as the original, but it is stated in different words. You must credit the source used even if you changed the wording, especially if the information is new to you, and is not considered common knowledge. The use should be acknowledged because although you are not using exact words, you are borrowing ideas.

Languages change all the time for social or political reasons, such as war or the movement of populations. ("Changing Voices")

Plagiarism By contrast, almost all the words in a plagiarized sentence are exactly the same as those of the original and there is no citation to indicate that these ideas are not the writer's, but are from an outside source.

All languages change as a result of social or political pressures, including invasion, colonization, or immigration.

Speaking Strategies

ORAL PRESENTATIONS

During your English course, you will be asked to present information and opinions in front of other students and your teacher. According to research, 74 percent of people are afraid of speaking in public. That's three out of four people! So if you are feeling nervous, it's completely normal. Following the steps below will help you feel more confident about giving a successful oral presentation.

Preparing for a Presentation

Being well prepared reduces your anxiety and boosts your confidence, so take time to prepare your oral presentation carefully.

- Review the guidelines for the oral presentation and ensure you understand exactly what you have to do.
- Refer to the evaluation grid to determine evaluation criteria.
- Do research if necessary.
- Prepare an outline for your presentation that includes an introduction, body, and conclusion (see the sample outline on page 132). Don't write all the details in your outline, just write key words.
- Presenters are often required to take questions from the audience at the end of an oral presentation. As part of your preparation, ask yourself what type of questions might be asked and try to be prepared with answers.

Using an Outline

A general outline for an oral presentation is similar to an essay outline because it has an introduction, body, and conclusion. Creating an outline will help you to structure your presentation. Remember, don't write everything on your outline; use key words only.

Elements of an Oral Presentation Outline

Introduction

- attention-getting statement or short anecdote
- presentation of topic and main idea

Body

Provide information that supports your topic such as specific details, explanations, or descriptions. (Confirm with your teacher how many details are required.)

- explanation and detail of example #1
- explanation and detail of example #2
- explanation and detail of example #3

Conclusion

- summary statement—summarize all the main points of your topic
- suggestion or prediction

Sample Outline

> **Presentation about Cellphone-Related Accidents**
>
> **Intro**
>
> - road injuries—one of the leading causes of teen death around the world (WHO study, 2012)
> - cellphone distraction is very high: 11 teens/day die b/c of texting & driving
>
> **Body**
>
> Cellphone distractions
>
> 1. taking eyes off the road
> 2. reduced concentration
> 3. taking hands off the steering wheel
>
> **Conclusion**
>
> - 5 seconds to answer a text: at 45 km/h, that's enough time to travel the length of a hockey rink!
> - Drivers should concentrate on the road, the flow of traffic, and the other drivers around them.

Using Cue Cards

Once you have completed your outline, preparing cue cards is a simple and effective way to get ready for your oral presentation.

Use a separate card for each element and number each card in order.

CARD 1

Intro

Did you know 11 teens die/day?

- 2012 World Health Organization
- Road injuries #1 adolescent death

CARD 2

Body

- Cellphone distraction high
- eyes off the road/concentration/ hands off wheel
- 5 seconds answer text = hockey rink @ 45 km/h

CARD 3

Conclusion

Concentrate on road/traffic, other drivers

CARD 4

Closing statement

Be smart/turn off phone/focus/stay safe

Questions?

Practise

- Practise, practise, and practise again. Practise your presentation in the shower, in your car, wherever you can, whenever you have a few free minutes! Record your presentation on your phone, tablet, or computer and watch it with someone who can give you feedback and help you improve.
- Make sure you know and respect the time required for the presentation.
- Don't memorize your entire presentation because when you say it out loud it will not sound natural.

Delivering Your Presentation

Introduction

- Use an attention-getting statement or anecdote to begin your presentation.

  > Did you know 11 teens die every day because of texting while driving?

- State the topic or main idea of your presentation. But never say ~~I am going to talk about car accidents related to using cellphones.~~ Instead speak about the topic of the presentation.

  > In this presentation you will learn about car accidents related to cellphones.

Body

- Use your cue cards to help you stay focused.
- Use visuals (pictures, photos, PowerPoint, and so on) to make your presentation more interesting.
- Speak clearly and naturally. Use intonation (emphasis) to help you communicate your message.
- Make eye contact with your audience to create a personal connection. Move your eyes across the whole audience, including your teacher.

Conclusion

- Summarize the main points of your topic or assignment.

  > In conclusion, using a cellphone while driving is very dangerous and a key cause of death in teenagers. It increases the risk of accidents because it takes your eyes off the road and reduces your concentration.

- Conclude with a suggestion.

  > Be smart, turn off your phone, and focus on safe driving.

- Expect—or invite—questions from other students and be prepared to answer them.

Reading Strategies

IDENTIFYING THE MAIN IDEA

One of the most important reading skills is identifying the main idea of a text. Knowing the main idea will improve your overall comprehension of the text and give purpose to your reading. To determine the main idea of the text, skim the introduction, conclusion, and the first sentence of each paragraph. Find answers to the Wh- questions: Who? What? Where? When? Why? How? Finally, write a concise statement that incorporates all this information.

ACTIVATING PRIOR KNOWLEDGE

Take a few minutes to think about your knowledge or experience related to the subject or theme of the text before you read it. This will help you understand more fully when you read. It's like warming up before you exercise and makes your reading more effective.

TRY IT OUT

Try activating prior knowledge next time you read a text.

- Ask yourself a few questions or make notes before you start reading.
  - » What do I already know about this subject?
  - » What vocabulary do I associate with this subject or theme?
  - » Do I know anything about the writer, publication, or site?
  - » What kind of text is this—news report, opinion, narrative, fiction, or another genre?

- Discuss your thoughts on and knowledge of the subject with other students

PREVIEWING

This simple strategy involves seeing what you can learn from the titles, subtitles, introductory and concluding paragraphs, or words that are emphasized (e.g., bold, highlighted, or underlined) to gain an overview of the content and organization. Previewing takes very little time and improves your concentration, understanding, and retention of the text. It also gives you a sense of the main idea of the text and its structure *before* you read.

TRY IT OUT

There are a few key steps to previewing a text:

- Read the title and subtitles (if there are any) and ask yourself what you already know about the subject. This is a way to activate prior knowledge.
- Read the first paragraph and last paragraph. The first paragraph develops the main idea of the text and the last paragraph usually contains a summary of the text. You can also read the first line of each paragraph if you need more information.
- Read any words in bold.
- Look at any images, graphs, or charts that accompany the text as they may help you clarify an idea.
- Look at any comprehension and vocabulary questions that follow the text. Looking at this information before reading gives you an idea of what information is most important in the text.

SCANNING

Scanning is reading a text quickly, but with the focused objective of locating the specific fact, date, or answer you need, or to see if the text mentions a subject you are researching.

For example, you check a website's Entertainment page, find the movie you want to see, and make a note of the time and place it is playing. This is scanning. You pick up a dictionary, flip quickly to the section for words beginning with *C*, and search for the word *competent*. This is also scanning.

SKIMMING

This reading strategy is useful when you are reading a text to get a general idea of the subject. When you skim, you ignore the details and look for the main ideas. Main ideas are usually found in the first and last paragraphs as well as the first sentences of each paragraph.

People use skimming strategies frequently, but they don't always realize they are doing it.

For example, you check an online news site and click through the main items quickly to get a general overview of the events happening in the world. This is skimming. You want to see a specific movie, so you quickly read a movie review without looking at all details, to determine if the review is generally positive or negative. This is also skimming.

If you can find the correct answers to these five questions in the text below in less than 30 seconds you are scanning successfully! Read all the questions first and then read the biography of Steve Jobs.

Questions

1. Where was Steve Jobs born? _____

2. What was one of his hobbies as a boy? _____

3. Did he finish college? _____

4. With whom did he found Apple? _____

5. When did he die? _____

Short Biography of Steve Jobs

Steven Paul Jobs, co-founder of Apple, was born on February 24, 1955, in San Francisco, California. He was adopted at birth, because his biological parents were unable to marry.

As a boy, Steve worked on electronics in the family garage, taking apart and reassembling televisions and radios, a hobby that was to inspire Jobs in his future career. He dropped out of college after only six months, although he took some classes in calligraphy, which he enjoyed and which influenced his interest in design.

He co-founded Apple with Steve Wozniak after building their first computer in Jobs's parents' spare room. Apple went on to create the Mac, iPod, iPad, and iPhone, all iconic products that revolutionized the electronics industry.

Steve Jobs died of complications from pancreatic cancer on October 5, 2011.

INFERRING

Inferring is sometimes called *reading between the lines* or *making an educated guess* because it involves making connections and drawing conclusions from the evidence in the text and your own experience and understanding of the subject. For example, if you're at the checkout at a store, and you see woman suddenly look in her wallet and say "oh no," you might infer that she has no money or has lost her credit card. Inferring while you read is often necessary because writers do not always explain everything directly.

SUMMARIZING

Summarizing is a practical strategy that is used to reduce an entire text to its most important points—main ideas—using as few words as possible. When you write a summary, use your own words; **do not** copy the original text. **Do not** include your opinion in a summary. When summarizing, identify the title and source of the material that you are referring to. (Ask for your teacher's requirements.) Summarizing helps you focus on the important information in a text. It also improves your ability to retain what you read.

Listening Strategies

Use the following listening strategies to improve your understanding of audio and video clips.

LISTENING FOR THE MAIN IDEA

When listening for the main idea, your goal is to determine the general purpose and main points of the listening clip. It is *not* essential to understand every word spoken. Use these suggestions for finding main ideas *before*, *while*, and *after* you listen.

Before You Listen

- Use predicting strategies to prepare yourself to listen. *Predicting* means making an educated guess about the content of the clip before you listen to it. Read the introduction if there is one. What do you already know about the subject?
- Look for clues that might help you understand the content. For example, the title and the introduction to the listening, as well as any images that go with it, will provide important information about the general content.
- Read the comprehension questions. Highlight the key words in each question. This will provide information about the content and help prepare you to listen. While listening, focus your attention on the specific information you need to answer the questions.
- Relax, breathe deeply, and get ready to pay attention to the listening.

While You Are Listening

- Accept that you will *not* understand every single word. If there are words you don't understand, use your knowledge of the subject as well as the context to help you understand the meaning.
- Pay attention to key words and facts. Speakers often use transition words such as *firstly*, *secondly*, and *in conclusion*, and other signal words before introducing key information. Listen carefully to information following these or similar signal words.
- Listen carefully to the speaker's tone and emphasis to help you understand which information is more or less important. Speakers tend to emphasize important points.
- Take brief notes while you listen.

After Listening

- Think about the clip again. Did you understand the main points? Review your notes.
- Were you able to complete the related task correctly? If the activity is formative, review your answers with another student.
- Ask yourself what specific problems you had while listening. This will help you to become familiar with the type of difficulties you tend to have. When

listening a second time, focus on those areas that were challenging. You will be more successful the second time you listen.

LISTENING FOR DETAILS

Unlike listening for main ideas, listening for details requires you to listen for *specific* points (not *every* detail). These details may include key words, dates, or answers to questions.

- Before listening, look for clues that might help you understand the content. For example, the title and the introduction to the audio or video clip will provide important information about the general content.
- Before listening, read the comprehension questions. Highlight the key words in each question. This will provide information about the content and help to prepare you to listen.
- While listening, focus your attention on the specific information you are looking for.
- Listen for main ideas before listening for details. You will usually be more successful if you listen for details *after* you have identified the main details. Generally, listening for details requires listening a second time.

TRY IT OUT

- Go to Compass Online and listen to the audio "Branding Yourself: Emotional Intelligence" to practise your predicting skills.
- Read the introduction to the listening in your text (page 7) and highlight any words you think are important. From the description in the introduction, you know that the audio clip will discuss the relationship between emotions and personality. What about your emotions? What role do they play in your life? What do you expect to hear? What words can you think of related to the subject of emotions?
- There is always a comprehension activity following the audio listening in your text so read those questions carefully before you listen and highlight key words. This information will help you predict what the listening is about and make it easier to answer those questions.
- You haven't listened to the audio yet, but you already know a lot about it. After listening, ask yourself if the predictions you made before you listened were accurate.

INFERRING

When we listen, we make educated guesses about things that the speaker might not say directly. We can infer a lot from the context, the way something is said, and the tone of voice the speaker uses. To infer means to understand something that is not directly stated.

EXAMPLE   In a conversation with another student in the school library, you ask if she is available after class to prepare for the oral evaluation. You see that she is putting her notes and books into her bag and looking at her watch while you're talking. You probably infer that she is in a rush to get to her next class, and possibly doesn't have time to talk.

While listening to a discussion about the high salaries of star athletes, one of the speakers says

> Athletes spend more time working every day than people in most other jobs. They have to travel a lot and spend hours training every day. Additionally, athletes often have short careers and if they get injured, they may suddenly lose their career and salary.

Do you think the speaker is *for* or *against* athletes being paid high salaries?

If you guessed *for*, you inferred correctly that the speaker agrees that athletes' high salaries are justified by the long hours they work and train, and the fact that their careers are short. The speaker doesn't say directly that star athletes deserve high salaries, but provides enough information for you to make a good inference.

SUMMARIZING

The objective of summarizing is to identify the most important ideas and to ignore any information that is not directly related to a key idea. A summary does not include your opinion.

- While listening ask yourself the following:
  - » What are the main ideas?
  - » What are the most important details necessary for supporting the main ideas?
  - » What information is irrelevant or unnecessary?
- We often include the title and the source of the audio or video clip when presenting a summary. Ask about your teacher's requirements for identifying content and its source.
- Make brief notes in your own words. Do not copy what the speaker says word for word.
- Do not include your opinion.
- After the clip is finished, write a short one- or two-sentence summary. If the activity is formative, compare your summary with another student's summary and revise it as necessary.

TRY IT OUT

1. Which of the following best describes *summarizing*?
   a) Writing down everything you hear, copying the speaker's exact words, and trying not to miss any details.
   b) Writing down just the essential elements and the main ideas in your own words, and ignoring unnecessary information.
   c) Writing the main ideas, supporting ideas, and your own opinion.

2. Go to Compass Online and listen to the Unit 2 audio clip called "Laurentian Students Check Out Art Therapy." Which of the following paragraphs best summarizes that audio?

   a) This CBC Radio clip explains how art therapy classes can help students deal with the stress and anxiety they experience during the session, particularly at exam time. Everyone interviewed agreed that the workshops gave them an opportunity to relax and take a break from their busy schedules.

   b) "Laurentian Students Check Out Art Therapy," presented by Jason Turnbull on CBC Points North discusses the benefits of art therapy in helping students deal with stress. More and more students juggle part-time work, full-time study, and a social life—all these obligations can affect students' mental health. Laurentian University has organized art workshops to help students find an outlet for their stress, and all the participants interviewed spoke of the benefits of the program.

   c) The main idea of the audio "Laurentian Students Check Out Art Therapy" on CBC Radio is that art can help students deal with stress at exam time. They interviewed the leader of the session and some participants to get their opinion. I think the idea is really fun and wish that we had a similar program in my college.

Grammar Guide

Chapter 1
Plural Nouns

Go to Compass Online for additional activities using plural nouns.

A noun is the name of a thing, idea, place, or person. Most nouns in English take -s at the end to make the plural form.

one door, two doors; one boy, two boys

There are some exceptions to this rule.

Words ending in	Plural	Examples
-s, -ch, -sh, -x, -z	Add -es	class → classes inch → inches dish → dishes box → boxes buzz → buzzes
-o	Add -es, generally Add -s, for certain words (exceptions that you will have to memorize)	tomato → tomatoes photo → photos kilo → kilos radio → radios piano → pianos
-f or -fe	Remove -f or -fe, and add -ves	shelf → shelves knife → knives
consonant + -y	Remove -y, and add -ies	personality → personalities

IRREGULAR PLURAL NOUNS

Memorize the plural forms of the irregular nouns below.

Singular → Plural	Singular → Plural
man → men woman → women	child → children ox → oxen
mouse → mice	person → people
foot → feet tooth → teeth goose → geese	sheep → sheep fish → fish moose → moose deer → deer

 (homework)

Exercise 1

There are several errors with the plural nouns in the paragraphs below. Find the errors and correct them.

1. When my four childrens were very young, I taught them how to brush their tooths. *[teeth]* My daughters were especially small. They looked like two little mouses. *[mice]* I bought them footstools that looked like boxs. *[boxes]* With their little foots they would stand on the stools to reach the sink to wash their hands and faces, and to brush their tooths. *[teeth]* Now, they are grown ladys *[ladies]* and gentlemans *[gentlemen]* and have their own kids, and they are teaching their kids the same things.

2. We live our lifes *[lives]* away from animals and nature these days. Our ancestors were persons *[People]* who raised goats, sheeps, chickens, and gooses. *[gee]* They hunted deers and mooses, and caught fishes fresh from the rivers that ran by their farmes. *[3]*

Exercise 2

Fill in the blanks with the plural form of the words in the box.

> sheep   mouse   villain   leaf   kilo   wolf   thief
> radio   foot   hero   penny   quality

1. The police followed the _____ and arrested them.

2. The dogs chased the _____, which were trying to eat the _____.

3. Before TV was popular, people listened to hockey games on their _____.

4. Twenty-four inches is equal to two _____.

5. Two thousand grams is equal to two _____.

6. _____ love cheese and hate mint.

7. In western movies there are always _____ (good guys) and _____ (bad guys).

8. Some trees lose their _____ in autumn.

9. My uncle is very stingy. He always counts _____.

10. What _____ make up your personality?

COUNTABLE AND UNCOUNTABLE NOUNS

Countable nouns can be counted and can be made plural.

a boy, two boy**s**

Uncountable nouns cannot be counted and do not take a plural form.

Correct   the rain

Incorrect   a rain, two rains

Some categories of words are usually uncountable.

Category	Example
liquids and gases	rain, water, air, milk, tea, coffee
abstract nouns (e.g., ideas)	love, information, intelligence, advice, research
things that are too small and too many to count	sand, sugar, rice, salt, flour
collection of different items	furniture, equipment, baggage
some types of food	bread, butter, cheese, meat, chicken, fruit

Exercise 3

Correct the errors related to countable and uncountable nouns in the following paragraph.

> Pierre is going to the grocery store. He wants to buy some foods, including fruits and vegetables. He needs broccolis, carrots, breads, butters, chickens, rices, apples, milks, bananas, strawberry jams, and porks. After the grocery store, he will stop at the hardware store to buy some equipments to fix his broken furnitures. He also needs a lock for his luggages before his trip to Cancun. In the evening, he will do some researches online for informations or advices and tips on how to save monies during his trip.

Note To make an uncountable noun countable add a unit, such as

A piece of → bread, advice, information, furniture

A slice of → cheese, bread, ham, salami

A bar of → chocolate, soap, granola, gold

A drop of → rain, blood, water

A bag of → flour, sugar, rice

A cup of → coffee, tea

A glass of → milk, water

Exercise 4

Match the units on the left with the items on the right. Check your dictionary if necessary.

1. a loaf of _____
2. a slice of _____
3. a drop of _____
4. a means of _____
5. an article of _____
6. a carton of _____
7. a flash of _____
8. a package of _____

a) lightning
b) clothing
c) transportation
d) bread
e) rain
f) cookies
g) pizza
h) milk

ARTICLES

Articles come before nouns. They can be definite (*the*) or indefinite (*a, an, some*). Indefinite articles come before countable nouns that are mentioned for the first time (*I saw **a** baby today*) or are one of many (*He picked **an** apple/**some** apples from the basket*).

The definite article (*the*) is used with a specific countable noun—something that is unique (***the** moon*), or previously discussed or understood (***the** baby I told you about*). *The* is also used with uncountable nouns.

Article	Use	Examples
a	before countable nouns that start with a consonant sound	a book, a university
an	before countable nouns that start with a vowel sound	an apple, an umbrella
some	before uncountable nouns and plural countable nouns	some water, some apples
the	before both singular and plural countable nouns, and before uncountable nouns	the sun, the man next door, the information

Note 1 Use no articles when you speak in general about a category.

> The lions in this zoo are majestic. (specific lions in a specific zoo—use an article)

> Lions are majestic animals. (lions in general as a category—do not use an article)

Note 2 Use no articles before proper nouns such as names of countries, provinces, or cities. Also, do not use articles for sports or for languages.

> I live in **Canada**, in **Quebec**, in **Rimouski**.

> I speak **French** and I love **hockey**.

Exercise 5

Fill in the blanks with *a, an, some,* or *the*. Leave the space blank if you don't need an article.

There's ____a____ cafeteria in our college. There's ____an____ open salad bar in ____the____ cafeteria. They sell ____✗____ pasta, ____✗____ boiled eggs, and different kinds of vegetables. Yesterday, I bought ____Some____ lettuce, which unfortunately wasn't very fresh. I asked for ____a____ manager and complained to her. She looked at ____the____ lettuce and said, "There's nothing wrong with this." I returned ____some____ food and went to ____the____ coffee shop near ____the____ college. There were ____Some____ people in line before me. After standing in line for ____a____ quarter of ____an____ hour, I ordered ____an____ angus burger, ____Some____ apple pie, and ____Some or ✗____ fries and ate ____an____ unhealthy meal.

DETERMINERS

Determiners show the number or amount of a noun. Some determiners are used only with countable or uncountable nouns; others can be used with both groups.

Determiner	Used with	Meaning	Example
much	uncountable nouns	a lot of (often used in negative statements)	I don't have much patience.
many	countable nouns	a lot of	I have many bad habits.
several	countable nouns	more than two but not very many	He became angry several times.
a lot of/ lots of	both countable and uncountable	a lot of	There was a lot of rain, but we had to visit a lot of people, so we went out.
a little	uncountable nouns	not much	Max has a little experience with volunteering.
a few	countable nouns	not many	Max has a few good qualities.

Exercise 6

1. Fill in the blanks with *a little* or *a few*. If the answer is *a few*, make the noun plural.

   EXAMPLE

   rain → **a little** rain; book → **a few** book**s**

   a) _____ water

   b) _____ cup

   c) _____ information

   d) _____ love

   e) _____ tooth

   f) _____ furniture

   g) _____ dollar

   h) _____ bread

   i) _____ equipment

   j) _____ fruit

   k) _____ money

   l) _____ banana

   m) _____ suggestion

   n) _____ advice

   o) _____ coin

   p) _____ child

   q) _____ help

   r) _____ hour

   s) _____ song

   t) _____ music

2. Working with the same list of nouns, fill in the blanks with *how much* or *how many*. If the answer is *how many*, make the noun plural.

a) _____ water

b) _____ cup

c) _____ information

d) _____ love

e) _____ tooth

f) _____ furniture

g) _____ dollar

h) _____ bread

i) _____ equipment

j) _____ fruit

k) _____ money

l) _____ banana

m) _____ suggestion

n) _____ advice

o) _____ coin

p) _____ child

q) _____ help

r) _____ hour

s) _____ song

t) _____ music

Exercise 7

Fill in the blanks with *a little, a few, much,* or *many*.

1. How _____ times have I asked you not to put too _____ water in the bathtub? Only _____ days ago we had this same conversation. Please show _____ more consideration.

2. Is it too _____ to ask for _____ minutes of your time to help me do _____ bit of painting around the house?

3. _____ people have so _____ money that they don't know what to do with it while others have almost nothing. Giving just _____ bit of money can help move _____ people out of poverty.

4. There's too _____ violence on TV. I'd like to see _____ movies with _____ less violence.

THERE IS AND *THERE ARE*

The word *there* comes at the beginning of a sentence to introduce information or to show that something exists. It is usually followed by the verb *be* (*is, are, was, were*).

There is a café on the sidewalk.

There are people sitting at the tables and there are pedestrians walking by.

There are cars parked in front of the hotel.

There is an umbrella on the patio.

The singular forms (*There is/There was*) introduce **uncountable nouns** (water, milk) or **singular countable nouns** (banana, apple).

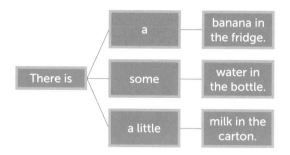

The plural forms (*There are/There were*) introduce **plural nouns**.

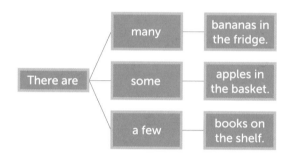

Affirmative	Negative	Question
There is . . .	There isn't . . .	Is there . . .?
There are . . .	There aren't . . .	Are there . . .?
There was . . .	There wasn't . . .	Was there . . .?
There were . . .	There weren't . . .	Were there . . .?

Exercise 8

Fill in the blanks with *there is*, *there are*, *is there*, *are there*, *there isn't*, or *there aren't*.

1. _____ many positive personality traits that I admire, but _____ only one that I find essential.

2. _____ any good Chinese restaurants around here?

3. _____ lots of options on the menu?

4. I'm thirsty, but _____ any juice in the fridge. _____ a can of pineapple in the cupboard, but _____ any can openers in the house.

5. _____ some fresh eggs in the fridge and _____ also some salad.

6. _____ many factors that shape our personality type.

Communicative Activity

Work in pairs. Take turns asking and answering the following questions.

Student A

1. How many planets are there in our solar system?

2. How much sugar is there in one can of Coke?

3. Are there any personality traits that you cannot tolerate?

4. Was there any soap in the Middle Ages?

5. Are there any common character traits among psychopaths?

Student B

1. How many French-speaking countries are there in the world?

2. Were there any Europeans settlers in Canada before the 15th century?

3. How much electricity is there in a single flash of lightning?

4. If there was one thing you could change about yourself, what would you choose?

5. Is there a city in Quebec with a population of more than 2 000 000?

Chapter 2
Simple Present and Present Progressive

Go to Compass Online for additional activities using simple present and present progressive.

Use the simple present to talk about facts and generalizations.

> The earth **revolves** around the sun.

> Birds **migrate** to the south every winter.

Also use the simple present to talk about repeated actions (e.g., routines and habits).

> David **works** at a grocery store.

> I **visit** my grandparents every Christmas.

Use the present progressive for things that are happening now or at the time the speaker is talking.

> I **am teaching** now.

> David **is working** at the moment.

> The students **are learning** grammar now.

Use the present progressive to talk about a temporary routine.

> I usually drive to school (regular routine), but **I'm taking** the bus this week (temporary routine).

Simple present		Present progressive	
Affirmative		**Affirmative**	
Use the base form of the verb except in third person singular. For third person singular, add -s (*walks*) or -es (*pushes*). **EXCEPTION** *to be* (am/is/are)	I walk. You walk. He walks. We walk. You walk. They walk.	Use *am/is/are* + the -ing form of the verb.	I am walking. You are walking. It is walking. We are walking. You are walking. They are walking.
Negative		**Negative**	
Add *don't* (*do not*) before the verb except in third person singular. For third person singular, add *doesn't* (*does not*) before the verb and change the verb to base form (remove -s or -es). **EXCEPTION** *to be* (am not/is not [isn't]/are not [aren't])	I don't walk. You don't walk. She doesn't walk. We don't walk. You don't walk. They don't walk.	Use *am not/isn't/ aren't* + the ing form of the verb.	I am not walking. You are not walking. It is not walking. We are not walking. You are not walking. They are not walking.

Simple present			Present progressive		
Question			**Question**		
Add *do* before the subject except in third person singular. For third person singular, add *does* before the subject and change the verb to base form (remove -s or -es). **EXCEPTION** *to be (Am I . . . /Is he . . . /Are you . . .)*		Do I walk? Do you walk? Does he walk? Do we walk? Do you walk? Do they walk?	Move *am/is/are* before the subject. Don't change the -ing form of the verb.		Am I walking? Are you walking? Is she walking? Are we walking? Are you walking? Are they walking?

Note 1 Always use the present form of the verb *to be* (*am*, *is*, *are*) for the present progressive.

Correct	I am working now
Incorrect	~~I working now.~~

Note 2 When speaking, we almost always use the short negative form.

You aren't working instead of *you are not working.*

He doesn't work instead of *he does not work.*

Am doesn't have a short negative form, so we contract *I am not* to *I'm not.*

Note 3 Do not use the present progressive with stative verbs.

Verbs that show actions are called action verbs. Verbs that show states are called stative verbs. Use the present progressive only for actions. When using a stative verb (for example with feelings, relationships, physical descriptions, beliefs, or possessions), use the simple present even when talking about something occurring right now.

EXAMPLE

Incorrect	~~Are you seeing the airplane? Yes, I'm seeing the airplane now.~~
Correct	Do you see the airplane? Yes, I see the airplane now.
Incorrect	~~I am knowing the answer now.~~
Correct	I know the answer now.

 For a list of stative verbs, see Grammar Appendix 1 on page 220.

THIRD PERSON SINGULAR: -S AND -ES

Spelling: -s or -es

Add -s to the third person singular for most simple present verbs.

walk → walks, talk → talks

Add -es to the third person singular for verbs that end in -s, -x, -sh, -ch, -o, and -z.

guess → guesses, box → boxes, push → pushes, punch → punches, go → goes

When a verb ends in -y, add -s if there's a vowel before the -y. Change -y to -ies if there's a consonant before the -y.

play → plays, study → studies

Exercise 1

Add -s or -es to each verb. Change the spelling where necessary.

1. discuss_____
2. wash_____
3. say_____
4. multiply _____

5. tear_____
6. echo_____
7. reply _____
8. reach_____

9. buz_____
10. mix_____
11. add_____
12. enter_____

Pronunciation of third person -s

The third person -s can be pronounced as /s/ as in *writes*, or /z/ as in *drives*, or /iz/ as in *watches*. Check your dictionary if you are not sure of the pronunciation of a word.

Exercise 2

Put the correct pronunciation (/s/, /z/, or /iz/) next to each verb.

1. squashes _____
2. drags _____
3. races _____
4. sleeps _____
5. drinks _____
6. strives _____

SPELLING OF -ING VERBS

For most short, one-syllable verbs ending in consonant-vowel-consonant (CVC), double the last letter before adding -ing.

swim → swimming, run → running

For most multisyllabic verbs ending in CVC, double the last letter *if* the last syllable is stressed. Do not double the last letter if the last syllable is not stressed.

begin → beginning **but** whisper → whispering

For verbs ending in a silent -e drop the -e, then add -ing.

shake → shaking

For verbs ending in -ie, change -ie to -y, then add -ing.

die → dying

Exercise 3

Add -ing to the following verbs. Change the spelling where necessary.

1. cut_____
2. act_____
3. prefer_____
4. star_____

5. clear_____
6. answer_____
7. lie _____
8. bake _____

9. ship_____
10. cope _____
11. cup_____
12. be_____

Exercise 4

Fill in the blanks with the correct choice. Then answer the question.

EXAMPLE

Question _____ (Do/Does) Sunday follow Monday?

Answer Does Sunday follow Monday? No, it doesn't. Monday follows Sunday.

1. _*Does*_ (Do/Does/Is/Are) a week have six days?
   No, it doesn't. A week has seven days.

2. _*Does*_ (Do/Does/Is/Are) water boil at 80 degrees Celsius?
   No, it doesn't. Water boil at 100 degrees C.

3. _*Do*_ (Do/Does/Is/Are) most birds migrate to cold places in winter?
   No, they don't. Most birds migrate to warm place (in winter)

4. _*Are*_ (Do/Does/Is/Are) your parents waiting for you outside now?
   Yes/No, they are/aren't

5. _*Is*_ (Do/Does/Is/Are) the earth getting closer to the sun at this time of the year?
   Yes, it's. No, it's not

Communicative Activity 1

Work in pairs. Each person creates five questions with *do* and *does* similar to the questions above. Then you and your partner take turns asking and answering the questions.

INFORMATION QUESTION WORDS

Yes/No questions require either a *Yes* or *No* answer but information questions require specific information in response. Words such as *who, what, when, where, why,* and *how* are used to ask for information.

Pay attention to the structure of each type of question.

Question type	Structure
Yes/No	Auxiliary (A) + Subject (S) + Verb (V) + . . . Do + you + like + . . .
Information	Question word (Q) + Auxiliary (A) + Subject (S) + Verb (V) + . . . How + do + you + like + . . .

Note When you create information questions, make sure they follow the formula Q+A+S+V.

EXCEPTION When you ask a question about the subject of a sentence, you don't need an auxiliary.

John lives here. → **Who** lives here?

List of question words

Question word	To ask about	Example
who	people	Who do you live with?
what	things, animals, actions, or states	What does she think about you?
when/what time	time	When does he come home from work?
where	place	Where do you live?
why	reason	Why do you live there?
how	manner	How do you go home?

Exercise 5

There is an error in each of the following questions. Find the error and correct it.

1. Who does live here? _Who lives here?_

2. What does your sister thinks about this problem? _____
   What does your sister think about this problem

3. What you doing now? _What are you doing now?_

4. Where you are going now? _Where are you going now?_

5. Why does Mary and her friend look at me like that? _do_ _____
   _____

6. How is she feel now? _does_ _How is she feeling now?_

Communicative Activity 2

Work in pairs. Each partner will write seven questions using the following question words: why, where, when, what, who, how, what time. Take turns asking and answering the questions.

EXAMPLE why

Student A: Why do you look so tired?

Student B: I have trouble sleeping at night.

QUESTION WORDS FOLLOWED BY NOUNS

Some question words are often followed by nouns.

> How many **jobs** does he have?

Here are some question words that are often followed by nouns.

Question word	To ask about	Example
How much	amount	How much **money** do you have?
How many	number	How many **friends** do you have?
Whose	possession	Whose **dress** do you like?
Which	choice/order	Which **car** do you want?

Exercise 6

Complete the following questions in your own words. Then answer the question.

1. How much patience _____?

2. How many dependable friends _____?

3. Whose personality _____?

4. Which type of personality _____?

ADVERBS OF FREQUENCY

Adverbs of frequency show how often something happens or is repeated.

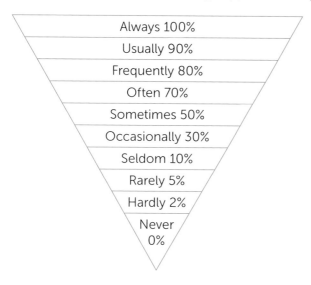

Always 100%
Usually 90%
Frequently 80%
Often 70%
Sometimes 50%
Occasionally 30%
Seldom 10%
Rarely 5%
Hardly 2%
Never 0%

Look at the position of the adverb (adv) in relation to the verb (v) in these two sentences.

> Melanie is always late for class.
>   v. adv.

> France never comes to class late.
>   adv.   v.

Adverbs of frequency come after auxiliary verbs (e.g., *am*, *is*, *are*) and before main verbs (e.g., *come*, *work*, *write*). When a sentence has both auxiliary (or modal) and a main verb, the adverb comes between the two.

> France <u>can</u> **never** <u>arrive</u> on time.

In questions, the adverb comes immediately after the subject.

> Does <u>France</u> **always** come to class late?

Exercise 7

There is a misplaced adverb in some of the following sentences. Find the error and correct it. If there is no error, write *correct* next to the sentence.

1. We like rarely dishonest people. _We rarely like dishonest people._

2. He often was rude. _He was often rude_

3. I sometimes feel lazy in the evenings. _____

4. Maurice Richard often is considered one of the best hockey players of all time.

   _____

5. Does always your sister make you angry?

   _____

Communicative Activity 3

Work in pairs. Ask your partner how often he or she does each of the following activities.

go to the cinema, drink juice, miss class, play hockey,
take a bath, travel abroad, eat fish

EXAMPLE   smoke

Student A: How often do you smoke?

Student B: I never smoke.

Exercise 8

As you learned in this chapter, the simple present is used for facts and repeated actions while the present progressive is used for actions that are in progress (right now). However, the simple present is used for stative (non-action) verbs even when they are in progress.

Fill in the blanks with either the simple present or the present progressive form of the verbs in parentheses.

1. How much exercise you _are doing_ (do) now is not as important as how much exercise you _do_ (do) on a regular basis.

2. At the moment, he _is think_ (think) about why his sister always _picks_ (pick) on him.

3. I _know_ (know) that you _are tryir_ (try) to control your anger now.

4. Listen! I _try_ (try) to do these exercises, but I can't concentrate because you _are making_ (make) too much noise.

5. _Do_ you _understand_ (understand) the question now?

6. _Am_ I _doing_ (do) this exercise correctly now?

Communicative Activity 4

Work in pairs. Each of you should choose five classmates you know very well. Describe to your partner what each of those five people is doing now. Then talk about some of those classmates' habits. Remember to take turns.

Marie is playing with her cellphone now. She seldom plays with her phone in the classroom.

Chapter 3
Simple Past and Past Progressive

Use the simple past to talk about something that happened in the past and is now finished.

Use the past progressive to explain that the action was in progress at a specific time in the past.

> Aurelie wrote a poem around 8:00 last night.
> (Her poem was complete around 8:00.)

> Aurelie was writing a poem around 8:00 last night.
> (She was still working on her poem around 8:00. Her poem was not complete by then.)

Note In English, the simple past is used to describe past habits. Do not use past progressive for habits.

| **Correct** | I biked to work when I was younger. |
| **Incorrect** | ~~I was biking to work when I was younger.~~ |

Go to Compass Online for additional activities using simple past and past progressive.

Simple past		Past progressive	
Affirmative		**Affirmative**	
Regular verbs take -ed in the past. Irregular verbs have special past forms. (*come* → *came*)	I arrived late last night. You arrived late last night. He arrived late last night. We arrived late last night. You arrived late last night. They arrived late last night.	Use *was/were* + the -ing form of the verb.	I was watching TV. You were watching TV. She was watching TV. We were watching TV. You were watching TV. They were watching TV.
EXCEPTION *to be* has two past forms: *is/am* → *was* *are* → *were*	I came home late last night.		
Negative		**Negative**	
Add *didn't* (*did not*) before the verb and change the verb to base form. **EXCEPTION** *was* → *wasn't* *were* → *weren't*	I didn't arrive late last night. You didn't arrive late last night. He didn't arrive late last night. We didn't arrive late last night. You didn't arrive late last night. They didn't arrive late last night. I didn't come home late last night.	Change *was* and *were* to *wasn't* (*was not*) and *weren't* (*were not*).	I wasn't watching TV. You weren't watching TV. She wasn't watching TV. We weren't watching TV. You weren't watching TV. They weren't watching TV.

Simple past		Past progressive	
Question		**Question**	
Add *did* before the subject and change the verb to base form.	Did I arrive late last night? Did you arrive late last night? Did he arrive late last night? Did we arrive late last night? Did you arrive late last night? Did they arrive late last night?	Move *was* and *were* before the subject. Don't change the -ing form of the verb.	Was I watching TV? Were you watching TV? Was she watching TV? Were we watching TV? Were you watching TV? Were they watching TV?
EXCEPTION *to be* Was she late? Were they late?	Did you come home late last night?		

SPELLING OF REGULAR PAST TENSE: -ED ENDINGS

Add -ed to most regular verbs to make the simple past. However, there are some variations. There are some spelling rules you have to observe for certain past tense regular verbs. If the verb ends in -e, add -d.

> live → lived
> hope → hoped
> paste → pasted

If the verb ends in a consonant + -y, delete the -y, and add -ied.

> study → studied
> try → tried
> copy → copied

If there's a stressed vowel before the final consonant, double the consonant, and then add -ed.

> prefer → preferred
> plan → planned
> omit → omitted

Exercise 1

Change each sentence to the past tense. Change the simple present to simple past, and the present progressive to past progressive. Keep the form the same (affirmative, negative, question). If you are not sure about irregular past verbs, see Grammar Appendix 2 on page 221.

> He goes home. → He went home.
>
> He is going home. → He was going home.
>
> He doesn't go home. → He didn't go home.
>
> Is he going home? → Was he going home?

1. Do you understand? _Did you ~~nte~~ understand?_

2. Are you listening to me? _Were you listening to me?_

3. They pay tax. _They paid tax._

4. He doesn't believe me. _He didn't believe me._

5. I'm not singing. _I wasn't singing._

6. He prefers classical music. _He prefers classical music._

7. I deny everything. _I denied everything._

8. Is he there? _was he there?_

9. We fall. _We fell._

10. I don't know. _I didn't know._

11. Birds fly. _Birds flew._

12. He cleans windows. _He cleaned windows._

13. It means a lot to me. _It meaned a lot to me._

14. I scan the document. _I scaned the document._

15. They aren't dancing. _They weren't dancing._

Exercise 2

Rewrite the following paragraph in past tense.

> Every Saturday, I wake up at 8:00. I brush my teeth, wash my face, and eat breakfast. Then I get dressed and go to the community centre near our house to practise hockey. After practice, I take a shower and have lunch at the cafeteria with a couple of my teammates. I come back home and change. Then I pick up my boyfriend and go to the cinema. After the movie, we drive to a nearby restaurant and have supper. I return home around 11:00, drink a glass of milk, and read a novel until I fall asleep.

You can start your paragraph with *Last Saturday* . . .

Communicative Activity 1

Work in pairs. Use the simple past tense to tell your partner what you did last weekend. Include as much detail as possible.

EXAMPLE

I woke up at . . .

I had . . . for breakfast

Communicative Activity 2

Work in pairs. Take turns asking and answering questions in the past tense about your partner's life. Use the clues below to help you think of questions to ask. You may add your own questions after you have used all the clues.

EXAMPLE

Which/primary school/go? → Which primary school did you go to?

1. Which/high school/go?

2. How many close friends/have/in high school?

3. When/graduate/high school?

4. What/do/last summer?

5. When/learn/to ride a bike?

6. What/eat/last night for supper?

7. What time/go to sleep/last night?

8. When/wake up/today?

9. Which city/visit/on/last trip?

10. Which movie/see/at the cinema/last time?

Communicative Activity 3

Work in pairs. Take turns. Tell your partner some of the things you wanted to do but did not do when you were younger and explain why you didn't. For example, consider talking about visiting new places, going to a concert, or doing something artistic such as singing, dancing, writing, painting, and so on.

EXAMPLE

I didn't go to Disneyland when I was a kid because I was afraid of flying.

Exercise 3

Rewrite the following paragraph in past tense.

Right now, I am sitting at my desk and I am checking photos on Instagram. There's a stupid movie on TV. A young man and a woman are trying to escape from evil witches who are looking for them, and they are killing a lot of innocent people in their way. One of the witches is running after small children. Another one is setting everything on fire. The third witch is creating a storm with her breath. The storm is destroying buildings. I am thinking "who watches such stupid movies?" My eyes are getting heavy. Am I dreaming all of this?

You can start your paragraph with *Last night at this time* . . .

SIMPLE PAST AND PAST PROGRESSIVE

Very often the past progressive is used in the same sentence with the simple past. In such cases, the simple past usually describes the main action. The past progressive describes what is going on in the background.

When Marc entered the food court, the cleaners were mopping the floors.
(The main action is Marc's entry. The cleaning was happening in the background.)

Sometimes the simple past (the shorter, main action) interrupts the past progressive (the longer, background action).

I was watching TV when the phone rang.
(The phone interrupts the TV watching.)

Two actions in progress

We can use the past progressive to talk about two actions that were in progress at the same time in the past.

> While he was washing the dishes, she was talking to her sister on the phone.
> (He was washing and she was talking at the same time.)

Remember that simple past is used to describe past habits. Do not use past progressive for habits.

Exercise 4

Fill in the blanks with the simple past or past progressive of the verbs in parentheses.

1. I _was drawing_ (draw) her portrait when she _fell_ (fall) asleep.

2. When I _entered_ (enter) the class, the teacher _was discussing_ (discuss) Tom Thomson's art.

3. He _interrupted_ (interrupt) me several times while I _was writting_ (write) a story.

4. She _was holding_ (hold) the phone with one hand while she _was talking_ (take) notes with her other hand.

5. After I _gave_ (give) her the portrait, she _jumped_ (jump) for joy.

6. When I was a student, I _sold_ (sell) newspapers in the mornings and _worked_ (work) at a bookstore in the evenings every weekend.

7. I _went_ (go) to sleep while you _were reading_ (read).

8. _Were_ you _singing_ (sing) while you _were taking_ (take) a shower?

Communicative Activity 4

Work in pairs. Take turns explaining what you were doing at the following times:

> At this time yesterday
> At this time last week
> At 8:00 PM last Sunday
> Last year at this time
> The last time your phone rang
> When the teacher entered the classroom today
> The last time you received some very bad or very good news
> When you had a creative idea (for example, a solution to a problem, an idea for a photo, a business idea)

Chapter 4
Future

Go to Compass Online for additional activities using the future.

The future tense tells what will happen in the future. The future tense is most commonly expressed with *will* or *be going to*.

Future with *will*	Future with *be going to*
Affirmative	**Affirmative**
will + base form of verb I will do it next week. It will snow tomorrow. They will sleep at a hotel tonight.	*to be* (*am/is/are*) + *going to* + base form of the verb I am going to do homework tonight. It is going to rain tomorrow. They are going to review the exercises next week.
Negative	**Negative**
Change *will* to *will not* (*won't*). I will (I'll) do it. → I will not (won't) do it. It will (It'll) snow. → It will not (won't) snow. They will (They'll) sleep → They will not (won't) sleep.	Change *am/is/are* to *am not/is not/are not*. I am not (I'm not) going to do homework. It is not (isn't) going to rain. They are not (aren't) going to review the exercises.
Question	**Question**
Move *will* before the subject. Will I do it? Will it snow? Will they sleep?	Move *to be* (*am/is/are*) before the subject. Am I going to do it? Is it going to rain? Are they going to review the exercises?

Note 1 In spoken English, we usually use contracted forms (e.g., *I'll* and *I won't* or *I'm going to* and *I'm not going to*) instead of full forms (*I will* and *I will not* or *I am going to* and *I am not going to*).

Note 2 In familiar spoken language, *going to* is sometimes changed to *gonna*. Do not use *gonna* in writing (or when speaking with people you are not close to).

He's going to do it. → He's gonna do it.

Exercise 1

Change the following sentences to the negative. Use the contracted form where possible.

1. I'll do the dishes. _____

2. We're going to dance tonight. _____

3. Will you help me boost my car battery? _____

4. I'm going to hit the play button. _____

5. Are you going to take a step back? _____

6. The snow will melt soon. _____

DIFFERENTIATING BETWEEN *WILL* AND *BE GOING TO*

Function	Form	Example
Predictions_ guess	*will* + verb	It will snow in January. It will rain tonight.
	be going to + verb	It is going to snow in January. It is going to rain tonight.
Spontaneous decisions	*will* + verb	What a mess! I will help you clean up. I'll call her right now.
Planned action in the future/intention	*be going to* + verb	We are going to finish at 11:30. I'm going to study harder next time.

Exercise 2

Underline the best answer. If both answers are possible, underline both.

1. Francois (will/is going to) solve the problem because he is a creative thinker. *Predictions* *both*

2. Why are you buying those art books? Because I (will/am going to) learn to draw.

3. The mail is here. I (will/am going to) get it.

4. What are your plans this weekend? We (will/are going to) visit the Tom Thomson exhibition at the gallery. *both*

5. Grandpa (will/is going to) be 90 years old this Sunday. *fact.*

6. What are you doing tonight? (I will/am going to) finish my biology exercises. I am behind in biology.

Communicative Activity 1

Work in pairs. Use *be going to* to tell your partner what your plans are for this weekend and ask about your partner's plans. You can use question words: *who*, *what*, *when*, *where*, *how*, and *why* to form your questions.

EXAMPLE   I'm going to take piano lessons Saturday morning. What are you going to do?

(handwritten margin note, top left) what I mean is that she is beautiful

Communicative Activity 2

Work in pairs. Use *be going to* or *will* to predict what the world will look like in 20 years.

> **EXAMPLE** We will all use self-driving cars. No one is going to be able to drive a regular car.

TIME MARKERS WITH FUTURE

Do not use the future after time markers (e.g., *when, before, after, as soon as, until,* or *for as long as*). Use the present tense instead.

Correct	I will get there tomorrow. I will rent a car.
Incorrect	**When** ~~I will get there~~ tomorrow, I will rent a car.
Correct	**When** I get there tomorrow, I will rent a car.

Exercise 3

Find the error with the verb tense in the following sentences and correct it.

EXAMPLE

Incorrect	I will call you when she ~~will arrive~~.
Correct	I will call you when she arrives.

(handwritten: time work)

1. As soon as I will know the answer, I will get back to you.

   _____

   (handwritten margin note: after the time work, we use present)

2. I will go to sleep when I will be tired. *(handwritten: am)*

   _____

   (handwritten margin note: By the time class is over, my coffee will be cold.
   My coffee will be cold by the time class is over.)

3. She will look for a job after she will graduate from art school.

   _____

4. Before the contractors will start work, I will cut off the electricity.

   _____

5. You will wait until everyone will leave.

   _____

6. The manager will hold a meeting as soon as he will arrive in the office.

   _____

7. I will not talk to you for as long as you will refuse to apologize to me.

   _____

Exercise 4

Complete each sentence in your own words.

> **EXAMPLE** I will think about the problem when . . .
>
> I will think about the problem when I have time.

1. I will help you for as long as . . . *(handwritten: You apologize to me)*
   (handwritten: ~~You~~ I finish my job)

2. When I . . . , I will not say anything. _____

3. My mother will never eat before . . . _____

4. He will brush his teeth after . . . _____

5. The students will not start the test until . . . _____

Simple present for scheduled future events

Use the simple present to refer to events in the future if they are scheduled. In this case, there must be a time signal (at 9:00 AM., in three hours, after lunch).

> My violin lesson starts after the lunch break.
>
> My flight leaves at 9:00 PM.
>
> The concert begins in two hours.

Communicative Activity 3

Work in pairs. Each partner prepares a schedule for the next three days. Include in-class and out-of-class activities. Exchange your schedules. Take turns using the simple present tense to read the schedules to each other.

EXAMPLE   Your biology class starts in an hour. Your first break is in 50 minutes. Your hockey practice starts at 6:00 tonight.

You may wish to set up a schedule like this one to show when your activities take place.

Time	Day 1 _____	Day 2 _____	Day 3 _____
6:00 AM	wake up		
7:00 AM	gym/spin class		
10:00 AM	biology class		
4:00 PM	dentist appointment		
7:00 PM	baseball game		

Present progressive for arrangements

Use the present progressive for things that have already been arranged. These planned events are often for the near future.

> What are you doing tonight? I am watching a movie with my friends.

Communicative Activity 4

Work in pairs. Use the schedule you prepared for Activity 3, but focus only on the out-of-class activities. Use the present progressive tense to tell your partner what you plan to do after class for the next three days.

EXAMPLE   I'm going grocery shopping today. I'm doing my math homework tonight. I'm meeting a friend at the cafeteria tomorrow at noon.

Review Exercise

Write the answers to the following questions. In your response, use the same tense used in the question (future [*will/be going to*], simple present, or present progressive).

1. Will you call 911 if you see a parent beating a child? Why?

2. Are you going to apply to university after you graduate from college? Why?

3. What are you doing today after class?

4. When does your next class start?

Chapter 5

Present Perfect and Present Perfect Progressive

PRESENT PERFECT

Go to Compass Online for additional activities using present perfect and present perfect progressive.

Form the present perfect with *have/has* + past participle of the verb.

The past participle of regular verbs is the same as their simple past form. They take -ed.

walk → walked   I have walked.
talk → talked   She has talked.

For the past participle of irregular verbs, see Grammar Appendix 2 on page 221.

drive → driven   They have driven.
go → gone   He has gone.

Affirmative	Negative	Question
I have (I've) written.	I haven't (have not) written.	Have I written?
You have written.	You haven't written.	Have you written?
He/She/It has written.	He/She/It hasn't written.	Has he/she/it written?
We have written.	We haven't written.	Have we written?
You have written.	You haven't written.	Have you written?
They have written.	They haven't written.	Have they written?

Exercise 1

Change the following sentences from past to present perfect. See Grammar Appendix 2 for any past participles that you do not know.

I left. → I have left.

1. Peter ate insects. _____

2. Miriam saw that movie three times. _____

3. My brother and I visited the food plant. _____

4. Peter and Miriam fell down. _____

5. 3D food printing began. _____

Using the present perfect: From past to present

Present perfect is a combination of past and present tenses. Present perfect can refer to an action that started in the past and continues to the present.

> She started teaching English in 1994. (past) She still teaches English. (present)

You can combine the ideas in the two sentences with the present perfect.

> She **has taught** English **for** more than twenty years.
> (taught in the past and teaches in the present)

Use the preposition *for* to indicate the length of time something has been happening.

> She has taught **for** twenty years.

Use the preposition *since* to indicate when the action began.

> She has taught **since** 1994.

Exercise 2

Fill in the first blank with the present perfect form of the verb in parentheses (add *have/has* + past participle) and use your own words to complete the second blank.

> I _____ (be) in this class since _____.
> I ___**have been**___ (be) in this class since ___**8:00 AM**___.

1. My parents _____ (live) in the same house for _____.

2. I _____ (have) a driver's licence since _____.

3. My sister _____ (not take) any vitamin supplements since _____.

4. We _____ (not see) a good movie for _____.

5. My mother _____ (work) for the same company since _____.

Communicative Activity 1

Work in pairs and take turns. Use *How long . . .* and one of the ideas from the box to ask your partner questions using the present perfect tense. The first suggestion has been completed as an example.

> you live in this city, you play hockey (or another sport),
> you know your best friend, you own a car, our teacher work at this
> school, we practise this tense, you sleep in the past 24 hours

Student A	How long have you lived in this city?
Student B	I have lived here for about four years.

Using the present perfect: Unspecified past

The present perfect can also be used to talk about actions that happened at an unspecified time in the past.

Compare these two sentences.

I **saw** that movie last night. (We know when in the past the event happened [last night]. The simple past is used.)

I **have seen** that movie. (We don't know when in the past the event happened. The present perfect is used.)

Communicative Activity 2

In pairs, take turns asking and answering questions. Student A asks a question beginning with "Have you ever . . ." and ends with one of the clues in the box. Student B answers. If the answer is *yes*, Students B explains how many times he or she has done the activity (using the present perfect) and explains when he or she did it for the last time (using the simple past).

> play basketball, break a bone, lose your wallet/purse, travel to the US, steal something, sleep more than ten hours straight, have food poisoning, catch a bad cold or flu, win anything

Student A Have you ever played basketball?

Student B Yes, I have played basketball several times. Actually, I played basketball with my friends last weekend.

Present perfect time expressions

The following time expressions are often used with the present perfect: *since, for, just, already, before, ever, never, so far, still,* and *yet.*

Exercise 3

Use each of the time expressions above with present perfect verbs in a sentence of your own. Check your dictionary for the expressions you do not know.

still → I still haven't finished my homework.

Simple past or present perfect?

Use the simple past for single or repeated actions, or states that are finished.

Use the present perfect if the single or repeated action or state, or its effect, is not finished

Pierre **taught** at Cégep de Sherbrooke for two years.
(He doesn't teach there now.)

Pierre **has taught** at Cégep de Sherbrooke for two years.
(He still teaches there.)

Use the simple past for actions or states at a specific time in the past.

Use the present perfect for actions or states at an unspecified time in the past.

Chantale **visited** Paris last year. (specific time)

Chantale **has visited** Paris. (unspecified time)

Exercise 4

Some of the following sentences contain the wrong tense. Find the tense errors and correct them. If the tense is correct, add a checkmark to the sentence.

1. He worked at this supermarket for six years.

   _____

2. He has worked at this supermarket for six years.

   _____

3. He has written a letter last night.

   _____

4. We worked here for the past two years.

   _____

5. I already ate, so I'm not hungry.

   _____

6. They didn't respond to our letter yet.

   _____

7. I didn't eat anything since this morning.

   _____

8. You have done this two years ago.

   _____

PRESENT PERFECT PROGRESSIVE

Like the present perfect, the present perfect progressive indicates an action that started in the past and continues to the present. Present perfect progressive focuses on the duration of the action and on the fact that the action is still going on uninterrupted (*I have been teaching for a very long time.*) or has very recently finished (*It has been raining here. The streets are still wet.*).

Present perfect progressive is formed with *have/has been* + verb + -ing.

> I have been teaching. She has been studying.

For the negative form, use *haven't* or *hasn't*.

> She hasn't been eating.

For the question form, move *have/has* before the subject.

> Has he been doing anything?

Compare the present perfect with the present perfect progressive.

> She has written a book. (The book is finished. The action is complete.)

> She has been writing a book. (The book is not finished. She's still working on it.)

In some contexts, with certain verbs (e.g., *work*, *live*, *teach*), there is very little difference in meaning between the present perfect and present perfect progressive.

> I have lived here for six years.

> I have been living here for six years.

Note 1 The present perfect progressive is generally not used with stative (non-action) verbs (see Grammar Appendix 1).

Incorrect	~~I have been hating ice cream all my life.~~
Correct	I have hated ice cream all my life.

Note 2 The present perfect progressive is not used for events in the unspecified past.

Incorrect	~~I have been visiting Japan before.~~
Correct	I have visited Japan before.

Exercise 5

Change the verbs in the following sentences from present perfect to present perfect progressive. If the change is not possible, write N/A.

EXAMPLE

He has worked here for a long time. → **He has been working here for a long time.**

1. They have lived in this town for ten years.

   _____

2. She has taught English in Japan for six months.

   _____

3. I haven't ever seen artificial meat.

   _____

4. We have investigated the food industry's secrets.

   _____

5. He has thought about food waste.

   _____

6. You have understood the difference between present perfect and present perfect progressive.

   _____

Communicative Activity 3

Work in pairs. Individually, make two lists of some of your past hobbies or habits (list A) and your present hobbies or habits (list B). Exchange the lists with your partner. Take turns asking how long each of you has been doing (present perfect progressive) or did (simple past) each hobby.

EXAMPLE

Past hobby	collected stamps
Student A	How long did you collect stamps?
Student B	I collected stamps for three years when I was in primary school.
Present habit	eat organic food
Student A	How long have you been eating organic food?
Student B	I have been eating organic food for the past two years. I started eating organic in the last year of high school.

Chapter 6

Pronouns and Possessive Adjectives

Go to Compass Online for additional activities using pronouns and possessive adjectives.

Pronouns refer to previously mentioned nouns or noun phrases. They are used to avoid repetition in sentences or paragraphs.

> I like Mike. Mike is nice. → I like Mike. He is nice.

SUBJECT AND OBJECT PRONOUNS

Subject pronouns replace subjects. Subjects usually appear *before* the verb (except in some questions).

> <u>I</u>   went on a fishing trip.
> subj.   v.

Object pronouns replace objects. Objects usually appear *after* the verb or *after* a preposition.

> Audrey   came   with   <u>me.</u>
> subj.   v.   prep.   obj.

Subject pronouns		Object pronouns
I		me
You		you
He		him
She	verb or preposition	her
It	+ +	it
We		us
You		you
They		them

Exercise 1

Underline the correct pronoun.

1. I like Anik and I respect (she/her).

2. Antoine came to class with Anik and (I/me).

3. Antoine and (I/me) went to class together.

4. Dominic tried an insect burger with (we/*us*).

5. (We/Us) had breakfast with Dominic.

THE POSSESSIVE FORM

Use -'s or *of* to show possession.

In general, we use *of* for things.

    the handle of the door

    the leg of the table

We use -'s for people, animals, or time.

    Jeremy's house

    the cat's nose

    today's special

Use -s' (instead of -'s) if the owner is plural.

    the girl's hands (one girl)

    the girls' hands (many girls)

However, there are instances when we use -'s for things and *of* for people. In some cases, we can use either form.

    Walmart's sale (~~the sale of Walmart~~)

    the son of God

    the name of the teacher or the teacher's name

Note Do not confuse the possessive -'s with the contracted *is* (as in **Joe is → Joe's**)

    Mary's food is cold. (possessive)

    Mary's a food critic. (Mary is a food critic)

Exercise 2

Some of the possessive forms below can be expressed better with -'s (or -s'). Change the possessive to -'s or -s' where appropriate.

    the hands of the girl → the girl's hands

    the hands of the clock → no change

1. the food of tomorrow ~~The food's~~ Tomorrow's food.

2. the children of the family The family's children.

3. a piece of the puzzle ____ ✗ ____

4. the rules of the game The game's rules.

5. a sample of the food ____ ✗ ____

6. the feelings of the people The people's feeling

7. the offices of the teachers The teachers' offices

8. the enemies of my friends The friends' enemies

9. the food allergies of a person The food's ✗ allergies. (person's)

10. the taste of the 3D food The food's taste. ✗ no change (The food's taste is awful.)

Exercise 3

Write V if the -'s represents a contracted verb and P. if the -'s shows the possessive.

EXAMPLE

V → Mary's an artist.

P → Mary's father

1. __P__ Jerry's restaurant . . .
2. __V__ Jerry's at the restaurant . . .
3. __P__ The chef's genius . . .
4. __V__ The chef's a genius . . .
5. __V__ Mike's here . . .
6. __P__ Mike's ear . . .

POSSESSIVE ADJECTIVES AND POSSESSIVE PRONOUNS

A possessive adjective is used with a noun to show who or what that noun belongs to.

Mary's book → her book

John's car → his car

Mary and John's children → their children

the bird's eyes → its eyes

Note In English, the gender of a possessive adjective is determined by the noun that the adjective refers to, not the noun that follows the adjective.

| **Correct** | <u>Mary</u> has a son. <u>Her</u> son is young. |
| **Common mistake** | ~~Mary has a son. His son is young.~~ |

A possessive pronoun replaces both the possessive adjective and its noun.

my car → mine

This is my car. → This is mine.

Possessive pronouns are used alone. Do not use a noun after them.

Do not confuse the possessive forms *its*, *his*, *your*, and *their* with contracted subject-verb forms *it's* (*it is*), *he's* (*he is*), *you're* (*you are*), and *they're* (*they are*).

Possessive adjectives	Possessive pronouns
my	mine
your	yours
his	his
her	hers
its	its
our	ours
your	yours
their	theirs

Exercise 4

Underline the correct word to complete each sentence.

1. I value (my/mine) life. I am sure you value (your/yours) too.

2. This pen is (her/hers). (Your/Yours) pen is over there.

3. We borrowed (their/theirs) tray. (Our/Ours) tray was old and cracked, but (their/theirs) wasn't perfect either.

4. Matthew and Vanessa are married. He loves (his/her) wife, and she loves (his/her) husband.

5. What day is it today? (Its/It's) Monday.

6. (They're/Their) going to the restaurant after (they're/their) class.

7. (He's/His) crazy about (he's/his) powdered food.

8. Now that (you're/your) here, give me (you're, your) opinion about (he's, his) leftover chicken recipe.

9. I hope you like this. (Its/It's) a gift from (our, ours) family to (your/you're/yours) family.

REFLEXIVE PRONOUNS

Use reflexive pronouns when the subject (the doer) and the object (the receiver of the action) are the same.

> John (subject) loves John (object). → John loves **himself**.

> Mary looked at Mary in the mirror. → Mary looked at **herself** in the mirror.

The reflexive pronouns are: *myself, yourself, himself, herself, itself, ourselves, yourselves,* and *themselves.*

Using *by* + reflexive pronoun means *alone.*

> Mary was eating by herself. (She was eating alone.)

> John lives by himself. (John lives alone.)

Reflexive pronouns can also be used to emphasize either the subject or the object in a sentence.

> I (subject) did it myself. (I did it, not you or anyone else.)

> I talked to the chef (object) himself. (the real chef, not a sous-chef or other lower-ranking kitchen staff)

Exercise 5

Some of the following sentences contain errors. Find the errors and write the sentence correctly.

1. I remember it because I told you myself. _____

2. I bought this 3D printer for me. *myself* _____

3. He went home by hisself. *himself* _____

4. John! How do you feel when you look at yourselves in the mirror? *yourself*

_____

5. We will eat by ourself. *ourselves* _____

6. I go myself to bed. I go to bed by myself.

7. She is going to tell him the truth. _____

8. They saw theirselves in the mirror. _~~themselves~~_ _____

9. Does he work for himself? _____ ✗ _____

10. My wife just retired. I will retire myself soon. _I will retire soon myself_

Communicative Activity

Work in pairs and discuss the following questions. Ask your teacher for help if you have trouble understanding any of the questions.

1. Do you give yourself a present if you do something that makes you proud of yourself?

2. What's the first thing you do if you cut yourself badly?

3. Have you ever felt really sorry for yourself? Explain.

4. Can you enjoy yourself if everyone else around you is miserable, or do you feel guilty if you enjoy yourself in such an environment?

5. Have you ever taught yourself anything?

6. Can you still believe in yourself when everyone around you stops believing in you? How?

Review Exercise

Correct the pronoun or possessive adjective errors. If the sentence is correct, add a checkmark.

1. Me and my brother want to meet with themselves.

   _____

2. This should stay between you and I.

   _____

3. How are you? I'm fine. And yourself?

   _____

4. There will always be war between us and them.

   _____

5. He should be ashamed of hisself.

   _____

6. I talk to me all the time. _____

7. My aunt and his boyfriend came to see us garden last week.

   _____

8. My pen is broken. Can I borrow your?

   _____

9. Those women often lie to herself. _____

10. I talked to my dad and he's friend. _____

Chapter 7
Modals

Like common auxiliary verbs (*be, do, have*), modals work with other verbs They add extra meaning—or modality (possibility, necessity, permission, etc.)—to the verbs they accompany.

The most common modals in English are *will, would, can, could, may, might,* and *must.*

	Affirmative	Negative	Question
Structure	modal + base form of the verb	modal + *not* + base form of the verb	modal + subject + base form of the verb
Example	He may go.	He would not (wouldn't) go.	Can they go?

Note 1 Modals do not change form. Never add -s or -ing or -ed to a modal.

Note 2 To make a modal negative, just add *not* (*will not, should not*)

Note 3 The base verb after the modal doesn't change. Never add *to*, -s, -ing, or -ed to a verb after a modal.

Incorrect	~~He must to go.~~
Incorrect	~~He must going.~~
Correct	He must go.

FUNCTIONS OF MODALS

Each modal can have several functions (modalities). In this chapter we look at the most common functions (ability, necessity and advice, permission, and possibility and probability).

Present and past ability (*can* and *could*)

Can and *could* are modals of ability. *Can* shows ability in the present and *could* shows ability in the past.

> I **can** drive now.

> Last year I **couldn't** drive.

Go to Compass Online for additional activities using modals.

Communicative Activity

Work in pairs. Write 12 sentences about your present (e.g., *can dance*) and past abilities (e.g., *could speak*). Make six of the sentences true and make six of them false. Exchange your sentences with your partner and try to guess which of your partner's sentences are true and which are false.

EXAMPLE

I could read when I was two years old. False

I can speak some English. True

Necessity and advice (*must, have to, should,* and *ought to*)

Must signifies necessity.

You **must** wear a seat belt. It is the law. (no choice)

Have to is a near synonym of *must*, but is less formal.

You **have to** apply for the job before the deadline.

However, the negative forms *don't have to* and *mustn't* are very different.

Mustn't means that you are not allowed to do something. It is forbidden.

You **mustn't** eat that! (Don't eat it!)

Don't have to means you can choose to do or not to do something. It's your choice.

You **don't have to** eat that! (You can eat it if you want to and not eat if you don't want to. You decide!)

Must doesn't have a past form. For past necessity, use *had to*.

I **must** write a report today.

I **had to** write a report yesterday.

To talk about past advice that was not followed, use *should have* + past participle of the verb:

You should have done your homework.
(Why didn't you do it?)

Should signifies advice.

You **should** get more rest. It is good for you. (only a suggestion)

Ought to is a near synonym of *should*. However, *ought to* is more formal than *should* and is more objective.

You **should** call your sister. (friendly advice)

You **ought to** pay attention to your environment. (more formal advice)

Exercise 1

1. Make a list of six things you must and mustn't do when driving a car.

2. Make a list of six things you should and shouldn't do as a responsible citizen.

Exercise 2

Every teacher has rules for his or her classroom. Compare two of your teachers. Start by writing a list of some things you *have to do*, things you *don't have to do*, and things you *mustn't do* in each of the two classes. Then write the rules in the form of sentences.

	Teacher A	Teacher B
have to do	1.	1.
	2.	2.
	3.	3.
don't have to do	1.	1.
	2.	2.
	3.	3.
mustn't do	1.	1.
	2.	2.
	3.	3.

EXAMPLE

In Mrs. X's class, we don't have to leave our cellphones outside the classroom, but we have to turn them off and we mustn't use the phones during the course.

We have to leave our phones in our lockers for Mr. Y's class. We absolutely mustn't bring a phone to his class.

Permission or polite requests (*may*, *would*, *could*, and *can*)

The following modals are used for polite requests, permissions, offers, or desires.

The modals on the left (*may* and *would*) are very formal. The ones on the right (*could* and *can*) are less formal and are used with close friends or relatives.

most formal ⟶ most informal

　　　may　　　　would　　　　could　　　　can

Note *May* is almost always used with *I* (May I . . . ?) and *would* is most often used with *you* (Would you . . . ?) in requests.

Look at the following requests. Who do you think the person is talking to? Is it someone he or she knows?

1. May I ask for a loan?

2. Would you please give me a loan?

3. Could you lend me some money?

4. Can you lend me some money?

Exercise 3

Use modals to make the following requests politely.

1. (to your brother) Give me the salt! _Could you give me the salt?_

2. (waiter to customer) What do you want to eat? _What would you want to eat?_

3. (student to teacher) I want to go to the washroom. _May I goto the washroom?_

4. (teacher to student) Close the door behind you! _Could you please close the door behind you?_

5. (to your classmate) I want to borrow your pen. _Could I borrow you pen?_

Possibility and probability: Present and future (*must*, *can*, *could*, *may*, and *might*)

Modals are also used to show different degrees of possibility or probability.

Use *is* or *are* when you are absolutely sure that something is true. (100%)

My brother **is** here with me.

Use *must be* when you are almost sure because you are drawing a logical conclusion. (80–90%)

My brother **must be** at work now. He is almost always at work at this time.

Use *may*, *might*, *can*, or *could* when you are not sure. (50% or less)

My brother **might** be at home, or he **could** be at work. I'm really not sure where he is.

Use *can't* or *couldn't* when you are almost sure that something is not true. (80–90%) This is used as the opposite of *must be*.

My brother **couldn't** be at home now. He is almost always at the gym at this time.

Exercise 4

Fill in the blanks with modals of possibility and probability (*must be, can be, could be, may be, might be, can't be, couldn't be*). Use each modal once only.

I'm not sure if it is raining now. → It may be raining now.

1. He is drinking a huge bottle of water! He _must be_ very thirsty.

2. No one knows where Tony is. He _might / could be_ at home.

3. It's impossible for this story to be true. This story _cannot / couldn't_ true.

4. I've never met my uncle. That man looks like my dad and is the same age as my uncle. He _might / may / could be_ my uncle.

5. It's almost impossible for me to be any happier than this. I _couldn't / can't_ be any happier than this.

6. If you see a mushroom with red dots on it, don't eat it. It _may / might / could be_ poisonous.

7. It won't be easy, but it is possible to fix this machine. This machine _can_ fixed.

Possibility and probability: Past (*must have*, *could have*, *may have*, or *might have*)

Use *have* + the past participle of the verb to change modals of possibility or probability into past tense.

He must be at home now. → He **must have been** at home yesterday.

He may be there now. → He **may have been** there yesterday.

Exercise 5

Change the following sentences from present to past.

1. We could save the oceans. _We could have saved the oceans._

2. Kelvin may become a DJ. _Kelvin may have become a DJ._

3. One Drop Foundation might find a solution to the problem of access to clean water.

have found

_____

_____

4. This can take place anywhere. _____
   could have taken

5. They couldn't be doctors. _____
   have been

6. This can't be his job. _____
   couldn't been

Modal expressions (had better, would rather)

The expression *had better* is used for making suggestions—it is a near synonym of *should*. Generally, *had better* is used more in speaking than writing. It describes the best option in a particular situation and often expresses the consequences of the alternative.

You'**d better** (had better) drive carefully or we will get into an accident.

You'**d better** not make that noise. It makes me angry.

Would rather is used to express preference. It shows which of two alternatives the subject prefers. _would prefer_

I'**d rather** (would rather) eat vanilla ice cream than chocolate.

I'**d rather** not go to the cinema with you. I'**d rather** read a book instead.

Review Exercise

Write a sentence with each of the following:

1. may I (polite request) _____

2. may (present/future possibility) _____

3. may have (possibility in the past) _____

4. might (present/future possibility) _____

5. might have (past possibility) _____

6. can (polite request) _____

7. can (present/future ability) _____

8. can (present/future possibility) _____

9. can't (impossibility) _____

10. can't have (past impossibility) _____

11. could (polite request) _____

12. could (past ability) _____

13. could (possibility) _____

14. could have (past possibility) _____

15. couldn't (impossibility) _____

16. couldn't have (past impossibility) _____

17. would you (polite request) _____

18. would rather (preference) _____

19. should (suggestion/advice) _____

20. ought to (suggestion/advice) _____

21. had better (suggestion/advice) _____

22. must (necessity) _____

23. had to (past necessity) _____

24. have to (necessity) _____

25. mustn't (prohibition) _____

26. don't/doesn't have to (option) _____

27. must be (deduction) _____

28. must have (past deduction) _____

Chapter 8
Spelling and Word Choice

COMMONLY CONFUSED WORDS

Go to Compass Online for additional spelling and word choice activities.

Certain word pairs or trios are often confused by English language learners. This chart contains a short list of commonly confused words, along with their meanings.

Word	Meaning or function	Example
than	to show comparison	Malala was tougher *than* her enemies.
then	to show order	Kelvin first made a generator, and *then* started a radio station.
very	intensifier used before adjectives or adverbs, but not verbs	Zea is *very* smart.
really	intensifier used before verbs, adjectives, or adverbs	Zea is *really* smart. Zea *really* did it.
some	used mostly in affirmative sentences, sometimes in questions	I have *some* ideas. Do you have *some* thoughts about the issue?
any	used mostly in negative sentences (with *not*) and in questions	I don't have *any* idea. Do you have *any* thoughts?
no	used in negative sentences (without *not*)	I have *no* idea.
hear	to take in sound without planning or making an active effort	I *heard* Malala's voice.
listen to	to take in sound while consciously paying attention	I *listened to* Malala's speech.
see	to take in something visually without planning or making an active effort	I *was watching* TV when I *saw* a shadow on the wall. I *looked at* it for a few seconds before I noticed there was someone behind me.
watch	to choose to experience something visually (a changing scene or action)	
look at	to choose to experience something visually (a fixed scene)	

Word	Meaning or function	Example
learn	to take in and understand new information (Students *learn* from their teachers.)	I *learned* so much from Malala.
teach	to provide information to someone so that they understand something (Teachers *teach* their students.)	Malala *taught* me so much.
hear	to take in sound without planning or making an active effort	Did you *hear* the thunder?
here	adverb of place (opposite of *there*)	Come *here*!
to	preposition of place	Kelvin went *to* America.
too	intensifying adverb	The oceans are *too* polluted.
two	a number (2)	I have *two* solutions.
die	(verb) to lose life	Hadiya *died* young.
death	(noun) being without life	Her *death* made RaSia sad.
dead	(adjective) not alive	Hadiya is *dead* now.
fun	enjoyable, entertaining	We had a *fun* trip to Disneyland.
funny	humorous, comic	The stand-up comic told a *funny* joke.
say	to express something with words *say something* (to someone)	I *said* something stupid (to my teacher).
tell	to express something with words to a specific person (or group) *tell someone* **EXCEPTIONS** tell time, the truth, a lie, a story, a fortune	I *told* Tom what time we were meeting.
win	to be successful in a competition, get a prize	I *won* $1000 in a lottery.
earn	to get money for your labour or service	I *earned* $1000 through hard work.

FALSE COGNATES (FALSE FRIENDS)

False cognates are words from two different languages that look or sound similar, but are used differently or have partially or completely different meanings. For example, the expression *assister à* means *attend* in English while the French verb *attendre* means *wait* in English and the English verb *assist* means *to help*.

The following chart contains words in English that have commonly confused false cognates in French.

Word	Meaning or function	Example
leave	to go away from a place or person	He *left* the house at 6:00 AM.
quit	to stop a bad habit or give up a job	He *quit* his job. *Quit* smoking!
library	a place to borrow books	I borrowed two bestsellers from the *library*.
bookstore	a place to buy books	I bought two self-help books at the *bookstore*.
note	short record/written message	Could I borrow your math *notes*?
mark/grade	points earned on an exam or assignment	What was your *mark* on the test?
arrive	to get to a destination	Who *arrived* last night?
happen	to take place, occur	What *happened* last night?
assist	to help	The TA *assisted* the professor in class.
attend	to be present at, to go to	I *attended* a conference yesterday.
rest	to relax	They *rested* in the evening.
stay	to remain, not to go	I *stayed* at the school after class.
sensible	logical, wise	His answer was *sensible* and rational.
sensitive	emotional, delicate, easily affected by something	My skin is *sensitive* to soap.
resume	to begin again	I *resumed* work after lunch.
summarize	to abridge, to condense	I *summarized* the book in two pages.
history	past events	I studied *history* at college.
story	anecdote, fiction	She tells funny *stories*.

Exercise

Underline the correct choice to complete the sentence.

1. I'm (here/hear) to (here/hear) what you have to (say/tell) to me.

2. These (to/too/two) boxes are (too/to/two) heavy. They are much larger (then/than) I expected.

3. He (died/dead) a slow (dead/die/death). He (really/very) suffered.

4. I will (teach/learn) you how to (win/earn) more money by working less, but you cannot (say/tell) anyone else.

5. If you (see/watch/look at) my tutorial, I will (teach/learn) you how (to/too/two) improve your (notes/marks) on your English tests.

6. I borrowed (two/to/too) audio books from the school (bookstore/library). One was the (history/story) of an imaginary land and the second was an academic (history/story) of Ancient Rome. I (heard/listened to) both of them last week.

7. I don't have (no/any/some) money left. Let me (say/tell) you what (arrived/happened). Last week I worked hard and (won/earned) $50, but I went to the casino on the weekend and gambled. At first, I (won/earned) $10, but very soon I lost everything. Gambling is not (fun/funny).

8. Please (resume/summarize) this report and give it to me before I (quit/leave) for Paris tomorrow. Do not discuss the (sensitive/sensible) material in it with (no one/anyone/someone) else.

COMMONLY MISSPELLED WORDS

The following is a short list of words that students often misspell.

absence	believe	height	public
accidentally	deceive	immediately	responsible
address	development	independence	restaurant
advice	disease	misspell	technology
aggressive	enemy	movement	though
analysis	example	optimism	through
analyze	familiar	peculiar	tough
apartment	future	personal	traditional
argument	government	personality	vacuum
beginning	grammar	professional	

Communicative Activity

Work with a partner. Take turns dictating the words on the list for the other person to write on a piece of paper. Give the paper to your partner to mark.

Review Exercise

Underline 22 errors in the paragraph and correct them.

When we arrived at Eric's apartment, he started saying us a history about what arrived to him last week. Monday night was touhg; it was not a funny experience. He couldn't sleep because his two sensible teeth ached, so he decided to look at a movie. It was a stupid movie about the futur when technologie rules people's lives—gouvernment robots were attacking humans to stop the freedom mouvement and a lot of people dead. He than decided to read a book he had recently bought at a small library. It was full of advise that claimed to learn people how to be more professionnel and responsable at work. He didn't like nothing about the book. He left reading the book and closed his eyes when he suddenly listened to a loud bang. One of the agressif robots from the movie was standing in his bedroom! It shot a laser beam at his face. His teeth burned and he rolled off the bed. It was just a bad dream. There was no robot. There was only the burning sensation in his teeth.

Chapter 9

Adjectives and Adverbs— Comparatives and Superlatives

ADJECTIVES AND ADVERBS

Adjectives modify nouns. In other words, adjectives describe or give more information about nouns.

Tall trees (*tall* describes the height of the trees)
adj.   n.

Note 1 In English, adjectives normally come before nouns (**good** *student*, **tall** *woman*, **happy** *people*).

Note 2 Adjectives can also come after a linking verb (e.g., *be*, *look*, *seem*, *feel*, *appear*, etc.).

He is **young**. It feels **soft**. She looks **tired**.

Note 3 Adjectives never take a plural form (*one **happy** dog, ten **happy** dogs*)

Adverbs can modify verbs (**he reads *slowly***) or adjectives (***really** slow*) or other adverbs (***really** slowly*).

Adverbs are normally formed by adding -ly to adjectives.

real → really

slow → slowly

Some adverbs have the same form as their adjectives.

hard → hard
Providing clean water is <u>hard</u> work. → One Drop is working <u>hard</u> to provide clean water.
                              adj.   adv.

fast → fast
He is a <u>fast</u> runner. → He runs <u>fast</u>.
          adj.   adv.

early → early
Zea isn't an <u>early</u> adopter of technology. → Zea doesn't adopt technology <u>early</u>.
                adj.   adv.

Go to Compass Online for additional activities using adjectives and adverbs—comparatives and superlatives.

Some adverbs have their own unique form. For example, the adverb form of *good* is *well*. Some other adverbs with unique forms are: *soon, very, just, quite, perhaps,* and certain adverbs of frequency (*always, often, never, seldom*).

Note Some adjectives end in -ly. Be careful not to confuse these adjectives with adverbs: *costly, friendly, lonely, lovely, lively,* and *likely*.

Exercise 1

Find the best place in the sentence for the adjectives or adverbs in parentheses.

Remember Adjectives come before nouns and after linking verbs. Adverbs come as close as possible to the verb, adjective, or adverb that they modify. Adverbs of frequency come before main verbs and after auxiliaries.

EXAMPLE

I am a student. (good) → I am a **good** student.

I have worked. (never) → I have **never** worked.

1. Kelvin's village had a reliable electricity supply. (seldom) *[seldom]*
2. Kelvin is a dedicated person. (really) *[really]*
3. He isn't home right now. (probably) *[Probably]*
4. He bought the suit anyway. (expensive) *[expensive]*
5. People in Kelvin's village have a life. (simple) *[simple]*
6. Magalie studies hygiene at a college. (dental) *[dental]*
7. He goes there on Sundays. (only) *[only]*
8. The answer to ocean pollution isn't clear. (perfectly) *[perfectly]*
9. Rene likes hair colours. (bright) *[bright]*
10. I have one friend at this school. (just) *[Just]*

Exercise 2

Underline the best choice to complete the sentence.

1. Zea Tongeman worked (hard/hardly) to solve the problem and she (final/ finally) found a (good/well) solution.

2. Guy Laliberté wants everyone at his company to feel (safe/safely). He is a (real/ really) (careful/carefully) manager.

3. The (loud/loudly) noise scared me. I (sudden/suddenly) stood up and ran (quick/quickly) toward the exit.

4. The presenter spelled Malala's name (correct/correctly), but she pronounced it very (bad/badly). It made everyone in the audience laugh (loud/loudly).

Communicative Activity 1

Work in pairs. Each partner chooses either 1 or 2 below and writes questions using the jumbled words. Then take turns asking each other the questions you wrote.

Student A

1. Have you/lived/ever/in a/small/really/town?

   _____

2. How many times/eat/do you/usually/food/healthy/per week?

   _____

Student B

1. When/lonely/do/you/feel/usually/truly?

   _____

2. Would you/on a/very/like to/long/go/trip?

   _____

Comparative forms of adjectives and adverbs

The comparative form is used to compare only two categories or items (people, things, ideas, etc.). To compare more than two items, see superlative adjectives and adverbs on page 190.

Comparative form	Example adjectives and adverbs	Example sentences
Add -er after short adjectives (monosyllabic and some two-syllable adjectives).	young → younger slow → slower	My sister is *young*, but your sister is *younger*. Tuesdays are *slow*, but Mondays are *slower*.
Add *more* before long adjectives (some two-syllable and all three-or-more-syllable adjectives) and before all -ly adverbs.	careful → more careful carefully → more carefully slowly → more slowly	My sister is *careful*, but your sister is *more careful*. My sister drives *carefully*, but your sister drives *more carefully*. Tuesdays pass *slowly*, but Mondays pass *more slowly*.
EXCEPTIONS Some adjectives have completely different comparative forms	good → better bad → worse little → less far → farther much/many → more	I'm *good*, but you're *better*. He's *bad*, but she's *worse*. You know *little*, but I know *less*. I live *far* away, but you live *farther*. I have *many* friends, but he has *more*.

Note 1 When comparing two things in the same sentence use the word *than* after the comparative form.

> Your sister is younger **than** my sister.

> Quebec City is colder **than** Montreal.

> My sister drives more carefully **than** your sister.

Note 2 The opposite of *more* is *less*. We can compare longer adjectives or adverbs with either *more* or *less*.

> Your dog is **more** intelligent **than** my dog. My dog is **less** intelligent **than** your dog.

> My dog runs **more** quickly **than** your dog. Your dog runs **less** quickly **than** my dog.

Note 3 When forming the comparative with short adverbs that don't end in -ly, generally follow the rules set out for short adjectives: add -er to form the comparative.

> My sister will arrive **soon**, but your sister will arrive **sooner**.

> Your sister will arrive **sooner than** my sister.

Superlative forms of adjectives and adverbs

The superlative form is used to compare three or more items or categories (people, things, ideas, etc.) or to compare one item in a category against all other items in that category.

Superlative form	Example adjectives and adverbs	Example sentences
Add *the* + adj + -est after short adjectives (monosyllabic and some two-syllable adjectives).	young → the youngest	I have three sisters. Mary is *the youngest*.
Add *the most* before long adjectives (some two-syllable and all three-or-more-syllable adjectives) and before all -ly adverbs.	careful → the most careful carefully → the most carefully slowly → the most slowly	Your sister is *the most careful* person I have ever met. Quebec City is *the most beautiful* place I have lived in. Of all the students, Josée responded to the questions *the most slowly*.
EXCEPTIONS Some adjectives have different superlative forms.	good → the best bad → the worst little → the least far → the farthest much/many → the most	This is *the best* class this semester. He is *the worst* person I know. We had *the least* amount of snow in December. Neptune is *the farthest* planet from the sun. I love my youngest brother *the most*.

Note 1 It is possible to replace *the* with possessive adjectives (*my, your, his, her* . . .) in superlative form.

> the youngest sister → my youngest sister

Note 2 Superlative adverbs usually come before <u>the past participle</u> (a verb used as an adjective).

> the most beautifully <u>decorated</u> house ⤳
>
> the most slowly <u>processed</u> application ⤳
>
> the most carefully <u>selected</u> candidate ⤳

Note 3 When forming the superlative with short adverbs that don't end in -ly, generally follow the rules set out for short adjectives: add -est to form the superlative.

> Everyone in the class worked hard on the project, but I worked **the hardest**. ·

Equality (the equative form)

To show equality for adjectives or adverbs, use the structure *as* + <u>adj/adv</u> + *as*.

> My car is **as slow as** yours.
>
> My car moves **as slowly as** yours.

Exercise 3

Fill in the blanks with the comparative, superlative, or equative form of the adjectives or adverbs in parentheses.

> *King Lear* is one of the _most **beautifully**_ (beautifully) written tragedies in the English language. It was written by William Shakespeare, who is perhaps _the most famous_ (famous) playwright in the world. The main character, the elderly King Lear, who is getting _older_ (old) every day, decides to divide his kingdom among his three daughters. The _best_ (good) and _the largest_ (large) part of the country will go to the daughter who loves him _the much most_ (much). Lear's _oldest_ (old) daughter, Goneril, and his second daughter, Regan, are _as dishonest as_ (dishonest) each other and they both compliment their father _more excessively_ (excessive). Cordelia, the king's _youngest_ (young) and his favourite daughter remains silent. The king asks how much she loves him. Cordelia says, "I love your majesty _as much as_ (much) it is my duty, not _more_ (much) and not _less_ (little). Hearing this, the king becomes angry and renounces Cordelia. He then divides his kingdom between Goneril and Regan, giving each a piece _as large as_ (large) the other, and he retires.

Communicative Activity 2

Go online and find a summary of King Lear. Read the rest of the story. Write the rest of the story in your own words and discuss the story with your classmates.

Chapter 10
Prepositions

Go to Compass Online for additional activities using prepositions.

Prepositions (e.g., *at*, *on*, *in*, *to*) are words that come before nouns or pronouns and indicate place, direction, time, and so on.

PREPOSITIONS OF PLACE

Preposition	Image	Examples
at		at 60 Main Street, at home, at Uber's head office
on		on Main Street, on the second floor, on the desk
in/inside		in Gatineau, inside the car, in the picture, in my hand, inside the hotel room
over/above		over my head, over the door, above the fireplace
under/below		under the umbrella, under the roof, below the line
between		between two people, transaction between suppliers and consumers
among		among three other people, among friends, among trees, among strangers
against		against the wall, against my skin, against the wind
behind		behind me, behind the wall

Preposition	Image	Examples
in front of		in front of me, in front of the house
across (from)		across from me, across the room
beside/by		beside me, by the river
near/close to		near my house, close to school
far from		far from my house, far from everyone

Note 1 We use *on* for radio/TV/ phone/Internet, although *on* does not really refer to a place in this usage.

> He is on the phone with his friend.
>
> There is a great program on TV/the radio.
>
> I spent a lot of time on the Airbnb website yesterday.

Note 2 We use *above* and *below* to refer to temperatures that are higher or lower than the freezing point.

> I put my sandals away when the temperature dropped below zero.
>
> The streets are wet and slushy when it gets above zero in the winter.

Exercise 1

Fill in the blanks with prepositions of place. Use all the prepositions above. Use each preposition once only.

I live ___at___ number 186 ___on___ rue des Alpes ___in___ Sherbrooke. My house is halfway ___between___ a school and a grocery store. There is a gas station on the other side of the street right ___across___ my house. I live ___near___ downtown, but I am ___far from___ our college. I live the farthest from the college ___among___ all my classmates. There are two bedrooms in my house. The small bedroom is on the first floor ___beside___ the bathroom, and the master bedroom is on the second floor, right ___above___ the kitchen. In the master bedroom, there is a mirror on one wall and a bookshelf stands ___against___ the opposite wall. If you stand ___in front of___ the mirror, you can see the reflection of the bookshelf ___behind___ you. There is a small table ___under___ the mirror.

PREPOSITIONS OF DIRECTION

Preposition	Image	Examples
toward(s)		toward the finish line, toward the sun, toward the future
to		to the gym, to the ocean, to Gaspé
from		from Montreal, from the left, (coming back) from a run.
away (from)		three kilometres away from, away from home, away from danger
into		walked into the ring, looked into the distance, put into the fridge
out of		out of the hockey rink, out of my car, out of sight
through		through the hoop, through the forest, through traffic

Exercise 2

Fill in the blanks with prepositions of direction from the table above. Use each preposition only once.

The luxury car passed __through__ the gate and moved __toward__ the main entrance. Loud music boomed __from__ the car stereo. The chauffeur parked the car a few metres __away from__ the main door. A young woman and her dog got __out of__ the back seat, walked __to__ the door and marched __into__ the foyer.

PREPOSITIONS OF TIME

Preposition	Meaning	Examples
at	a specific time	at noon, at midnight, at night, at 6:00
on	one day	on Sunday, on my birthday, on Labour Day
in	more than one day; part of a day	in January, in 2017, in a century in the morning/afternoon/evening
from . . . to	marking the beginning and end of a time period	from 6:00 to 7:00, from Monday to Friday, from January to June
until	up to a certain time or another action	until she arrived, until noon, until tomorrow, until then
before	earlier than	before her brother came, before supper, before marriage
after	later than	after his sister left, after breakfast, after university
for	all the time in a given period	for two years, for a month, for six hours
during	at some point in a period of time	during his time as captain, during university, during work hours

Exercise 3

Fill in the blanks with a preposition of time from the table above. Use each preposition only once.

1. Wash your hands __after__ going to the washroom and __before__ eating!

2. __at__ 12:30 PM, I finally woke up.

3. We always go to Ottawa __on__ Canada Day.

4. I hope to graduate __in__ 2017.

5. We learn __from__ birth __to__ death.

6. I will remember this __for__ a very long time.

7. He didn't say anything __during__ lunch.

8. Two hours left __until__ dawn!

FIXED PREPOSITIONS AFTER VERBS, NOUNS, AND ADJECTIVES

Many verbs, nouns, and adjectives always take the same prepositions. The best way to learn these fixed combinations is simply to memorize them together. A few examples are shown here.

Adjectives + Prepositions	Nouns + Prepositions	Verbs + Prepositions
afraid of	approval from someone for something	agree with somebody
interested in	an attack on	apologize to somebody for something
ashamed of	congratulations to someone on	arrive in/at/on
good at	something	believe in
proud of	demand for	decide on
similar to	emphasis on	depend on
tired of	excuse for	participate in
responsible for	key to	rely on/upon
bored with/by	lack of	suffer from
excited about/by/for	reason for	take care of
	success in/with	

Exercise 4

Fill each blank with the correct preposition. Work from memory. Do not look at the preceding table until you have completed the exercise.

1. I am ashamed __*of*__ myself and feel responsible __*for*__ my actions. I have no excuse __*for*__ what I did. I sincerely apologize __*to*__ all of you __*for*__ my stupid reaction.

2. Congratulations __*to*__ you __*on*__ your upcoming wedding. I am proud __*of*__ both of you and excited __*about*__ being your best man. I wish you happiness in your life together.

3. I agree __*with*__ you that Marc suffers __*from*__ certain superstitious beliefs. He believes __*in*__ ghosts and is afraid __*of*__ them. I am very tired __*of*__ listening to his ghost stories.

Phrasal verbs

Some verb + preposition combinations are idiomatic (i.e., the meaning of the verb changes completely based on the preposition that follows it). These combinations are called *phrasal verbs*.

Here are some common phrasal verbs that include *get*, *take*, and *put*. Notice how the meaning of the phrasal verb changes when the preposition changes. Again, the best way to learn phrasal verbs is to memorize them in context.

Idiom	Meaning	Example
get along	have a good relationship	The taxi industry and Uber don't get along very well.
get away with	do bad without getting caught	He got away with murder.
get by	survive (financially)	We don't make much money but we get by.
get over	recover from	I got over the flu.
get on/off	enter/leave a bus/ship/plane	I got on the bus at 6:00 and got off at 7:00.
get up	leave bed	I woke up at 7:00 and got up at 7:15.
get in(to)/out of	enter/leave a place/a situation	I get into and out of debt all the time.
take after	look or behave like (a parent)	I take after my father.
take in	take care of/adopt	She took in a stray cat.
	trick or fool	He took in all the investors and stole millions.
take off	remove clothes /leave the ground	I took off my jacket after the plane took off.
take on	accept responsibility	I took on more work after the holidays.
take out	invite to restaurant, etc.	I took my wife out for her birthday.
take up	start a habit or hobby	I took up tennis in college.
take over	take control	My friend was tired so I took over driving.
put away	tidy or organize	My room is nice! I put everything away.
put down	criticize	He always tries to put me down.
put off	postpone, do later	I put off my meeting until next week.
put on	get dressed in something	He put on his jacket and his glasses.
put out	extinguish	The firefighters put out the fire.
put up with	tolerate	I can't put up with cold weather.
put across	communicate	I tried to put my plan across.

Exercise 5

Fill in each blank with the correct preposition(s) to form phrasal verbs.

1. She takes __after__ her mom in appearance and behaviour.

2. A nasty virus took __over__ my computer and deleted my files.

3. He has taken __on__ more responsibility than he can handle.

4. It took some time but she got __over__ her ex-boyfriend.

5. He thought he could get __away with__ cheating on the test, but the teacher noticed.

6. I have a dog and a cat. They get __along__ very well with each other.

7. Please put __out__ your cigarette. This is a no-smoking zone.

8. I have to put __off__ my medical appointment until next month. I'm too busy now.

9. Sometimes, Airbnb hosts have to put __up with__ very bad guests.

Chapter 11
Conditional Sentences

Go to Compass Online for additional activities using conditional sentences.

The conditional is used to describe possible or probable situations in the present and near future, situations that are unlikely to happen in the near future, and situations in the past that did not happen.

Conditional sentences have two main parts or clauses: an *if clause* that sets a condition and a *main clause* that shows the result or consequence of the condition.

If the conditional sentence starts with the *if* clause, it is followed by a comma. It can also start with the main clause, in which case no comma is needed. The sentences have the same meaning no matter which clause comes first.

If I study harder this semester, I will certainly pass this course.
   condition (*if* clause)   result (main clause)

I will certainly pass this course if I study harder this semester.
   result (main clause)   condition (*if* clause)

Types of conditional sentences

There are many types of conditional sentences. The chart below shows the three most common types.

Type	*If* clause	Main clause	Example
1. possible or probable condition in the present or future	*if* + present tense	future	*If* you *do* the exercises, you *will understand* the lesson. (You will probably do the exercises and will therefore understand.)
2. unlikely condition in the present or future	*if* + past tense	*would* + base form of verb	*If* you *did* the exercises, you *would understand* the lesson. (You probably won't do the exercises and therefore won't understand.)
3. condition that did not happen in the past	*if* + *had* + past participle	*would* + *have* + past participle	*If* you *had done* the exercises, you *would have understood* the lesson. (You didn't do the exercises and therefore didn't understand.)

Note 1 In formal type 2 conditionals, use *were* instead of *was*.

If I were rich, I would buy you a house. (instead of ~~if I was rich~~)

Note 2 The *if* clause cannot include *will* or *would*.

~~If I would know the answer, I would tell you.~~ → If I knew the answer, I would tell you.

Exercise 1

Fill in the blanks with the correct tense of the verbs in parentheses.

Type 1 conditionals

1. If she ___does___ (do) a good job, she will receive a bonus.

2. If I ___am___ (be) lucky, I will find a good deal on Craigslist.

3. If he arrives early, he ___will call___ (call) the Airbnb host to bring him the keys.

4. If he ___finds___ (find) the time, he ___will send___ (send) me the files.

Type 2 conditionals

5. If I ___had___ (have) time, I would certainly help you.

6. If I ___were___ (be) you, I wouldn't use Uber.

7. If I knew the answer, I ___would give___ (give) it to you.

8. If he ___told___ (tell) you the truth, you ___would get___ (get) angry.

Type 3 conditionals

9. If I ___have seen___ (see) you yesterday, I would have said hello.

10. If I ___had had___ (have) that kind of money when I was younger, I wouldn't have accepted a job like that.

11. If I hadn't broken my leg, I ___would have become___ (become) a professional hockey player.

12. I don't know how long it ___would have taken___ (take) me to finish the job if you had not helped me.

Exercise 2

Read each sentence and write a conditional sentence based on it. Follow the examples provided.

Type 1 conditionals

I will (probably) see you, and I will talk to you. → If I see you, I will talk to you.

1. They will (probably) need money, and I will give them some.

    ___If they need money, I will give them some.___

2. You will (probably) see him, and you will be shocked.

    ___If you see him, you will be shocked.___

3. The Uber driver will (probably) arrive, and will text me.

    ___If the Uber driver arries, he will text me.___

4. She will (probably) need a drill, and her neighbour will lend one to her.

    ___If she needs a drill, her neighbour will lend one to her.___

Type 2 conditionals

I am afraid of animals, so I don't buy a dog. → If I weren't afraid of animals, I would buy a dog.

5. I don't have wings, so I don't fly.

   If I had wings, I would fly.

6. I don't sleep well, so I don't have a lot of energy.

   If I slept well, I would have a lot of energy

7. He isn't very rich, so he doesn't own things.

   If he were rich, he would own thing.

8. We have children, so we stay home a lot.

   If we didn't children, we wouldn't stay hom→

Type 3 conditionals

I didn't take care of my car, so it broke down last week. → If I had taken care of my car, it wouldn't have broken down last week.

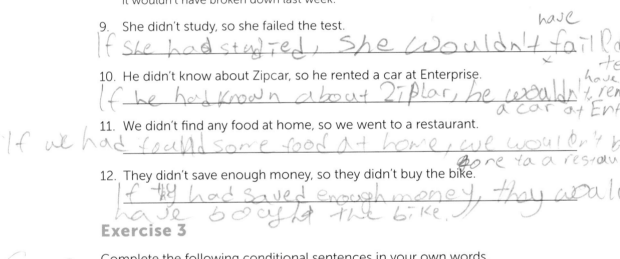

9. She didn't study, so she failed the test.

   If she had studied, she wouldn't fail(have)ed tes-

10. He didn't know about Zipcar, so he rented a car at Enterprise.

    If he had known about Ziplar, he wouldn't(have) rente a car at Enter

11. We didn't find any food at home, so we went to a restaurant.

    If we had found some food at home, we wouldn't be-(go)ne ta a restaura

12. They didn't save enough money, so they didn't buy the bike.

    If thy had saved enough money, they would have bought the bike.

Exercise 3

Complete the following conditional sentences in your own words.

(future)

1. If I have to choose between Uber and a traditional taxi, _I will choose Uber._

2. If I graduate from college, _I will have a Vacation._

3. If I had a million dollars, _I would have a farishi Car_

4. If I were a bird, _I would want to die'._

5. If I had been born in a different country, _I would have spoken anoth language_

6. If I hadn't eaten so much, _I would have energy._

Communicative Activity 1

Complete this activity as a class. The first student or the teacher creates a conditional sentence. The next student changes the main clause of the first sentence into an *if* clause and completes the second sentence. The game continues until all students have made at least one sentence.

EXAMPLE

Student A   If I were a bird, I would fly.

Student B   If I flew, I would go south in the winter.

Student C   If I went south in the winter, I would swim in the ocean.

Communicative Activity 2

Work with a partner and take turns asking and answering these questions.

1. If you rent your house on Airbnb and the guest destroys your furniture, what will you do?

2. If you don't learn today's grammar lesson, what will you do?

3. If you could travel in time, which year would you go to? Why?

4. If you could choose to have any superpower, which power would you choose? Why?

5. If you had one month to live, how would you spend your time?

6. If you could change one thing about the past, what would you change?

7. If you hadn't come to college, what would you have done instead?

8. If you had been born a different gender (boy instead of girl or vice versa), how would your life have been different?

Exercise 4

Fill in the blanks with the correct tense of the verbs in parentheses. Use all three types of conditionals.

1. If you think hard, you _____ (find) the answer, but if you _____ (not try) hard enough, you _____ (not find) the right answer. You can also call Charles. If he _____ (know) the answer, he will definitely tell you.

2. He wouldn't have lost all his money if he _____ (not invest) everything in the same company. If only he had listened to me and _____ (diversify) his portfolio, he _____ (make) a lot of money.

3. If I _____ (know) how to take tests better, I would be a more successful student and _____ (get) better marks today.

4. If it _____ (snow) too much tomorrow, I _____ (not go) to school. If I _____ (drive) this car in bad weather, I _____ get (get) into an accident for sure.

5. If I _____ (be) in your position, I _____ (listen) to the teacher's advice, but you make your own decision.

Exercise 5

Find and correct the errors. There might be more than one way to correct some of the errors.

1. If we had known, we would help you yesterday.

   _____

   _____

2. If I had more money, I would have bought a new car.

   _____

   _____

3. If my neighbour rented her house on Airbnb, I will be annoyed.

   _____

   _____

4. If I would have seen him, I would have told him.

   _____

   _____

5. If I will arrive on time, I will call you.

   _____

   _____

6. What would you do if you would get into an accident?

   _____

   _____

Chapter 12

Combining Sentences, Punctuation, and Capitalization

COMBINING SENTENCES

Coordination

Coordinating conjunctions (*and, but, so, or,* etc.) can be used to join two or more complete ideas that are related in meaning. The result is a compound sentence. In compound sentences both ideas are equally important.

Handwritten margin notes:

FANBOYS

Comma is a optional.

Capital only
Proper nouns = I, name, tittle, Counties, cities, etc.

Conjunction	Function	Two ideas	Combined ideas
and	links ideas may show order of events	John knocked. His mom opened the door.	John knocked, *and* his mom opened the door.
but	shows contrasting ideas	John knocked. His mom didn't open the door	John knocked, *but* his mom didn't open the door.
so	expresses a result	John was tired. His mom offered him her seat.	John was tired, *so* his mom offered him her seat.
or	expresses an alternative	Did John call his mom? Did his mom call John?	Did John call his mom, *or* did his mom call John?

Note 1 Use a comma (,) before coordinating conjunctions, except when using *and* to combine two things when the order is not important.

> I like cats and dogs. (no comma)

> I adopted a dog, and then two cats. (*and* shows order of events)

Note 2 The capital letter at the beginning of the second sentence changes to lower case (if it is not a proper noun).

Go to Compass Online for additional activities combining sentences and using punctuation and capitalization.

Exercise 1

Use coordinating conjunctions (*and, but, so, or*) to connect each pair of sentences below. Remember to change capitalization and punctuation where necessary. Use each conjunction once.

1. Michael wanted to volunteer in Belize. He couldn't because of his medical condition.

   _____

   _____

2. Michael became sick. He couldn't to go to Belize.

   _____

3. Michael went to Belize. He helped build a school there.

   _____

4. Michael can go to Belize as a volunteer. He can go to Kenya instead.

   _____

Subordination

Use subordinating conjunctions (*although, as soon as, when, if, because,* etc.) to join a complete thought (independent clause) with an incomplete one (dependent clause). The result of subordination is a complex sentence. In complex sentences, one idea (independent clause) is more important than the other one (dependent clause).

> When it rains, I stay in.
>
> I stay in. (independent, more important)
>
> When it rains, (dependent, less important)

Note If a sentence starts with a subordinating conjunction, use a comma (,) after the first (dependent) clause.

> Although I studied hard, I didn't pass the test.

There is no comma (,) if you start the sentence with the independent clause (i.e., if the subordinating conjunction is in the middle of the sentence).

> I didn't pass the test although I studied hard.

Exercise 2

Join each set of sentences with subordinating conjunction (or *subordinators*) from the box. Use correct punctuation and capitalization. The first sentence has been completed as an example.

> if, because, although, while, until, ~~as soon as~~

1. I will call you. I receive the test results.

   I will call you as soon as I receive the test results.

   As soon as I receive the test results, I will call you.

2. He travelled abroad to work as a volunteer. He was sick.

   _____

   _____

3. He was sick. He didn't work as a volunteer.

_____

_____

4. You do not feel good. You should not volunteer.

_____

_____

5. He was volunteering in Belize. He met his future wife.

_____

_____

6. He ignored the pain. He fell unconscious.

_____

_____

Relative pronouns

Relative pronouns can sometimes be used for subordination. The relative pronoun replaces a repeated noun or noun phrase. In the following example *the man* is repeated in both sentences.

> This is the man. The man helped me.

The second use of *the man* can be replaced with *who* to join the two sentences.

> This is the man **who** helped me.

Here's a list of relative pronouns and what they replace.

Remember to delete the repeated element.

Correct This is the man who helped me.

Incorrect ~~This is the man who he helped me.~~

Pronoun	Function	Example
who	replaces people (subjects)	This is the man. The man helped me. This is the man *who* helped me.
whom	replaces people (objects) (can be used immediately after a preposition)	This is the man. I gave my money to the man. This is the man *to whom* I gave my money.
which	replaces things or animals (can be used after a comma or preposition)	We can go to Tony's restaurant. Tony's restaurant serves vegetarian food. We can go to Tony's restaurant, *which* serves vegetarian food.
that	replaces people, things, animals (cannot be used after a comma or preposition)	This is the idea. The idea changed the world. This is the idea *that* changed the world.
where	replaces a place	This is the store. I met my wife at the store. This is the store *where* I met my wife.
when	replaces a time	This is the day. I celebrate my birthday on that day. This is the day *when* I celebrate my birthday.
whose	replaces a possessive	This is the man. The man's son helped me. This is the man *whose* son helped me.

Note 1 Do not confuse *whose* (possessive relative pronoun) with *who's* (who is).

> The girl whose mom is here . . .

> The girl who's (who is) here . . .

Note 2 In informal English *who* is sometimes used for objects if the preposition is not right before the pronoun.

This is the man **who** I gave my money to.

Exercise 3

Join the sentences with relative pronouns. There might be more than one way to join some of the sentences.

1. We are making complex sentences. ~~The~~ sentences contain adjective clauses. *that or which*

    _____

2. She saw a dog. *Whose* The dog's tail was blue.

    _____

3. I was born in 1998. A ~~massive~~ *huge* snowstorm hit Quebec in 1998.

    I was born in 1998, when a massive snow storm hit Quebec.
    I was born in 1998, in which a massive snow storm hit Quebec.

4. I was born in Quebec. Celine Dion was also born in Quebec.

    I was born in Quebec, when or in which Celine Dion was also born.

5. Steinman was a Canadian scientist. He received the Nobel Prize after his death.

    Steinman was a canadian scientist who received the Nobel Prize after his death.

6. She is a close friend. I trust her.

    She is a close friend who I trust.
    that I trust.

Exercise 4

Fill in the blanks with the correct word from the box. Use each word once.

> who, whom, which, that, when, where, whose, who's

1. This is the concert hall ___*that*___ I told you about.

2. This is the school ___*where*___ my sister is going to teach as a volunteer.

3. This is the area in ___*which*___ I backpacked.

4. This is the nurse ___*who*___ volunteers in Haiti.

5. This is the guy with ___*whom*___ I worked as a carpenter.

6. This is the organization ___*whose*___ mission is to move people out of poverty.

7. This is the man ___*who's*___ going to Guatemala as a volunteer.

8. This is the day ___*when*___ I started volunteering.

PUNCTUATION AND CAPITALIZATION

Apostrophes (')

1. Contraction

Apostrophes are used to

For more examples of contractions, see Grammar Guide Chapters 2, 3, 4, 5, and 7.

- contract a subject and its verb

I am → I'm	you will → you'll
he is → he's	they have → they've
we are → we're	I had/I would → I'd

- contract a negative auxiliary

is not → isn't	will not → won't
are not → aren't	cannot → can't
were not → weren't	had not → hadn't

- contract a number

    class of 1990 → class of '90

2. Possession

For more examples of possessives, see Grammar Guide page 173.

Apostrophes can also be used to show possession. Singular nouns and irregular plurals take an -'s, while plural nouns and nouns ending in -s take an apostrophe after the final s.

Singular	The book belongs to that girl. → that girl's book
Plural	The book belongs to those girls. → those girls' book
Singular	The book belongs to that woman. → that woman's book
Irregular plural	The book belongs to those women. → those women's book
Singular noun ending in -s	The book belongs to Mr. Jones. → Mr. Jones' book/ Mr. Jones's book

Periods (.)

Periods are used

- to mark the end of a complete sentence (statement)

    I live here. You live there.

- to mark an abbreviated title

    Dr.   Mr.   Mrs.   Jr.

- to mark other (lower case) abbreviations

a.m. (morning)	e.g. (for example)
p.m. (afternoon/evening)	p.s. (note at the end of a message)
i.e. (that is)	

Commas (,)

Commas are used

- to separate three or more items in a series

    I volunteered in Toronto, Burlington, Ottawa, Montebello, and Montreal.

- to separate a city from its province or state

    Interesting! You live in Burlington, Ontario. Your brother lives in Burlington, Vermont.

- before coordinating conjunctions

    You live in Ontario, but your brother lives in Vermont.

- after introductory subordinating clauses

    Although I was tired, I continued to work.

- before and after appositives (non-essential information in the middle of a sentence)

    Joel, my sister's husband, works for Médecins Sans Frontières.

- after an introductory phrase before a quotation

    Mary said, "Give me the book!"

Note Never separate two complete sentences with a comma (,).

| **Incorrect** | ~~Wendy is a real jerk, she broke my phone.~~ |
| **Correct** | Wendy is a real jerk. She broke my phone. |

It is possible to use a semicolon [;] to separate two complete sentences with a related meaning.

Correct   Wendy is a real jerk; she broke my phone.

Capitalization

Capitalize the following:

- the first word of a sentence

    Cars break down. Accidents happen.

- proper nouns and all the words in addresses and place names

    Xavier Ménard, Lake Ontario, Cabot Square, Main Street, Herzing College

- the pronoun *I*

    My sister and I travelled together.

- days of the week, months, and holidays

    Monday, February, Christmas Eve, Labour Day, Fête Nationale

- languages, nationalities, and religions

    Canadians might be Christians, Muslims, Jews, or Buddhists, or they may have other beliefs. They might speak English, French, Algonquin, Hindi, Mandarin, or many other languages.

- titles of individuals, courses, books, and articles

    Professor Tremblay, Coach Therrien, Chemistry 101, The Heart of the Matter

Note Articles and prepositions in the middle of a title are not capitalized.

Exercise 5

Punctuate the following sentences.

1. While I was going to my brothers home I saw the two sisters car.

   _____

2. I have an appointment with Dr. Smiths assistant Mrs. Tremblay at 4 pm.

   _____

3. Winters are dull. I hate winters long, dark and cold nights.

   _____

4. I think Ill go somewhere warmer where there isnt any snow in the winter.

   _____

Exercise 6

Correct the capitalization errors.

1. my sister jasmine and i were both born on monday, april 7, 1997, to hindu parents in india. we speak gujarati and english, but not much french.

2. uncle tom teaches german at carleton university in ottawa. he bought a house on queen elizabeth drive last Summer. his house is close to dow's lake. we will visit him on new year's eve.

3. they wrote an article called "the problem with our nation" for the *montreal gazette*.

Chapter 13
Word Forms

Go to Compass Online for additional activities using word forms.

GERUNDS AND INFINITIVES

A gerund is an -ing form of a verb that functions as a noun.

I enjoy <u>books</u>. → I enjoy <u>reading</u>.
      n.   gerund

An infinitive is *to* + the base form of the verb. Infinitives function as nouns as well.

I want <u>books</u>. → I want <u>to read</u>.
      n.   infinitive

When a verb immediately follows another verb, the second verb appears in the infinitive most of the time.

I refuse **to leave**.

I am planning **to travel**.

He intends **to write**.

There are a few verbs (e.g., *finish, deny, delay*) that are always followed by a gerund rather than an infinitive.

She finished **writing**.

He denies **cheating**.

We delayed **leaving**.

Here are the 10 most common verbs or verb phrases that are followed by gerunds in English. Memorize these—you will need to use them as you continue this chapter.

avoid → I avoid volunteering in war zones.
be worth → This book is worth reading.
consider → Will you consider cancelling the exam?
discuss → We discussed buying a new house.
dislike → I dislike talking about that subject.
enjoy → I enjoy watching movies.
feel like → Do you feel like going out tonight?
finish → He finished eating dinner.
miss → I miss playing hockey.
risk → They risked losing their money.

The verbs on the next list can be followed by either a gerund or an infinitive with minimal change in meaning.

begin, start, continue, like, love, hate, prefer

I began to cry.

I began crying.

If a verb form appears immediately after a preposition (e.g., *in, on, from, by*, etc.), use a gerund.

Correct   I am interested in studying biology. (gerund after preposition)

Incorrect   ~~I am interested in to study biology.~~ (infinitive after preposition)

Exercise 1

Fill in the blanks with the correct form (gerund or infinitive) of any verb that best completes the meaning. There might be more than one correct answer.

I enjoy _____ in the evenings.

I enjoy __reading__ in the evenings.

I learned _____ when I was in high school.

I learned __to drive__ when I was in high school.

1. I feel like __going out__ right now.
2. This issue is not worth _____ to consider about every day.
3. The police officer asked __me to show__ my licence and registration.
4. I began __to going__ to bed early.
5. Many people avoid __going outside__ in bad weather.
6. I intend __to find__ a good job after I graduate.
7. Many Canadians enjoy __playing__ hockey.
8. I never delay __saying__ what is important.
9. My friend offered __to lend__ me some money.
10. I have finished __writing__ my homework.

Exercise 2

This exercise contains some prepositional expressions you learned in Chapter 10. Fill in the blanks with a gerund of your choice that best completes the meaning of the sentence.

1. I am tired of _____ homework.
2. I am proud of _____ from high school.
3. I apologize to you for not _____ your phone call.
4. I always put off _____.
5. I have no good excuse for _____ that mistake again.
6. I congratulate you on __doing__ such important volunteer work.
7. Are you afraid of _____ after dark?
8. I am bored with __sitting__ at a desk all day.

Work in pairs. Ask each other what things you love or hate to do, what you enjoy or dislike doing, what you would consider doing, and what you absolutely refuse to do.

ACTIVE AND PASSIVE

When the sentence starts with a subject (the person or thing that does the action), the sentence is *active*.

The paramedics **took** the man to the hospital.

When the sentence starts with the object (the person or thing that receives the action), the sentence is *passive*.

The man **was taken** to the hospital.

The passive voice is formed by the verb *to be* (in the appropriate tense) plus the past participle of the main verb. See the chart below for verb changes.

Active	Passive
They *take* him.	He *is taken*.
They *took* him.	He *was taken*.
They *will/can take* him.	He *will/can be taken*.
They *are taking* him.	He *is being taken*.
They *were taking* him.	He *was being taken*.
They *have taken* him	He *has been taken*.
They *are going to take* him.	He *is going to be taken*.

Exercise 3

Fill in the blanks with the correct passive verb form based on the active sentence next to it.

They punished him. → He ___**was punished**___.

1. They served lunch. → Lunch _____.

2. They are breaking the law. → The law _____.

3. Jim will do the job. → The job _____.

4. We must obey the law. → The law _____.

5. He has forgotten everything. → Everything _____.

6. We buy cars every day. → Cars _____ every day.

7. She was spending a lot of money. → A lot of money _____.

8. You should pay taxes soon. → Taxes _____ soon.

9. They are going to close the doors. → The doors _____.

10. He could do it. → It _____.

Exercise 4

Underline the correct (active or passive) form.

1. The two voluntourists paid/were paid the company $10 000 for a three-week volunteer experience.

2. Voluntourists (take/are taken) to Central America.

3. We (are playing/are being played) hockey now.

4. Some jailed volunteers (will free/will be freed) soon.

5. Antibiotics (should take/should be taken) regularly.

6. We (have watched/have been watched) the police.

7. We (have watched/have been watched) by the police.

8. We (were taking/were being taken) individually.

9. We (made/were made) the transaction by credit card.

Communicative Activity 2

Work with a partner. Take turns using the passive voice to describe a country or a city. Your partner has to guess which place you are talking about based on your clues.

The Olympic Games <u>can be traced</u> back to this country. Answer: Greece

The inventor of the radio <u>was born</u> in this country. Answer: Italy

PARTICIPLE ADJECTIVES (ACTIVE AND PASSIVE)

Active participle adjectives are formed by adding -ing to the verb.

To amaze → amazing: That volunteer doctor has an **amazing** <u>resume</u>.
adj.   noun

To freeze → freezing: The liquid reached the **freezing** <u>point</u>.
adj.   noun

Passive participle adjectives have the same form as the past participle of the verb.

To amaze → amazed: The **amazed** <u>audience</u> watched the singer's performance.
adj.   noun

To break → broken: She fixed the **broken** <u>window</u>.
adj.   noun

Active participles have an active meaning. In other words, the noun that follows these adjectives is the doer of the action

amazing voice: the voice amazes the audience

freezing point: the temperature point freezes the liquid

Passive participles have a passive meaning. The noun that follows the adjective is the receiver of the action.

amazed audience: the audience is amazed by the singer

broken window: the window is broken by someone

Exercise 5

Underline the correct participle form.

1. The (satisfied/satisfying) customer paid the (advertised/advertising) price for the (interested/interesting) product.

2. I read an (inspired/inspiring) book about a (fascinated/fascinating) young nurse who decided to change her (bored/boring) job and embark on an (excited/exciting) voyage across the ocean to volunteer in Africa. The book has a (complicated/complicating) style and some parts of the story are (confused/confusing). The ending is a bit (disappointed/disappointing), but I found the message of the book (encouraged/encouraging).

3. You should have seen my (surprised/surprising) look when my classmate told that (embarrassed/embarrassing) joke. The rest of the students thought the joke was really (insulted/insulting).

Chapter 14
Review Exercises

Verb tense review

Tense	Use	Key time markers	Examples
Simple present	1. habits, repeated actions 2. facts 3. scheduled future tasks 4. description of current situations with stative verbs	adverbs of frequency (*often, usually, sometimes, etc.*), *every day/month/year, today*	1. I brush every day. 2. The sun revolves around the earth. 3. Your flight takes off at midnight. 4. This food smells great.
Present progressive	1. current actions (happening now) 2. arrangements (planned events for near future)	*now, at the moment, currently, these days, nowadays*	1. I am studying grammar now. 2. He is leaving the country soon.
Simple past	1. one-time action completed in the past 2. repeated action completed at a specified time in the past.	*yesterday, ago, last night/week/month/year*	1. I taught grammar last week. 2. I taught grammar for 10 years.
Past progressive	1. action in progress at a specific time in the past 2. action in progress in parallel with another action 3. action in progress and interrupted by another action	*while, as, during, when, at* + specific time	1. I was studying for high school exams last year at this time. 2. I was washing dishes while she was sleeping. 3. I was watching TV when the phone rang.
Future (*will*)	1. facts, certainties, predictions in the future 2. spontaneous decisions	*tomorrow, next week/month/year, soon, later, some time*	1. We will graduate next year. 2. I'll have some ice cream, please.
Future (*be going to*)	1. firm decisions for future 2. predictions	*tomorrow, next week/month/year, soon, later, some time*	1. I'm going to work harder. 2. It's going to rain.
Present perfect	1. action that started in the past and continues to the present 2. action that happened at an unspecified time in the past	*since, for, already, yet, still, ever, never, so far, up to now/the present*	1. I have been here since this morning. 2. I have already eaten lunch.

Review Exercise: Verb Tenses

Fill in the blanks with the correct tense of the verb in parentheses.

Right now, I _am sitting_ (sit) at home and I _am watching_ (watch) TV. My mother and sister _left_ (leave) the house an hour ago. They _____ (go) to the grocery store to do some shopping. Mom _____ (go) shopping every Saturday. My sister _____ (not go) with her very often, but today she _____ (decide) to go because she _____ (need) a ride to her friend's house. I _____ (not go) to the grocery store for a couple of months because the last time I _____ (go) there, I _____ (get) into an accident. I _____ (drive) around a curve when I _____ (see) a deer on the road. I _____ (try) to avoid hitting the deer and I _____ (go) into the ditch. Now, I _____ (not like) that road. The next time I _____ (go) to the store, I _____ (take) a different road. Also, I _____ (drive) more slowly and _____ (watch) for deer on the road.

Review Exercise: Passive Forms

Fill in the blanks with the passive form of the verbs in parentheses. Key words are in bold to help you identify the correct tense of the verb.

1. **Right now** in my city a new highway _is being developed_ (develop), so many trees _are being cut_ (cut) and natural habitats _are being destroy_ (destroy).

2. **Yesterday** in class, I _was told_ (tell) by my teacher that penicillin _was discovered_ (discover) by accident in 1928. **Since then** millions of lives _have been saved_ (save) and several diseases _have been eradicate_ (eradicate).

3. **In the future** cars _will be driven_ (drive) automatically by computers. Wars _will be fought_ (fight) by robot soldiers and several of today's incurable diseases _will be cured_ (cure) easily.

4. **Today** in some societies, the number 13 _is considered_ (consider) unlucky; therefore, very often, the 13th floor in high-rise buildings _is omitted_ (omit). Sometimes the 13th floor _is skipped_ (skip) and sometimes it _is renumbered_ (renumber). Sometimes hotel rooms _are numbered_ (number) to avoid having a room 13.

Modal review

Modal	Use	Example
would	1. polite request (formal) 2. desire	1. Would you please close the door? 2. I would like tea please.
can	1. polite request (informal) 2. ability 3. possibility (50%)	1. Can you close the door? 2. I can swim. 3. It can snow at this time of the year.

Modal	Use	Example
could	1. polite request (semi-formal) 2. past ability 3. possibility (50%)	1. Could you close the door please? 2. I could swim when I was four years old. 3. It could snow in April.
should	advice	You should rest more.
may	1. polite request (very formal) 2. possibility (50%)	1. May I close the door? 2. It may snow in April.
might	possibility (50%)	It might snow tomorrow.
must	1. necessity 2. probability (90%)	1. You must have a passport for travel. 2. She must be at home now.
ought to	advice	You ought to be more careful.
had better	advice	I had better go or I won't get there.
would rather	preference	I would rather get cash than credit.

Add *have* + past participle to certain modals to form past modals (*should have/ could have/may have/might have/must have* + past participle).

Review Exercise: Modals

Underline the errors and rewrite the sentence correctly.

1. Would I go to the washroom please?

   <u>May/can/or could</u>

2. I can't walk when I was six months old.

   <u>I can't couldn't</u>

3. You would rather leave now before it gets dark.

   <u>You had rather</u>

4. I'm not sure! Marie must be home or she must be at work.

   <u>May/migh/could</u>

5. You must to hand in your homework on time.

   <u>must/should/have to</u>

6. I should like to have a cup of coffee.

   <u>Would</u>

7. I'm pretty sure he <u>may</u> have closed the door.

   <u>Must</u>

8. We must brush our teeth when we were children.

   <u>had to</u>

9. You ought be more careful in the future.

   <u>ought to or should.</u>

10. May you leave the room please?

    <u>Would you/can/could</u>

Review Exercise: Conditionals

Complete the following conditional sentences in your own words. Use the correct verb tense.

1. If I don't find a job after I graduate, _____

   _____

2. If I had a million dollars today, _____

   _____

3. If I hadn't come to this school to continue my education, _____

   _____

Review Exercise: Prepositions

Fill in the blanks with the correct prepositions.

1. I hear the same things every day _____ TV, _____ the radio, even when I'm _____ the phone with my friends. I feel surrounded by the media at all times during the day: _____ the morning, _____ the afternoon, even _____ night.

2. I live _____ number 25 _____ rue Taschereau _____ Gatineau. I live close _____ Ottawa, but far _____ Vancouver.

3. I am interested _____ cats, but I'm afraid _____ dogs. I'm ashamed _____ my bad deeds, and proud _____ the good ones. I'm excited _____ the future, but bored _____ the present. I take care _____ myself and I rely _____ myself, but I also depend _____ my family.

4. At night, before sleep, I put _____ the fire, put _____ my fishing gear, take _____ my pants, put _____ my pyjamas, get _____ my tent, close my eyes, and go to sleep like a baby.

Review Exercise: Gerunds and Infinitives

Complete the following sentences in your own words. Start each blank with a gerund or an infinitive form, as appropriate.

1. Today, I don't feel like _____

2. My parents are interested in _____

3. I refuse _____

4. I am planning _____

5. I often put off _____

6. In winter, I always avoid _____

7. Today in class, I learned _____

8. If there is a need, I am prepared _____

Review Exercise: Articles and Determiners

Underline the best choice. If an article or determiner is not needed, underline the X.

(Some/An/The/X) other day, I saw (some/a/an/the/x) man walking along (some/a/an/the/x) Highway 40 during (some/a/an/the/x) rush hour. (Some/A/An/The/X) man was clearly in distress. He was talking to (some/a/an/the/x) imaginary person. (Some/A/An/The/X) cars slowed down and drivers showed concern. Others didn't pay (many/much/some/a little/a few) attention. (A/An/The/A little/A few) minutes later (a/an/the/some) police cruiser arrived on (a/an/the) scene. (A/An/The) officer got out of (a/an/the) cruiser and started talking to (a/an/the) man. (A/An/The) officer asked him (a few/a little/x) questions. He then led (a/an/the) man to (a/an/the) cruiser and drove away. (A little/A few/Much/Many) hours later, I saw (a/an/x/the) incident reported on (x/the/an) evening news.

Review Exercise: Pronouns and Possessive Adjectives

Underline the best choice.

(My/Mine/Me) brother and (I/me/myself) bought a car together last month. We love (our/ours/us) car and are proud of (us/ours/ourself/ourselves) for buying it. (Its/It's) an old car, but (its/it's) engine is in great condition. We saved (our/ours/us) money for two years.

When we had enough money, I asked (my/mine/me) brother to give me (his/he's) share of the money. I added (my/mine/me) to it and I bought the car for (our/ours/us).

Review Exercise: Adjectives and Adverbs

Find and correct the errors. You can delete, change, or move adjectives and adverbs.

1. I work very hardly but I make littler money than my more old brother who doesn't very often work.

2. My car is more comfortabler than my sister's although her car is much expensive than my car.

3. I live farther from school than Joe does. Joe lives more close. If Joe rents the apartment next to mine, he will be as farther from school as I am.

4. Joe and I are both badly drivers, but he is badder than me. He drives horrible.

Grammar Appendix 1
Stative Verbs

Present progressive is used only for actions. If the verb is not showing action (for example, when talking about feelings, relationships, physical descriptions, beliefs, or possessions), the simple present is generally used even when talking about the moment of speaking.

Verbs that show actions are called action verbs. Verbs that show states are called stative verbs.

Stative (non-action) verbs usually express senses, emotions, mental states (thoughts and opinions), ownership/relationship, or measurement. Here are the most common stative verbs by category.

Category	Examples
senses	see, hear, smell, taste, feel, appear, look, sound
emotions	love, hate, like, dislike, desire, want, need, prefer, appreciate, seem, deserve
mental states	believe, imagine, suppose, think, know, remember, recognize, understand, doubt, mean, wonder
ownership/ relationship	own, belong, have, contain, consist, involve, include, depend
measurement	measure, weigh, equal, cost, fit

Note Some of the verbs above can be used in more than one way, and can have an action meaning as well as a non-action (stative) meaning.

EXAMPLE

think

Action meaning: to use your mind to solve a problem; to perform the act of contemplating

> Don't interrupt me. I am thinking.

Non-action meaning: to have an opinion; to believe

> I think there's someone at the door.

Grammar Appendix 2
Irregular Verbs

Base form	Past	Past participle	Base form	Past	Past participle
arise	arose	arisen	forget	forgot	forgotten
be (am/is/are)	was/were	been	forgive	forgave	forgiven
beat	beat	beaten	freeze	froze	frozen
become	became	become	get	got	gotten
begin	began	begun	give	gave	given
bend	bent	bent	go	went	gone
bet	bet	bet	hang (up)	hung	hung
bite	bit	bitten	have	had	had
bleed	bled	bled	hear	heard	heard
blow	blew	blown	hide	hid	hidden
break	broke	broken	hit	hit	hit
bring	brought	brought	hold	held	held
build	built	built	hurt	hurt	hurt
buy	bought	bought	keep	kept	kept
catch	caught	caught	know	knew	known
choose	chose	chosen	lay	laid	laid
come	came	come	lead	led	led
cost	cost	cost	leave	left	left
cut	cut	cut	lend	lent	lent
dig	dug	dug	let	let	let
do	did	done	lie (down)	lay	lain
draw	drew	drawn	light	lit	lit
drink	drank	drunk	lose	lost	lost
drive	drove	driven	make	made	made
eat	ate	eaten	mean	meant	meant
fall	fell	fallen	meet	met	met
feed	fed	fed	pay	paid	paid
feel	felt	felt	put	put	put
fight	fought	fought	quit	quit	quit
find	found	found	read*	read	read
fly	flew	flown	ride	rode	ridden

*The pronunciation of *read* in the present is different from the pronunciation in its past and past participle forms. In the present form, *read* rhymes with *need*. In the past and past participle, it is pronounced the same as *red* (the colour).

Base form	Past	Past participle
ring	rang	rung
rise	rose	risen
run	ran	run
say	said	said
see	saw	seen
sell	sold	sold
send	sent	sent
set	set	set
shake	shook	shaken
shine	shone	shone
shoot	shot	shot
shrink	shrank	shrunk
shut	shut	shut
sing	sang	sung
sink	sank	sunk
sit	sat	sat
sleep	slept	slept
slide	slid	slid
speak	spoke	spoken
spend	spent	spent

Base form	Past	Past participle
spin	spun	spun
stand	stood	stood
steal	stole	stolen
stick	stuck	stuck
sting	stung	stung
swear	swore	sworn
sweep	swept	swept
swim	swam	swum
take	took	taken
teach	taught	taught
tear	tore	torn
tell	told	told
think	thought	thought
throw	threw	thrown
understand	understood	understood
wake	woke	woken
wear	wore	worn
win	won	won
wind	wound	wound
write	wrote	written

Index

-es in third person, 151–2
-ing verbs, 152–3
misspelled words, 186
stative (non-action) verbs, 151, 220
stress, 34, 35
subject, gerund as, 32
subject pronouns, 172–3
subordinating conjunctions, 204–5
summarizing, 136, 139–40
superlative adjectives, 89, 190–1
superlative adverbs, 190–1
supporting details, in paragraphs, 117, 118–19

teenagers, and changing the world, 61–4
the, 145
there is/there are, 147–9
thesis statement
checklist, 121
in essay, 121–2, 123–4
and introduction, 47–8
as main idea, 121–2
vs. topic sentence, 121, 122
use of, 47–8
third person, 14, 151–2
Thomson, Tom, 36
3D printing of food, 42, 50–2
time, prepositions for, 195
time expressions and markers, 9, 164–5, 169
to, 109, 210
to listen to, 23
Tongeman, Zea, 62–3
topic sentences
checklist, 118

in essay, 121, 122–3
in paragraphs, 15, 117–19, 120
vs. thesis statement, 121, 122
trading zone in class, 91
transition words, 127–8

uncountable nouns, 143–4, 145, 146, 148
urban farming, 41, 45–7
URLs, meaning of, 129
Usher, David, 31, 32, 33

verbs
action and stative, 151, 220
and conditional, 106–7
and gerunds, 32, 210
of movement, 109
passive and active voice, 81, 212–13, 216
and prepositions, 196–7
pronunciation, 28
spelling of, 152–3
verb tenses
irregular verbs, 221–2
review of, 215–16
and time, 9, 164–5, 169
see also each verb tense
vocabulary
cognates and false cognates, 6
and context, 24
farming and food, 45
in listening activities, 7, 34–5, 91, 104–5
personality traits, 4
in reading activities, 10–11, 24, 31, 40, 60, 68, 83, 88, 99
slang, 88

in watching activities, 16, 45, 85, 111
word families, 65–6
volunteering and volunteer work
effects of, 107–10, 111–12
exercises, 98–9, 110
voluntourism, 100–3, 105–6, 107–10, 111–12

watching, strategy for, 72
water, in 21st century, 69–70
Wikipedia, 130
will and *be going to*, 52–3, 162–4, 215
wish, 31
word families, 65–6
words
confusing words, 183–4
in dictionary, 49
forms of, 65–6
meaning of, 23, 49
word stress, 103–4
would, 106–7, 179
would rather, 181
writing
of essays, 120–6
ideas for, 116–17
online research, 128–9
of paragraphs, 15, 117–20
and prior knowledge, 41
sources and plagiarism, 129–30

yes/no questions, 153
your and *you're*, 25
Yousafzai, Malala, 60, 76

"z" sound, 14, 152
ZipCar, 81

Credits

Unit 1

Photo Credits

1   iStock.com /Borut Trdina
2   iStock.com /PeopleImages; igmit/Thinkstock
3   Weekend Images Inc.,/Shutterstock.com
5   Africa Studio/Shutterstock.com
6   Dirk Ercken/Shutterstock.com
7   © Kiosea39 | Dreamstime.com
9   iStock.com/urbancow
11   Franzi/Shutterstock.com; Broccoli Photography / Alamy Stock Photo
15   BrianAJackson/Thinkstock
16   David Sacks/Digital Vision/Thinkstock
17   iStock.com/SolStock
20   iStock.com/manley099

Literary Credit

11   What Disney Pixar's Film Inside Out Teaches Us about Emotions by Kristen Lee. *Psychology Today*. Reprinted by permission of the author.
18   eqrocks.com Emotional Intelligence Quiz. Reprinted by permission of Matt Perelstein.

Audio Credit

7   Branding Yourself. Mark Connolly, CBC Edmonton AM. © CBC
16   www.MargieWarrell.com

Unit 2

Photo Credits

21   iStock.com/Manakin
22   kenzon/Thinkstock
23   iStock.com/Zzvet; Golubovy/Shutterstock.com
24   © Mauro Mancini | Dreamstime.com; Martinan/Thinkstock
26   iStock.com/annebaek
27   wavebreakmedia/Shutterstock.com
28   michaeljung/Shutterstock.com
29   Anthony Correia/Shutterstock.com
30   iStock.com/PeopleImages; iStock.com/pjhpix
31   iStock.com/as3d
33   iStock.com/MarianVejcik; iStock.com/Fat Camera
34   iStock.com/mediaphoto
35   Zinkevych/Thinkstock
36   bmcent1/Thinkstock
37   iStock.com/Kokkai Ng

Literary Credit

24   7 Awesome Ways Music Makes Life A Hell Of A Lot Better by Bill Protzmann. www.yourtango.com
31   "Yes, Creativity Can Be Taught," from fresh gigs.cs blog. Reprinted with permission of Advicetap Digital Inc.

Audio and Video Credits

28   Henry Responds to Music from His Era. Alive Inside. Reproduced with permission from Alive Inside LLC
35   Laurentian Students Check Out Art Therapy. Jason Turnbull CBC Points North. © CBC

Unit 3

Photo Credits

39   monticello/Shutterstock.com

41–3 By permission of Space 10. A project by Bas Van de Poel, Kaave Pour, Simon Perez, Lukas Renlund, Karin Borring and Simon Caspersen.
44   Edith65/Thinkstock; DarcyMaulsby/Thinkstock
46   iStock.com/FangXiaNuo
48   © Aaneela | Dreamstime.com
50   tinxi/Shutterstock.com
55   dpa picture alliance/Alamy Stock Photo

Literary Credits

41   By permission of Space 10. A project by Bas Van de Poel, Kaave Pour, Simon Perez, Lukas Renlund, Karin Borring and Simon Caspersen.
50   Is 3D Printing the Future of Global Food? By Sylvain Charlebois. *The Globe and Mail*. Reprinted by permission of the author.

Audio and Video Credits

46   Why We Should Be Urban Farming. The Good Stuff. Reproduced by permission of Craig Benzine, The Good Stuff.
55   Sustainable, Efficient, and Slightly Nutty—What It's Like to Eat Insect Burgers. Nora Young. CBC Spark. © CBC

Unit 4

Photo Credits

59   Lukasz Janyst/Shutterstock.com
62   Global Minimum, Inc.
64   Donatas Dabravolskas/Shutterstock.com
67   monkeybusinessimages/Thinkstock; Ververidis Vasilis/Shutterstock.com
68   s_bukley/Shutterstock.com
73   mihtiander/Thinkstock; The Ocean Cleanup Project; The Ocean Cleanup Project
76   © Mikobagus | Dreamstime.com
77   Press Association via AP Images; © Monkeybusinessimages | Dreamstime.com
78   © Mangostock | Dreamstime.com

Literary Credits

61   Beyond Malala: Teenagers Changing the World. Reprinted with permission from The Guardian/ www.theguardian.com
68   www.onedrop.org

Audio and Video Credits

72   "One Night for One Drop." www.onedrop.org
73   Ocean Cleanup Project. © PBS
74   Paying It Forward. David Gray and Jennifer Lee. CBC Calgary Eyeopener. ©CBC
77   "One Drop Foundation featuring In-Q." www.onedrop.org

Unit 5

Photo Credits

79   Montri Nipitvittaya/Shutterstock.com
80   iStock.com/VisualCommunications; Megapress / Alamy Stock Photo
84   © Stephanie Swartz | Dreamstime.com
86   iStock.com/monkeybusinessimages
87   iStock.com/andipantz
88   Marta Iwanek/Toronto Star via Getty Images
90   DaLiu/Shutterstock.com
91   Agencja Fotograficzna Caro/Alamy Stock Photo

92   iStock.com/vgajic
95   iStock.com/Leonardo Patrizi
96   © Marie Velde | Dreamstime.com

Literary Credits

81   The Sharing Economy By Terry O'Reilly. Under the Influence, CBC.ca. Reprinted with permission from Terry O'Reilly, www. terryoreilly.ca
88   Facebook Flea Market Has Just One Rule:No Cash Allowed. By Geoffrey Vendeville. From Toronto Star, October 23, 2015 © 2015 Toronto Star Newspapers Limited. All rights reserved. Used by permission and protected by the Copyright Laws of the United States. The printing, copying, redistribution, or retransmission of this Content without express written permission is prohibited.

Audio and Video Credits

86   How the Sharing Economy Is Catching On. Chris Brown. CBC News. ©CBC
92   The Pitfalls of Collaborative Consumption. Nora Young. CBC Spark. © CBC

Unit 6

Photo Credits

97   hxdyl/Shutterstock.com
99   Monkey Business Images/Shutterstock.com
100   Valeriya Anufriyeva/Shutterstock.com
101   © Khunaspix | Dreamstime.com
103   Monkey Business Images/Shutterstock.com
105   Agencja Fotograficzna Caro / Alamy Stock Photo
107   AP Photo/Dieu Nalio Chery
111   Monkey Business Images/Shutterstock.com
115   iStock.com/starman963
141   iStock.com/Radachynskyi
144   monticello/Shutterstock.com
146   iStock.com/rue015
148   monticello/Shutterstock.com
156   iStock.com/manley099
160   Megapress/Alamy Stock Photo
171   monticello/Shutterstock.com
180   mihtiander/Thinkstock
205   iStock.com/SolStock
206   David Sacks/Digital Vision/Thinkstock
213   AP Photo/Dieu Nalio Chery

Literary Credits

100   The Voluntourist Dilemma. By Pippa Biddle reprinted By permission of GoOverseas
107   The Downside of Overseas Volunteering. By Bob Hepburn. From Toronto Star, January 4, 2012 © 2012 Toronto Star Newspapers Limited. All rights reserved. Used by permission and protected by the Copyright Laws of the United States. The printing, copying, redistribution, or retransmission of this Content without express written permission is prohibited.

Audio and Video Credits

105   Volunteer Tourism. By permission of Jason Moore, Zero to Travel.
111   The Voluntourist: Is Voluntourism Doing More Harm than Good? Reproduced by permission from The Voluntourist, Chloé Sanguinetti, 2015